Praise for *Frankie's Place:*

"This is a beautiful memoir, giving a glimpse not just of a person but of a time and a place worth noting. This is a work suffused with love of every stripe, from the romantic kind to the kind one might feel for a place, a way of life and a really good dinner."

—*Publishers Weekly* (starred review)

"*Frankie's Place* is a memoir almost audacious in its normalcy: it's the story of a middle-aged white guy with no obvious dysfunctions or ghosts in his closet. What Jim Sterba does have—and has in abundance—is charm, humor, and a wonderful gift for capturing the rhythms and pleasures of July days whiled away on the Maine coast. Sterba is great company on the page, and *Frankie's Place* succeeds, like no other book I know, in getting the quotidian glories of a New England summer between two covers."

—Michael Pollan

"*Frankie's Place* is quite simply a joy to read—a portrait of a place, a way of life, and a marriage, by a reporter who turns out to be the world's last extant romantic. Not to mention a great natural cook—who gives us, in addition to everything else, his recipes."

—Joan Didion

"A whimsical memoir that will tickle the fancy of those who have always dreamed about escaping the real world to the coast of Maine. Sterba is . . . very funny. He leaves the reader smiling to himself time and again. Perhaps the most touching episode in the book comes near the end when Sterba discovers he isn't fatherless after all. His natural father [whom he hasn't seen in some fifty years] gets in touch with him. The story of how they get together is a gripping account."

—*The Kent Tribune*

"Jim Sterba's *Frankie's Place* has tremendous natural charm, the witty and wonderfully observed narrative of a summer's action Down East. It should fit very nicely into anyone's beach bag, though it helps if you're attracted to islands, Maine lore, lost fathers, the absurdities of the reporter's trade, and love stories."

—Ward Just

"Jim Sterba has found his own American Arcadia, his own Walden Pond and, in the process, himself. He records his quest with a loving honesty, never sentimental, never cloying . . . a man taking stock of his life at a certain time of life." —Morley Safer

"A bucolic memoir of two middle-aged writers . . . hiking, swimming, doing chores, taking turns cooking, growing increasingly irate at encroaching developers and wacky next-door neighbors intent on building a Maine version of Taj Mahal." —*The Washington Post*

"Its attention to details of nature . . . rivals Annie Dillard's in *Pilgrim at Tinker Creek* and Henry Beston's in *Outermost House*."
—*New York Sun*

"Jim Sterba made his name as a courageous foreign correspondent—a restless, gifted journalistic explorer. But in the middle of his odyssey the wind changed, and, most extraordinarily, he found his way home. We can't all be so fortunate, but we can do ourselves the favor of reading *Frankie's Place*." —Michael Janeway

"A perfect read for summer. Jim Sterba's Maine . . . [is] the Maine all of us dream about: a rustic cottage, drinks on a mosquito-attractive deck, cozy chowder dinners in front of the fire on a foggy night."
—*Ellsworth American*

"Celebrating Down East life, Sterba, a *New York Times* reporter, depicts halcyon summers in which he and Pulitzer Prize winner Frances FitzGerald abandoned their cramped Manhattan apartments for a rustic cottage and hikes through fern forests, dips in the bracing Atlantic, and foraging trips for chanterelles." —*Condé Nast Traveler*

"Sterba handles with . . . aplomb the love story that is the subtitle of *Frankie's Place*." —*Los Angeles Times*

"[Sterba] writes with an open heart, a charming voice and one eye on the fish stew. He may have not only cooked up a pleasing memoir, but also the perfect antidote for Mainers who sigh and quietly say, 'Here come the summer people.'" —*Sun Journal* (Lewiston, Maine)

"Equal parts love letter, history lesson and cookbook, Sterba's chronicle of one summer on Mount Desert Island is a slide show of life at its richest. Sterba's narrative keeps the pages turning, giving readers a sense of what it might be like to stop by for dinner at Frankie's place, crack open a lobster and listen to stories of a life well-lived."

—*San Francisco Chronicle*

"Every word of this wonderful love story speaks of solid, old-fashioned ideals. It is an honest, often hilariously funny book that tells a love story you'll not soon forget. A selection of curious, Down East recipes is an added lagniappe." —Peter Duchin

"Some people write for money, some for recognition, some for obscure personal motives or even revenge. Jim Sterba has written an ode to Mount Desert and summer living out of love."

—*Press Herald* (Portland, Maine)

"*Frankie's Place* . . . will find its place on the kitchen shelf of many homes, both as a retreat from demands of daily chores and as a source of ideas for many memorable meals." —*The Argus Press*

"The story of finding a place that fits, a home in the world. *Frankie's Place* is the anti-exposé, a revelation in kindness."

—*Chicago Tribune*

"Lyrical. [The] best recipe in Sterba's repertoire . . . is the recipe for the good life. To suss it out, you have to read between the lines in this cozy little book. Or, as they say in cookbooks, repeat as necessary. No need to worry, though, *Frankie's Place* will hold up for a second or third tasting."

—*Austin American-Statesman*

"The only real problem is that Sterba has made Mount Desert Island and life here sound a bit too appealing. He reminds us how special it all is in a way that is far more intimate and personal than your average guide or travel book." —*Bar Harbor Times*

FRANKIE'S PLACE

FRANKIE'S PLACE

A Love Story

JIM STERBA

Grove Press
New York

The author and publisher gratefully acknowledge the following
for the right to reprint material in this book.

Donald Malcolm's "Edible, But Not Recommended," originally
appeared in *The New Yorker* on June 28, 1958.

Lost Bar Harbor, by G. W. Helfrich and Glady O'Neil, published by Down East
Books, a Division of Down East Enterprise, Inc., Camden, Maine.

Poems by Russ Wiggins and the "Letter to the Editor" all originally
appeared in *The Ellsworth American,* Ellsworth, Maine.

Published simultaneously in Canada
Printed in the United States of America

FIRST GROVE PRESS PAPERBACK EDITION

Library of Congress Cataloging-in-Publication Data
Sterba, Jim, 1943–
Frankie's place / Jim Sterba.
p. cm.
ISBN 0-8021-4140-4 (pbk.)
1. Sterba, Jim, 1943—Relations with women. 2. FitzGerald, Frances,
1940—Relations with men. 3. Journalists—United States—Biography.
I. Title.
PN4874.S6846A3 2003
070.92'273—dc21
[B]   2002041676

Grove Press
841 Broadway
New York, NY 10003

04 05 06 07 08   10 9 8 7 6 5 4 3 2 1

For Frances

Acknowledgments

This story could not have been written without the kindness and generosity of the members of the FitzGerald and Peabody families.

Frankie's brothers and sisters and their children made me a part of their families, and I thank them: Desmond FitzGerald, Lucinda Ziesing, Pam Allen, Caitlin FitzGerald, Ryan FitzGerald, Alexander FitzGerald, Cooper FitzGerald, Joan FitzGerald, George Denny, Frances Denny, George Denny Jr., Amos Denny, Barbara Lawrence, Cuff Train, Michael Train, Elizabeth Train, Mike Cassidy, Penelope Tree, Ricky Fataar, Paloma Fataar, Stuart MacFarlane, and Michael MacFarlane.

Frankie's uncles and their families were equally welcoming and generous. They taught me a great deal and told me wonderful stories: George Peabody, Sam Peabody, Judy Peabody, Elizabeth Peabody, Mike Peabody, Pam Peabody, Carter Peabody, Payson Peabody, Karin Peabody, Claire Peabody, Nicholas Peabody, Chub Peabody, Toni Peabody, Bob Peabody, Laura Peabody, Sam A. Peabody, Emma Peabody, Barbara Peabody, Michael Cusick, Theo Cusick, and Isabel Cusick.

I am indebted to my brother Ken Sterba and his family, Patty Sterba, Anne Sterba, and Matthew Sterba, for their encouragement over the years and for their courage. I am thankful to Walter

Watts and Agnes Watts for reaching out to me and offering unconditional love.

I am grateful to those who read my manuscript as a work-in-progress and offered many useful comments and suggestions: Alice Arlen, Michael Arlen, David Greenway, J. B. Greenway, Sarah Catchpole, and Ken Wells. I am also grateful to the staff of the Northeast Harbor Library for helping me track down local resources and history.

Without the many talents of Robert Lescher, my literary agent, this project would have easily floundered. He took on other duties: hand-holder, writing coach, guidance counselor, wise man, and attending physician.

My thanks to my editor at Grove/Atlantic, Joan Bingham, and to others on the staff who helped: Lindsay Sagnette, Michael Hornburg, Judy Hottensen. Thanks also to Don Kennison, who copyedited the manuscript.

Finally, I owe my deepest thanks and love to Frankie. Without her, of course, I would not have a story, or this wonderful life.

FRANKIE'S PLACE

Introduction

Frankie never called what she did "writing," she called it "typing." For most of the year she "typed" in a tiny office on the Upper East Side of Manhattan overlooking the East River. Her office wasn't much bigger than a walk-in closet, but it was part of a book-lined one-bedroom apartment on the top floor of a five-story brick walkup built just after the Civil War. From her windows, she could look out on to the river and watch the city's water traffic. Tugboats growled up and down. Sight-seeing boats headed north on their New York City tours. Passenger ferries trudged back and forth from La Guardia airport. Private motor yachts cruised by, along with speedboats and the occasional sail-boat, their skippers waging tricky battles for control in the East River's muscular tidal currents.

Each summer, Frankie decamped around the first of July to another island named Mount Desert, on the coast of Maine. There, she typed in a small house in a forest overlooking a fjord called Somes Sound, which runs for some six miles up the middle of the island. On each side of the fjord rise forested mountains of pink granite rounded smooth by glaciers and grown up with cedars, spruce, and pines, patches of junipers and huckleberry, blueberry, and bayberry bushes, and hundreds of wildflowers, plants, and mushrooms that inhabit the northern forest. The mountains, many barren on top, are part of Acadia National Park. Here, Frankie's view, beyond the trees outside her window, was another waterscape, this one dotted with lobster-trap buoys and alive with seabirds.

Outside the house, just off the porch under a cedar tree, three old wooden lobster traps aged in a bed of pine needles. Out back, a tangle of blackberry bushes fought with ferns for sunlight. Under the house sat a stack of firewood and a green canoe with enough scratches to suggest a history of intimacy with barnacles on the granite ledges out front.

The walls inside the house were gray. The floors and slanted ceilings were walnut-colored, giving its rooms the dark feel of a cabin in the woods, or what, I learned later, other summer people called a camp. The shades on the windows were slatted rattan roll-ups. The centerpiece of the living room was a huge fireplace made of rough granite stones collected nearby. In front of the fireplace, a thick wooden ship's hatch served as a coffee table. On the back walls were shelves stuffed with books, above them was a loft with more shelves and more books, and in the ceiling above was a skylight.

A large kilim rug covered much of one wall. Below it, on a low table, sat a golden Buddha that had been rescued during the war in Vietnam. Its right torso was charred by fire. It was life-sized, it faced the front door, and it made an instant impression on anyone coming into the house for the first time. It made such an impression on the young children of Frankie's brother and sister that they came to call the place "Buddha's house."

Frankie first invited me for a visit over a long weekend in July of 1983. I had seen a lot of America and the world as a newspaper reporter. But I had never been north, or east, of Boston, and the Maine coast was completely new to me. I took an Eastern Airlines shuttle from New York to Boston, then hopped a tiny, twin-engine commuter prop jet for the Bar Harbor airport, which is in the village of Trenton on what I came to learn was referred to by islanders as "the mainland." There, Frankie picked me up in a decrepit 1966 Volvo station wagon and drove me onto the island of Mount Desert, which she pronounced "dessert."

What impressed me first about Frankie's place was its isolation. The house was situated on a peninsula, and to get to it she turned off the main road down a narrow winding lane, bumping over stones and ruts through half a mile of dense forest. From the small clearing where she parked, we could see the house tucked among the evergreens, its cedar siding weathered to a black-streaked gray. From the car we padded over exposed tree roots and a spongy carpet of pine needles flanked by beds of moss, lichen-covered granite, and patches of ferns and bayberry bushes. Three wooden steps led to a front porch, which overlooked water through more trees.

Inside, the house was dark but cozy. It felt like a nest. It was devoid of worldly distractions. There was no television, no radio. Indeed, except for a telephone, it was removed from all contact with other human beings that wasn't self-initiated. Of all the fantasies I'd had over the years of the perfect writer's retreat, none came closer than this. It turned out to be a great place to relax, too.

That wasn't what Frankie had in mind, though. I was a guest that first summer, and not the only guest. Two of her friends from New York, Kevin and Gail, arrived shortly after I did. As guests, in Frankie's view, we had to be entertained. That meant her typing had to stop temporarily. Kevin, a magazine editor, and Gail, a writer, had been guests in the past. They were wise to the drill and shrewdly opted out of much that lay ahead. Frankie's idea of entertainment included so-called walks up and down mountains that would have been called forced marches in many of the world's armies. There was "swimming," an anemic euphemism for the shock therapy that awaited us in the icy ocean waters of Somes Sound. Tennis meant putting oneself at the wrong end of a vicious forehand. Then came trips to smaller islands and walks around their rocky shores. Then sailing, which meant following orders, sorting out a tangle of ropes, being corrected for calling them ropes instead of lines and sheets, and pulling them and cranking winches until rarely used muscles burned and, later, ached. Then more mountains, more tennis, more "walking," more "swimming." I called it the FitzGerald Survival School.

Between these recreational ordeals, Frankie took me to the little village of Northeast Harbor. We drove down the eastern side of Somes Sound on one of the prettiest stretches of road I had ever seen. She showed me its snug harbor full of sailboats of every size and description. The harbor was flanked by steep, wooded hills dotted with large shingled cottages. She introduced me to Mr. Stanley, the fishmonger, and Bob Pyle, the librarian. She took me to McGrath's, the little store where she got the newspapers, to Brown's Hardware, and to the Pine Tree Market. She showed me the house in Aunt Hannah's pasture on Smallidge Point where she spent summers with her grandparents when she was small. She took me to the Fleet, a yacht club across the cove, where as a child she took rowing and sailing lessons. She told me a great deal about the history of the village and her family's long attachment to it; how her ancestors had arrived as summer rusticators three generations ago. I remember listening to this, but I don't remember paying much attention to it. I was trying to catch my breath, and to steel myself for the next event of the FitzGerald Survival School.

The accommodations at Frankie's place were spartan. Behind the living room were two bedrooms where guests stayed. The beds were plywood racks topped with firm foam-rubber slabs that served as mattresses. The end tables were made of unfinished plywood and had single drawers.

A third bedroom flanked the kitchen on the other side of the house. Besides a bed and two reading tables with lamps, the only other piece of furniture in it was a built-in L-shaped plywood desk that faced south and west out large windows and afforded a panorama of Somes Sound through the trees. Here, Frankie "typed" on a half-century-old Remington Noiseless manual typewriter that weighed a ton and sounded like thunder. In the late morning, the sun rose high enough over a dense stand of tall cedars to spill its rays into the room and onto her desk. In the afternoon, the sun beamed in over her right shoulder from beyond the front porch, high over the sound. That is, of course, if the sun shined at all. Sometimes it was cloudy. Sometimes it rained. More often the sun was obscured by a commodity of nature underappreciated by those who have not spent time on the Maine coast: fog. Sometimes the fog swooped in so densely that it completely obscured the water and made Frankie's place seem like it was cocooned in cotton.

Fog or sun, Frankie sat for the main part of each day "typing" in splendid isolation. Not that she was entirely alone. Squadrons of seagulls patrolled her vista. Ravens and crows squawked in the treetops. An osprey, with its singular high-pitched cry, perched much of the time atop half-dead spruces near the shoreline. A magnificent bald eagle lived in the neighborhood and made regular passes, occasionally stopping out front. There were forest birds and waterbirds—jays and thrushes, cormorants and loons. Chipmunks scampered over the porch. Red squirrels plied the trees.

Then there was me. How I joined the ranks of the fauna that were more or less permanent fixtures at Frankie's place is part of this story. It is, to tell the truth, something of a mystery. I know this much: I survived the FitzGerald Survival School that first weekend and then was invited back for another weekend in the fall. I survived that. The next summer, Frankie invited me for a week. Meanwhile, we began to spend more and more time together in New York.

Gradually, our commutes between Manhattan and Mount Desert became a habit. Each July, Frankie and I returned to Somes Sound, staying as long as possible, sometimes only a few weeks, sometimes a month, sometimes through Labor Day, and, occasionally, into October and beyond.

By mid-June, as Manhattan turned hot and sticky, our longing for Maine began to well up. Then on the appointed day we would fly to Bangor, and take a taxi to Ellsworth, where the old Volvo spent the winters. Reunited with this rusting hulk, we would stuff it with groceries and supplies and join a great caravan of vacationers headed for the coast. Along the way, we would begin to overdose on the green intensity of the forested landscape, with its many shades and hues. Finally, we would arrive at a clump of familiar lobster pounds, their outdoor pots steaming on both sides of the highway. Then it was up to a little causeway across the Trenton Bridge, over Thompson Island, and on to Mount Desert Island. In the middle of the bridge, as the smell of ocean brine filled our nostrils, Frankie would yell, "Whoopie!" It was a FitzGerald family tradition. It meant we were back.

There was a comforting sameness to the summers at Frankie's place. There was a stability and predictability in the permanence of place and ritual, in knowing that the rotten tree trunk out back was still there for picking over by the neighborhood woodpeckers. That the raccoon that prowled the peninsula would eventually pay a visit or two to the garbage can on the back porch. That the lane to the house would have grass growing between the furrows made by our tires, and that mushrooms would pop up along it beckoning to be turned into soup. That the tides would rise and fall twice a day, and that when they were low we could pick shiny, black mussels off the wet rocks and make a delicious meal of them. We could count on the weather changing rapidly, radically, and often. It would offer up light and color so crisp and clear, as Frankie liked to say, that it hurt. It would deliver stiff winds or dead calms. It would blow in storms that howled through the night, or bring rain, drizzle, and fog that hung around for days, keeping towels wet, clogging the saltshaker, and sending sodden vacationers fleeing like half-drowned rats.

There was a deep comfort in knowing that once we tucked ourselves into this tiny corner of the woods by the sea we were all by ourselves. We could work and play, read and cook, walk and swim, and be with each other just far enough beyond the edge of the world's clamor to feel momentarily out of harm's way. Or so we thought.

This story takes place in a summer that was the same as others in many ways, but in many ways not. Each summer began with a great sense of anticipation, a buildup of energy to splurge on a fresh interlude in the crisp, clean air and green, watery outdoors of the Maine coast. Then we would settle into a routine of writing punctuated by bouts of play. The days would fly by. Local soap opera fueled chatter at dinner tables and at sunset gatherings called porch-benders. Then it would be over, as quickly as the snap of a switch in a gaily lit room.

Some summers, singular events stood out in my memory: the sunny day I asked Frankie to marry me; our first porch crops; my first mackerel and striped bass; a new store in town. Others contained seasonal highlights: the damp summer when chanterelle mushrooms were everywhere; the chilly summer when tomatoes never got ripe.

There was the summer we bought our boat and began visiting outlying villages, exploring uninhabited islands, and watching seabirds and seal colonies; the summer we saw a mother skunk and five baby skunks parading beside the road into Northeast Harbor at sunset; the summer a cock pheasant and a fox turned up on Cedar Swamp Mountain, appearing before us at the same place along a trail almost every time we walked past.

There was the first time we went whale watching. As we neared Mount Desert Rock, a tiny island twenty-five miles out to sea, in a friend's little lobster boat, we spotted some humpback whales in the distance. But they submerged before we could get near them. When we arrived at where they had been, we cut the boat's engine and quietly drifted. Within minutes, two huge humpbacks came up alongside the boat, their snouts within inches of its hull, their eyes peering up at us, their blowholes exhaling the foulest breath in creation: eau de rotten shrimp. They stayed with us, circling, playing, diving under and around our little boat, for almost an hour.

The idea for this book began with recipes. Frankie is a by-the-book cook, and a good one. Whenever a reliable rendition of a classic Julia Child production was called for, Frankie got the assignment. I liked to improvise. Experimenting was part of what made cooking enjoyable for me. Sometimes I pushed too far.

Once I made a pâté out of mussels that even the seagulls avoided. On occasion my creations turn out not half bad. Sometimes I placed a new dish in front of Frankie and she sniffed, nibbled, and said, "You've got to write this down."

This was the summer I started writing down recipes. When I concocted a fish stew or a bean salad that we agreed was good enough to serve to dinner guests, I'd go to my computer and write down the recipe while Frankie did the dishes. I hated doing dishes. Washing and drying dishes, I learned early in life, was a task adults dreamed up to torture little boys. My boyhood interest in cooking was motivated in no small measure by a desire to avoid dirty-dishes duty. When I cooked, I was exempt from dishes, and I insisted on this exemption for life.

Since the recipes took only a couple of minutes to write down, I'd linger at the computer until Frankie finished. To fill the time, I wrote down the source of the ingredients for the recipes. I wrote about foraging in the woods for mushrooms and foraging in the village for groceries. My writing began to take the form of a journal. I put down the events of the day leading up to the meal and even my thoughts during the day. I wrote about what we talked about on walks. When we told stories about events from the past, I put those in too. I wrote down growing-up stories, cub-reporting stories, young-writer stories, war stories.

Quite early in this summer of recipe journalism, some very unusual things began to happen. As I included them in my journal, I thought that I might have the makings of a book. The book would be about a summer at Frankie's place. To write it, I realized, I would have to answer a question: What was so special about Frankie's place?

The question can be answered many ways. One answer has to do with location. Frankie's place is on the biggest island on the Maine coast. It is a beautiful island with an interesting history. I'd read several books about Mount Desert Island, Acadia National Park, and the Maine coast, but I didn't know enough. To supply this answer I set to work reading everything I could find about Mount Desert, from the history of its geology to the history of its inhabitants. Among those inhabitants were some of Frankie's ancestors, and they lured me deeper into the library stacks and through books that took me back to the Massachusetts Bay Colony and colonial Salem. All this became part of the story.

Another answer has to do with Frankie. Frankie's place couldn't be special to me without her. The cozy house, the woods and water, the lovely views, and the extraordinary island were part of a stage on which our relationship grew, and I knew that the story of that relationship would have to be part of my story as well.

Frankie's place was special to me for another obvious reason, but one I tried not to think about. Then one bizarre summer day I had no choice.

The day was August 23, 1991. It began at a small cemetery in the forest near Northeast Harbor where relatives and friends had gathered to bury the ashes of Frankie's mother. The morning, eight days after her death, was sunny, the wind still in the wake of a big storm that had battered its way up the coast and moved out to sea. The mourners, men in coats, ties, and white shirts, women in dark dresses, and children in shined shoes, gathered in clumps at the gravesite. The pastor said prayers. The mourners said their good-byes. One by one they turned spadefuls of dirt over a small tin box containing the ashes. Back at Frankie's place that evening, the phone rang. It was my uncle in Michigan. He said my father, my *real* father, was trying to find me. My uncle gave me a phone number. I called it as Frankie hovered at my shoulder.

"Hello," said the voice of a man I didn't know, a man who had disappeared from my life when I was two years old.

Discovering my father that night brought back painful memories. The life I told people I had lived was a kind of whirlwind of luck and adventure: growing up with relatives; then a stepfather on a farm; escaping to college and into journalism; travels to the far corners of the world as a foreign correspondent. It was exciting, but it wasn't the whole story. Something was missing: a home. I was a wanderer living in a suitcase.

Frankie's place let me unpack my socks, put them in the dresser, and feel at home.

One

The first thing we did that summer was jump into the sea naked. We tore off our travel clothes, grabbed a couple of old beach towels, and padded off the porch on tender feet.

We followed a pine-needle path that led through ferns and bayberry bushes, ouching our way over twigs and roots and then past a dwarf juniper to a lichen-encrusted granite ledge above Somes Sound. The path switched back over a series of smooth, descending ledges and down a rounded ridge to massive rocks matted with seaweed, encrusted with tiny white barnacles, and dotted with periwinkles. The tide was receding and the rocks and seaweed were wet and slippery.

At the water's edge we moved quickly. This wasn't a time for contemplation. The less brainwork the better. It was important not to think about the incoming tides that pushed enormous volumes of seawater up the sound from the open ocean. This was water that had found its way from the Arctic, branching off the Labrador Current and curling around Nova Scotia to the Maine coast.

The idea was to jump before ten thousand anticipatory nerve endings began a chorus of, "Don't be a Fool!" Keeping toes from making contact with the water was mandatory lest they send an urgent loony-alert message to the brain. Headfirst was best. The question was who would jump first. We giggled. We grimaced. Frankie feigned a leap. I took the bait and jumped.

It is difficult to describe in any quiet way the sensation of a pampered urban body, humming along metabolically at 98.6 degrees Fahrenheit, being swallowed up by an unruly monster of nature approximately forty degrees colder. But I felt two involuntary urges. One was to scream. The other was to get the hell out of there!

Doing either one, however, was extremely bad form. As the initial plunger, I was required by tradition to come to the surface nonchalantly and exhibit no signs of urgency. I couldn't lunge for shore. I had to pretend I had just jumped into the Caribbean. Frankie laughed knowingly, uttered an obligatory, "No way!" And jumped.

Now, an unspoken sense of solidarity came into play as we cheered each other and scrambled back onto the rocks, nerve endings in a welcome work stoppage.

"Not bad," I said.

"Nonsense, it's *never* been so cold," she said. "Brrrr!"

As we stood on the rocks, like a couple of walking goose bumps, wet and salty, I felt a warm glow inside. I felt the sun's warmth outside. I jumped again. Frankie followed. The water felt warmer this time. But it didn't feel that way for long, so we scrambled out. By this time millions of brain cells were on red alert, demanding an immediate halt to the proceedings. We wrapped ourselves in towels and padded up the rocks to the porch.

Thus the summer officially began.

It was a Saturday, the second day of July, and we spent much of it unpacking and settling in for a long stay. We planned a summer that would extend deep into autumn, beyond Labor Day when most summer people departed. We had brought enough work to keep us busy until the middle of October.

We emptied bags of groceries, filling the refrigerator and kitchen shelves. We introduced ourselves to an occupation force of tiny black ants busily liberating brown sugar we mistakenly thought we had sealed in a porcelain box the summer before. We trooped from room to room, each with its faint whiff of mildew and moth-balls, opening windows to pine-scented air. We unpacked boxes of books and files brought up for the summer's work. We de-ployed our work machinery—Frankie's typewriter, my laptop, printer, fax, and answering machine. Soon it felt as though we had been away for a long weekend instead of eight months. Once operational, we decided that there was no sense going to work prematurely. We'd go for an afternoon stroll.

The neighborhood around Frankie's place is a peninsula of eighty acres that pokes out into Somes Sound in a northerly direction toward the top of the fjord. In the late nineteenth cen-tury, the peninsula was part of a huge granite-quarrying opera-tion. To this day, slabs of its warm pink granite adorn buildings up and down the East Coast. It was an outdoor factory back then, and much of it couldn't have been pretty. But the quarry-ing gradually died out, and the forest slowly reclaimed the land. Frankie's place was halfway down a lane from the main road. The lane wound for a mile around granite and trees to the tip of the peninsula.

Frankie's place was really the FitzGerald family place, a hallowed plot of three acres that Frankie's father bought in 1947. When his children were growing up, Desmond FitzGerald brought them out from town to have picnics on the rocks by the sea. In 1972, six years after their father had died, the FitzGerald children, now young adults—Des, Joan, and Frankie—built a small house on the property. It was the first dwelling on the peninsula since the quarrying days. And it was a true camp, in the local sense of the word, being way out of town, deep in the woods, and not win-terized. Except for occasional picnickers and clam diggers, the FitzGeralds had the peninsula pretty much to themselves. In 1975 another cottage went in up the lane, closer to the main road. But it was tucked into the woods by the shore, virtually invisible. Two more houses went up in the late 1980s, but there was plenty of distance and forest between neighbors. The rest of the peninsula remained dense with woods and unmolested, with plenty of room to prowl.

We strolled north along the lane toward the end of the point, stopping by a couple of places where chanterelles had grown in years past. Chanterelles are treasures among the wild mushrooms of Mount Desert. We made a habit of keeping close track of chanterelle locations, so that when their chalky-orange bodies pushed out of the ground we would not miss them.

We wandered deep into the forest, where the bark on giant tree trunks was encrusted with blue-green lichens. Exposed roots were matted in moss. The afternoon sunlight pierced holes in the evergreen canopy in rich golden shafts of angled beams that hit the forest's pine-needle floor like spotlights. The gray carcasses of decaying trees, clumps of ferns, mats of moss, and red-capped russula mushrooms made the woods look like a primeval place where humans were strangers. Walking around wind-toppled trees and branches, we eventually came out on a granite bluff overlooking the sound a hundred yards north of the house. A startled cormorant flapped and splashed, taking off horizontally a few inches above the water. We made our way south along the granite shoreline back to the house.

Along the way, I noticed that the tide was low and pointed to the mats of seaweed and colonies of mussels crowded together just above and below the waterline. It was a perfect time to gather mussels for our first meal of the summer. I grabbed a pail and we headed down to the rocks, where these beautiful black-shelled bivalves clung to crevasses under the seaweed, sticking to one another and to the rocks with their natural Velcro.

The meaty body of a steamed blue mussel (*Mytilus edulis*) is almost too erotic for innocent eyes. Indeed, some history books reported religious objections by early Christians to consuming or having anything to do with these sexy bivalves. For a long time, they were thought of locally as trash-shellfish, no doubt because their shells clustered so ubiquitously on the lower tidal regions in these waters that they were available to anyone willing to bend a back to scoop them up. Julia Child called them "poor man's oysters." I became a devotee when I had my first heaping platter of *moules à la marinière* at a French restaurant in Bangkok in 1970. I became a devoted mussel gatherer as soon as I spied them clinging to the rocks in front of Frankie's place.

Timing is essential to the gathering process because the tides rise and fall every twelve hours and the mussels are easily accessible only when the tide is low. Along this part of the Maine coast, the sea rises and falls fourteen and a half feet during the twice-a-month spring tides, when the moon and sun are aligned and exert their peak gravitational pull on the earth. At other times, the tidal change is less. But even during weakest tides, called neap tides, which also occur twice a month when the sun and moon are at right angles to the earth, the sea rises and falls eight and a half feet.

I preferred to gather mussels when a low tide occurred in the middle of a cool sunny day, when mosquitoes and deerflies were less likely to attack. I made my way, pail in hand, down the rocks to the water's edge. There I usually stripped and jumped in. People have suggested that this is a strange way to approach mussels. One friend even wondered aloud whether I was trying to avoid "stressing" them the way a frontal land assault might. Since I couldn't confirm having seen a nervous mussel, let alone a stressed one, I said I didn't know.

In any case, it took less than fifteen minutes to fill the pail. I carried the mussels up the rocks to the porch and rinsed them with fresh water. We cleaned them and threw out a few mudders. (Mudders are closed shells filled with mud.) Using a clam knife, I scraped off the barnacles and pulled off their beards, then rinsed and rinsed again.

I believe that the simpler mussels are prepared, the better they are. I usually steam them or make stew. The recipe below evolved from the traditional French version because I found that mussels taken straight from the sea to the pot contain much more seawater than mussels from the fish market. That water, expelled when the mussels open, dilutes the broth and makes it salty. I wanted to reduce the liquid content of the broth in order to concentrate its flavor.

MOULES MARINIÈRE SOMES SOUND

In a small pot or skillet, melt 8 tablespoons of butter, add half a cup of olive oil, a cup of chopped green onions, 8 cloves of mashed garlic (house rule: never skimp on garlic), 2 cups of dry white wine, and a few sprigs of thyme.

Chop about 2 cups of parsley and/or cilantro and several sprigs of tarragon. (Try different combinations of fresh herbs, with more or less tarragon, basil, chervil, or oregano.)

In a big, covered lobster pot, bring a quart of water and/or dry white wine (enough to make about two inches of liquid in the bottom of the pot) to a vigorous boil and add about 90 cleaned mussels. (Leftovers are great in a tarragon vinaigrette.) Steam this mixture, pot tightly covered, for about 5 minutes, or until mussels open, shaking the pot once for even steaming. Drain out most of the liquid.

Pour the melted butter/oil/wine liquid combination over the mussels, toss in the chopped herbs, stir with a big spoon, and serve immediately in bowls with crisp, hot French bread to sop up the juice.

Before we sat down, I brought up some split logs from under the house and built a fire. Frankie uncorked a bottle of chardonnay and lit candles. As we feasted on our *moules,* the setting sun put on a show of pinks and blues, then turned the horizon a deep red. By nine o'clock we had finished off a salad, cheese, and the last of the wine. We rose and stood before glowing birch embers in the fireplace, formally toasted our arrival, and fell into a gleeful embrace. We were asleep within the hour.

The next morning I rolled over in the grand tradition of Sunday sloth, but the roar of a lobster boat, making its way from trap to trap on the water wouldn't let me sleep. Awake, I anticipated the opening day of the FitzGerald Survival School. I rose quickly.

Frankie stirred but showed few signs of life. I pulled drawstrings on the shades, rolling them up and letting the light pour in. The morning was sunny. A thin haze hung over the Sound.

Soon we were on the porch in T-shirts, shorts, and running shoes for a summer reveille regimen that almost never varied. We began bending, stretching, and flexing muscles that hadn't bent or stretched much in the last hectic weeks before we decamped from Manhattan. The idea was to feel out our bodies, testing how far they had retrogressed into lumpen disgrace, and then begin a glorious and virtuous comeback. I envisioned a sinewy September torso, with rock-hard abdominals. Next, we jogged half a mile up to the main road, and back, working up a sweat. Then came the ocean.

We jumped into Somes Sound almost every morning, rain or shine, wind or fog, from July through Columbus Day and beyond, morning after morning, and most afternoons, too, summer after summer, with a regularity that went beyond habit to the edge of addiction. I say "almost" because every now and then we would be awakened by an icy, pelting rain, and Frankie would refuse to budge. But most of the time, it was the morning dip that kick-started the day. Visitors and houseguests who ventured a finger or toe into the water thought we'd gone mad. We told them that Frankie's grandparents and uncles and aunts and cousins had been "swimming" in these waters for generations. And lots of summer people did the very same thing daily, in the name of character building, or cranial cobweb clearing. I don't know why we did it, other than that we had always done it.

The reward for this rigor was a clear head and a wonderful breakfast. Orange juice, bowls of fresh Maine strawberries and yogurt, toast made with sourdough bread, local blueberry jam, and coffee.

Maine is berry heaven. By the time we arrived each July, the fresh-picked local strawberries were being sold at roadside farm stands and by men out of the backs of their pickups. Then sometime in mid-July, strawberries disappeared, usually before I remembered to stock up on a few extra quarts to freeze for autumn desserts. In mid- to late July came raspberries. Then sometime in August, Maine's blueberry crop came rolling in. After that, the blackberries on bushes in back of the house ripened, yielding a quart or two of the sweet, seedy orbs.

On warm, sunny mornings, we'd eat on the porch table under a sun umbrella and read the morning papers, the *New York Times* and the *Wall Street Journal*. The fact that they weren't that particular morning's papers didn't bother us in the least. They didn't arrive in town each day until around noon, and we didn't go get them until late afternoon. Since we didn't feel like reading morning papers in the evening, we simply let them sit until the next morning and pretended they were hot off the presses. Since we didn't watch TV or listen to the radio, whatever was in the papers was still news to us whenever we got around to reading it— sometimes two or three days later. Unless it was big news. In that case, somebody usually mentioned it in town or on the phone. We got our local news from the *Bar Harbor Times* and the *Ellsworth American,* which came out on Thursdays.

Gradually, after second cups of coffee, we retreated to our desks. We worked through the core of each day, seven days a week, from about ten o'clock in the morning to three-thirty or four in the afternoon.

Living with a writer isn't easy. Writers go off into their own worlds and stay there for hours and hours. They must sop up enormous amounts of information, analyze it, and synthesize it in a new way. They exist during their writing hours in the world of their subject, tuning back in to the world that surrounds them and the people in it when necessary.

Living with a journalist isn't easy either. We're always dashing off to the scene of the next story. We're gregarious because it's a good work habit. We're constantly listening and observing the world around us. We talk on the phone a lot, asking the same questions of many different people, skimming off information, scribbling into notebooks, and scrambling to write a coherent, understandable, and error-free account of what we have learned.

Sometimes we have only a few hours or minutes to do all this before a looming deadline. Journalists exist in this final frenzy oblivious to anything but the story at hand.

I was on vacation in July, but I brought some *Wall Street Journal* files so I could continue working. I made lots of phone calls, took lots of notes. What made our coexistence possible was that Frankie's place was perfectly laid out for a writer and a journalist to work at the same time. Our work places were in bedrooms at opposite ends of the house. Frankie worked in the bedroom off the kitchen. I worked in a bedroom beyond the fireplace. We could close our bedroom doors and shut each other out.

I worked because Frankie worked. With unfailing discipline, she typed day after day at the other end of the house. To play while she was working was a recipe for guilt, or self-loathing. I wouldn't go so far as to say that I was strapped to my desk. If the phone rang at the right time, I could be talked into almost anything. My fishing rod stood ready. The post office and the hardware store beckoned. Sometimes an irresistible need popped into my head and wouldn't go away until it was satisfied. When that happened, I abandoned Frankie in a flash. I popped into town for some finishing nails, envelopes, eggs, or socks. I'd go mail a letter. But most of the time I stayed home and worked, or engaged in some facsimile of work.

Without looming deadlines I could thumb through a book in the guise of doing "research." And thumb and thumb. Or I could dive into another book on the shelf or table that caught my eye, temporarily abandoning the research-thumbing. Hours could pass.

Simply looking up a word could be an adventure because the dictionary in the house was a 2,798-page behemoth called *The New Century Dictionary of the English Language*. It was a 1927 edition published in two thick volumes (Volume One: A–pocket veto; Volume Two: pockmark–zymurgy) and contained all sorts of wonderful words and quaint definitions that had slipped from modern usage. For example: while "escutcheon" (a shield or shield-shaped emblem bearing a coat of arms) populates most modern dictionaries, the *New Century* gave me "inescutcheon":

"a small escutcheon borne as a charge upon a larger escutcheon."
It had an illustration of one, too. On page 1,630 alone, I came
upon "scolopendrid" (any of the myriapod family, including many
large and poisonous centipedes); "scombroid" (pertaining to the
mackerel family); "scololamine" (a depressant in crystalline alka-
loid form obtained from the rhizome of a European plant, *Scopo-
lia,* which produces a "twilight sleep" and sometimes is used to
extract confession from criminals); and "scorbutic" (pertaining
to scurvy). I had sat through entire lectures in college that im-
parted less information.

The *New Century* had more to say about lobsters than most
dictionaries: "Any of various large, edible, marine, stalk-eyed
decapod crustaceans of the suborder Macrura and esp. of the genus
Homarus, having two enormous claws and a long abdomen or so-
called tail; any of various similar crustaceans, as certain crawfishes;
also, a British soldier (colloq.: orig. in allusion to the armor of
cuirassiers, later, as also in 'boiled lobster,' to the characteristic
red coat); also, a gullible, foolish, or stupid person (slang)."

When book learning got to be too much of a strain, I turned
to another activity that fit in to my somewhat loose definition of
work: nature studies. When you sit in a room facing windows
overlooking a forest, nature studies are all but unavoidable. From
my windows, I saw far less water through the forest than Frankie
did from hers. But I saw far more of the antics of the birds and
squirrels in the nearby trees. Naturally, these creatures forced me
into deep empirical research into their habits, sometimes requiring binoculars and often prompting analytical thoughts that consumed great bites of the day.

By early afternoon the sun shot beams of light down through the
window and onto my desk. This was no problem in summers past
when I had pecked away on an Olivetti Lettera 32—my old foreign-
correspondent's portable typewriter, a workhorse that had served
me faithfully through wars and coups and natural disasters across
Asia. Now, however, I was high tech and typing on a Toshiba laptop
computer. This required me to unroll the reed window shade to

block the sunlight in order to see a rather dim computer screen. Being high tech, however, had its advantages in the procrastination department. It was so easy for me to delete words, revise sentences, and move paragraphs around that I often found myself crafting and recrafting the first few paragraphs of a story again and again and, thus, leaving the rest of my story unwritten. This was organizational softheadedness that Frankie managed to avoid, without knowing it, in eschewing the computer. She had to know pretty well what she wanted to say before she started typing, or else she faced the penalty of having to retype a whole page.

From Frankie's room came sustained bursts of thunder, like the muffled sound of popcorn exploding in a kettle in the distance. The eruption of the old Remington into action constantly reminded me that the search for deeper meaning in, say, a chipmunk's foraging patterns had its limits. I'd shut my door and go back to my laptop.

To leave Frankie's place in the afternoon was to venture out beyond the woods and into the larger world that was Mount Desert Island. At one hundred and eight square miles, it is the largest island on the coast of Maine, and the third largest island in the continental United States, behind Long Island, in New York, and Martha's Vineyard, in Massachusetts. It is an island of spectacular beauty, with mountains of pink granite rising dramatically out of the ocean.

This beauty and the riches of the sea around it attracted summer colonies going back to the Passamaquoddy Indians, who had clam feasts by the shore for centuries. European explorers found the place in the sixteenth and seventeenth centuries, and settlers moved in to fish, farm, lumber, and mine. The settlers and their descendants had the island pretty much to themselves until the nineteenth century, when landscape painters discovered its beauty and their works attracted summer rusticators. Soon, some of the wealthiest and most influential families in America were spending their summers on Mount Desert Island, among them the Astors, Carnegies, Fords, Morgans, Rockefellers, and Vanderbilts. Before the turn of the twentieth century, the island was one of society's most fashionable resorts. Its popularity almost destroyed it.

The task of saving Mount Desert from real estate speculators and developers, miners and lumber exploiters was untaken by a small group of summer residents led by Charles W. Eliot, the president of Harvard College, and George B. Dorr, his friend from Boston. They set out to protect parts of the island by creating a public park. John D. Rockefeller Jr. quietly bought up large tracts of land, much of which he later donated. The park grew into a national monument and then into Acadia National Park.

Among the early rusticators to arrive on Mount Desert were Frankie's ancestors on her mother's side, the Parkman clan from Boston, and, much later, the Boston Peabodys. They moved into the village of Northeast Harbor, a quiet little settlement founded by educators and clergy on the northeast side of the entrance to Somes Sound. In the years just before World War II, Frankie's father, Desmond FitzGerald, a New Yorker, came to Mount Desert and stayed with friends. One summer, he met Marietta Peabody; the result was marriage, and Frankie.

By the late twentieth century, all sorts of Parkmans and Peabodys, at least two and sometimes three generations of them, called Mount Desert home for parts of each summer. As did their friends, and their friends' friends. Which is to say that if we ventured up the lane from Frankie's place and on to the main road, it didn't matter if we turned left or right, the chances were excellent that we'd run into people we knew.

We ventured out daily, usually around four o'clock, for provisions and exercise. We foraged in nearby villages. To the south was Northeast Harbor, our newspapers, groceries, tennis courts, and some of our favorite walking trails. To the north was Somesville.

On the afternoon of our first full day on Frankie's place, we went to pick up our boat and seedlings for our summer "crops." This required a trip to the other side of Somes Sound, beyond Somesville and Southwest Harbor to a village called Manset. We stopped first at a greenhouse on Seawall Road called the Islandscaping Garden Center. It had herb seedlings and we loaded up the car with plastic trays of them, along with a couple of bags of potting soil.

Next we drove over to the Manset Town Dock to pick up our boat, a seventeen-foot Boston Whaler that we stored over winters at the Manset Boat House. I hitched a dinghy ride out to a buoy that Charley Bolger, the boathouse manager, had tied her to that morning and boarded. I lowered the engine, gave the rubber bulb on the fuel line a few squeezes, and turned the starter key. The engine gargled to life and settled into a purr. I signaled to Frankie on the dock and cast off. While Frankie drove the car home, I maneuvered the Whaler past the Southwest Harbor Coast Guard station and headed north up the Sound's main channel. I pushed the throttle forward; the engine's purr became a buzz and before long I was whizzing along at twenty knots, then twenty-five, dodging lobster buoys. By the time Frankie arrived, I had moored the boat and was rowing the dinghy back to a dock not far from Frankie's place.

The drive home was short, but not without excitement. As we bumped down the lane, we were ambushed. Something flashed toward us from the first cottage we passed. It was a muscular white terrier with brown spots. It leaped into the lane directly in front of us, growling and barking. There it stopped. I hit the brakes. Bentley was back for another summer of chasing cars. Bentley's technique was unique. Once he jumped out in front of the car, he stopped and just stood there, turning and looking at the driver. Stopping the car was his goal. Not running over him was mine. Bentley counted on me hitting the brakes. That meant I had lost the game and Bentley had won. Once that happened, he stood his ground, looking at the stopped car, head high—not much over a foot high, mind you—and casually walked to the side. "Swaggered" would be a better word. Bentley counted on drivers' instincts, then ridiculed them.

There was still plenty of daylight for the next task: putting in our crops.

I grew up on a farm that required milking cows, feeding pigs, shoveling manure, weeding vegetables, baling hay, and endless other chores that kept us going from before sunrise to beyond sunset. I let my agricultural skills lapse as soon as possible. Indeed, one of higher education's greatest virtues in my mind was that it might forever foreclose the possibility of returning to farm life in central Michigan, where dairy cows might again rule my life. Cows had to be milked twice a day. We did it by hand, which I had considered to be a form of slavery. We could not get away from the cows for more than twelve hours at a time, unless we hired someone else to milk them. Hired hands were expensive. Something very important would have to come up to justify hiring one, and in our family the only event important enough was deer season.

Many years later, I delighted in hearing people from the city talk about how "wonderful" it would be to get a little place in the country, grow vegetables, and keep some animals, maybe even a cow or a pig and a few chickens. They didn't have a clue, I thought. Actually, I didn't have a clue. I didn't know that people from the city with the means to buy a place in the country became farmers in the same way they became parents. They hired nannies. Child nannies. Animal nannies. Plant nannies. It never occurred to me that their idea of farming was supervising the hired help. This wasn't farming. This was recreation. To me, "farming" and "recreation" didn't belong in the same sentence. To me, the notion of farming as recreation had all the appeal that recreational camping had for ex-Vietnam grunts. "You gather some firewood, honey, while I set out the claymores."

It took more than a quarter century to turn me back into a farmer—a porch farmer. In the early years at Frankie's place, I experimented with various vegetable and herb seeds planted in tubs on the porch. But there simply wasn't enough time for seeds planted in July to sprout and grow to maturity before the short Maine summer was over. The head-start programs of the greenhouses made sense to me. So gradually I adopted seedlings.

As the sun began to redden and sink across the sound, I unloaded the seedlings and planted them in wooden barrels and trays arranged around the edges of the porch. In the center of the porch sat a cedar dining table, director's chairs, and a green and yellow Tusker Beer umbrella from Vanuatu.

I put sorrel seedlings into one wooden half-barrel, planted garlic chives, oregano, and basil into another, and installed peppermint, thyme, rosemary, sage, and tarragon into a third. Chives and thyme lived year-round in two wooden boxes, more or less reviving each spring before we arrived, depending on rainfall. Sometimes we found them dried out and scraggly. But it didn't take more than watering, fertilizing, and cutting to bring them back to health. The chives grew thicker with each trim and the thyme formed a carpet over the box and cascaded over its side like a little green waterfall. Finally, I put in two kinds of lettuce seedlings.

One summer early on in my porch-farming career I picked up a large bag of dried cow manure from the greenhouse and mixed generous portions of it into the potting soil in my wooden boxes and tubs before putting in my seedlings. Feeling virtuously organic, I gave this mixture its first good soaking with the hose. All went well until I began to notice an amber liquid from the planters dripping onto the porch, and along with it a smell I hadn't smelled in such pungency for decades. As the sun went to work on the porch, the full force of this smell—akin to a barnyard spreader freshly loaded with steaming cow manure—began to waft its way over the porch, through the open windows, and into the house. The porch reeked for days. I had nightmares about being back in the Michigan manure pile. With each watering, the amber run-off lightened. The smell finally leached away, but only after weeks of hosing down the porch and a couple of major downpours. Even so, we whiffed lingering residues all summer. After that I embraced Miracle-Gro.

The day after we got the boat and put in the crops was a national holiday for everyone, it seemed, but us. We spent the Fourth of July working, not out of any disrespect for Independence Day or a lack of patriotism. We did it because Frankie thought that it was important early each summer to establish good work habits lest we too easily succumb to what most other summer people came here in July and August to do: play.

"But this is the Fourth of July!" I objected before adjourning to my laptop, thinking, but certainly not admitting aloud, that she was right. Writers have to write.

As the hours passed I realized that we were working through a very beautiful day. I found myself looking at my watch nearly as much as my computer, and at exactly three-thirty I impulsively shouted, "Frances, let's go!"

We piled into the car and drove to Northeast Harbor. We parked on Main Street, a single block of old wooden storefronts, several occupied by art galleries and boutiques. Other stores on the street sold stuff people needed in their daily lives, and we made our way to each of them. There was McGrath's, a stationery and book store that also sold penny candy, where we got our newspapers. There was the Pine Tree Market, which in the summer supplemented all its grocery-store essentials with lots of fresh seafood, fancy cuts of meat, and expensive cheeses. There was Provisions, a tiny designer meat-pasta-lettuce-pâté place that could be counted on to have exotic meats, cheeses, herbs, and vegetables. There was Brown's Hardware, for lightbulbs and tools and toasters and fishing lures and nuts and bolts. There was the Holmes Store, for pants and socks and boat shoes and an annual tide chart.

Then there was Stanley's Fish Market. We stopped in not only to buy the evening's dinner but also to pay our respects to Mr. Stanley. He was as venerable a fishmonger as had ever inhabited the Maine coast and as essential a Maine character as a Down East village could have. He had been Frankie's grandmother's best friend in the village. A decorated veteran of infantry combat in the Pacific during World War II, Mr. Stanley was proud of his military service and he always led Mount Desert's Memorial Day Parade.

Stanley's Fish Market was distinct from the boutiques and galleries that tarted up the village in the summer. It didn't smell like aromatic soaps or candles. It smelled like fish, and you didn't have to go inside to get a strong whiff. Mr. Stanley wasn't much for "improvements," either. So when something new was added, it got noticed. Frankie admired the new screen door to his back room.

"Ahyup," he said. "Sa new one. You noticed it, did ya?" He sat at a cluttered old desk in the front of the store. It was piled high with old bills and other paperwork. On top was a radio on which he listened to his beloved Red Sox.

We picked up some crabmeat, paid Mr. Stanley, and jumped back in the car. Our town foray had taken less than half an hour, and we were ready for a walk.

"So, which one?" I asked.

"Let's do Norumbega," Frankie replied.

No one who spent summers on Mount Desert referred to tramping up and down the trails of Acadia National Park as "hiking." It was called "walking," and we went on walks of an hour or two in the late afternoon almost every day. There are fifty-seven miles of carriage roads in and around Acadia National Park and more than one hundred and twenty-five miles of marked walking trails requiring varying degrees of exertion and time. The far trails took twenty or thirty minutes to get to by car. The near ones were minutes away.

The trails were so abundant and varied that we could pick one to fit the weather, our mood, our guests, or all three. There were walks for sunny days that had great scenery, such as up and over Pemetic Mountain. There were walks for when it was hot, along shady, deep-forest trails and beside rippling brooks. There were walks, such as the one through fern glades on the back side of Beech Mountain, that were wonderful in pea-soup fog. Cedar Swamp Mountain had a variety of views and terrain, a good all-around walk for houseguests. For the FitzGerald Survival School, there were tough climbs, such as the west face of Cadillac Mountain or stretches of Dorr Mountain. Eliot Mountain was a paradise for wild mushrooms, especially after a warm, soaking rain. From the bald tops of the Bubbles, you could see half a dozen species of hawks plunge down the mountainside into the deep blue ice age gorge that is Jordan Pond.

Norumbega Mountain is on the edge of Northeast Harbor, near the golf course, and if we went up it from the golf course parking lot, up the west side, and came down the south slope to Lower Hadlock Pond, the walk took an hour and a half. We knew from experience that our chances of encountering other walkers were slim. It was amazing how few visitors to Acadia Park actually walked. Many summer residents of the island walked almost every day. Mountain bikers seemed to be discovering the carriage roads in increasing numbers. But Norumbega had no carriage roads, so we figured we'd have it more or less to ourselves.

Often we walked in silence, listening for birds and watching for squirrels and chipmunks and the odd porcupine and deer. Or thinking. Sometimes we talked about work in progress: Frankie's fourth chapter was almost done. Sometimes writing problems came up: I'd rewritten my third paragraph three dozen times and it still didn't work. About thirty minutes up Norumbega, we reached a plateau that led to its summit. We made our way over pine-needle carpets, up over massive faces of granite, along easy switchbacks and on to a shelf of solid rock. Toward the top we found ourselves in a very Japanese kind of landscape, among red pines stunted and gnarled into the shapes of man-sized bonzai trees and barren granite dotted here and there with solitary boulders.

We scrambled toward the summit, making our way through a tiny gorge and out onto bald granite where a signpost marked the summit elevation at eight hundred and fifty-two feet. It wasn't very high as mountains go, but it offered views in every direction. To the south, we could see small islands and the open sea. To the west was Acadia Mountain and, beyond it, Blue Hill on the mainland. To the north, a blanket of green forest stretched as far as we could see. We sat down on the granite and let the views soak in. After a while, we watched low clouds begin to envelop Sargent Mountain, to the east. The clouds were headed our way fast, but they seemed to be too low to be clouds and too high to be fog.

"Lost fog," I said.

The fog didn't stay lost for long. Suddenly we were enveloped in it, too. Our views vanished. It was nature's way of telling us who was in charge of the scenery. We felt closed into this cool, cottony haze, but in a very romantic sort of way—romantic enough to allow for some spirited canoodling, which was warming.

"What are you thinking?" she asked.

"About the first time we met," I said. "I thought it would be the last."

I was introduced to Frances FitzGerald in New York in 1982 at a party for a friend who was an editor at *Time* magazine and had gotten a promotion. It was one of those drop-by-after-work cocktail parties. I knew of Frankie, as her friends called her, as a journalist who had been to Vietnam and had written a famous book in 1972 about the war, called *Fire in the Lake.* I also knew she wrote for *The New Yorker.* She didn't know of me at all. If she had seen my byline on stories in *The New York Times,* she didn't remember it. She didn't read bylines, she said.

The first thought that popped into my head when I saw her was "Wow!" She was blond, tall, beautiful, smart, famous, and scary. She was glamorous, and glamour flummoxed me. Fame and power didn't faze me. As a newspaperman, I accosted prime ministers and generals fearlessly. I pestered them with impolite questions. I could be nice, demanding, insistent, or whatever it took to get the pen in my left hand writing down notes in the pad in my right hand. Without pen and notebook I felt like a shy boy, awkward in small talk. It was painful thinking about small talk with someone as attractive as Frankie. She had a kind of stage presence that sent me scurrying for the comfort of the back row of a darkened theater. Our conversation began:

"Hello, nice to meet you."

And ended:

"Good luck on your next book."

"Thanks."

"Thanks."

I didn't see her again for weeks. Then, our friends Kevin and Gail invited me to a small dinner party at their apartment. Frankie was there. We talked briefly but I don't remember the conversation. I was preoccupied with preparations for a long reporting trip to the Pacific. I was away for six weeks.

In the lost fog atop Norumbega, as I stood squeezing Frankie for warmth, I said, "What do you remember about the first time we met?"

"I thought you were kind of cute," she said.

Cute? This was not the word I was looking for. "Cute" wasn't a word that sprang to mind when I looked myself in the mirror. I was a professional newspaperman, a worldly foreign correspondent no less. I knew my way around. I had been through some scrapes. I could tell her a war story or two. What about handsome, sexy, and dashing? It was true that I was an inch or so shorter than she was. But cute?

The chill of the fog soon propelled us back down the mountain along a trail that led eastward, ending up at Lower Hadlock Pond. From there it was a short walk to the parking lot and a quick drive back to Frankie's place, where I set to work on turning the crabmeat we'd gotten from Mr. Stanley into crab cakes while Frankie fed the fireplace.

Local crabmeat is fresh, abundant, and useful in a variety of dishes, the most common of them being a homemade dip for crackers or chips with drinks before dinner. I loved to experiment with crab cakes, using a recipe I'd torn out of a magazine for general guidance, then winging it with fresh herbs and other seasonings. Fresh crabmeat is sold in half-pound or one-pound plastic containers, and I found that half a pound was quite enough for two people. Depending on the amount of crushed crackers I used for filler, I could make four cakes the size of small doughnuts or two cakes the size of cupcakes. I preferred the latter because while cooking they quickly form a crisp brown crust while staying moist and steamy inside.

CRAB CAKES, BASMATI RICE, AND FRESH PEAS WITH MINT

Crack 1 egg into a large bowl. Add 1 tablespoon of mayonnaise, 1½ tablespoons of mustard, 1 tablespoon of Worcestershire sauce, ½ teaspoon of freshly ground pepper, and 1 teaspoon of Old Bay seasoning. Stir. Add ¼ cup of chopped herbs/greens (cilantro, dill, basil, green pepper, green onions in any combination) and stir some more. Then blend in 12 small saltine crackers crushed by hand (not powdered). Finally, add ½ pound of fresh crabmeat, stirring in gently to avoid breaking up its chunks.

Cover a broiler pan with aluminum foil and paint it with olive oil. Using a shallow cup, mold the cakes, one at a time, turning the cup over and plopping them out into your hand or directly onto the foiled broiler pan.

Set oven to broil. Adjust oven trays so that the crab cakes end up 4–6 inches below the broiler coil (if the stove is electric), perhaps a bit more if you broil with gas. When the oven is hot, slip crab cakes into broiler. They take 10 minutes or less to get nicely browned on top. Remove from the oven, squeeze half a lemon over them, and serve immediately.

We usually serve them with plain basmati rice. The first peas of the season are a good match too. (Shucking peas is about as agricultural as Frankie gets, but she shucks with great enthusiasm.) Half a cup per person is about right. Dump peas and a sprig of fresh mint into a cup of boiling water for five minutes or so. Al dente is what you want. We followed with a salad and warm crisp bread.

The next morning, we went through our paces briskly—swimming, showering, and eating breakfast—in order to be ready to welcome our first visitor of the summer.

Two

Every three or four years Herb Watson paid a visit to Frankie's place. He worked as a physical education teacher most of the year, but in the summer he barbered the woods in these parts, and Frankie's woods needed a little trim. We had phoned for an appointment early, knowing his schedule would fill up fast as summer residents arrived. We were lucky. He had some free time, and he arrived promptly with his chain saw and, more important, his judgment.

It had been a cold, rough winter, he told us. Windstorms had uprooted and toppled trees all over the island and he had been exceptionally busy all spring cutting them up and hauling them away. The winter had been so cold, he said, that Somes Sound froze over and the ice got so thick that people drove across it on their snowmobiles from Somesville a good five miles down to the narrows just north of Northeast Harbor. While he told us this, he eyed Frankie's trees.

From the porch, the kitchen, and the front bedroom, Frankie's place had a lovely view to the southwest, down and across the sound toward Acadia and St. Sauveur mountains. But two young cedars had grown up to block part of that view and some branches on a big red pine and two spruces had grown out partway across it. Herb agreed with Frankie that the trees needed to be cut back.

There was a very nice view to the northwest toward the entrance to Somesville harbor. But that sight line had become partially obscured by a thicket of cedars. No problem, Herb said. He would thin out the cedars.

Directly in front of the porch stood another clump of cedars. These trees provided some natural privacy. Boats cruising by out in front got only the most fleeting glimpses of the house and the doings of its occupants on the porch. The trees also obscured the view across the sound to the village of Hall Quarry, where lots of houses dotted a hillside. Was it possible, Frankie asked Herb, to do just enough thinning there so that we could see a little more of the water directly down in front without seeing more of Hall Quarry farther up on the horizon? He said he'd see what he could do.

Herb fired up his chain saw and went about his magic. An hour later, we reassembled on the front porch for an inspection. Frankie's views up and down the Somes Sound had been restored, and we could see much more water down in front. With the cedar gone, we now had a good view of a big pine tree with several dead branches near the water and a dead spruce beside it. Should they be removed? Herb didn't think so. He told us he was a minimalist pruner, favoring the natural look, so that his cuts and trims weren't visible to someone who didn't know what was there to begin with. Lots of summer residents wanted every last dead tree and branch removed, and he'd bite his tongue and do it if they insisted. But he wasn't in favor of it. The resulting look, he said, was too manicured, and that wasn't what the Maine woods was all about. Besides, birds needed perches and dead branches and trees made good perches.

We sang Herb's praises later when a bald eagle alighted on a dead branch of the pine and when we found the neighborhood osprey perched on the top of the dead spruce.

That afternoon, Frankie and I drove into Acadia Park to walk up Pemetic Mountain. We passed Jordan Pond House, parked in a pull-off, and started along the trail. Pemetic was a favorite walk for us. It required plenty of exertion in the early stages, up through the forest and a series of granite-ledge lookouts. Then it opened onto a long, bald granite top with panoramic views. Besides, Pemetic Mountain was special. Near its summit one summer I asked Frankie to marry me.

Ours was a love affair that almost didn't get off the ground. After our chance meeting at our friend's promotion party and our second encounter at Kevin and Gail's dinner, I didn't see Frankie again for weeks. My Pacific reporting trip went well, and as it drew to a close I promised myself to ask her out when I got home.

"It took forever," she said later. "I thought you'd forgotten about me."

Not that she let on. The next time we met, I invited her to my apartment—along with five other single women and five of my editors at the *Wall Street Journal*. I did a lot of diving in those days and took underwater slides. Some of these people had expressed an interest in seeing them, and I took them at their word. I invited them over to see fish pictures. Some of the women were so impressed that I never heard from them again. I feared that Frankie had been similarly put off. When I finally got up the courage to call her, she said she loved the fish. They reminded her of how much she loved to dive. I asked her out. She accepted. Our first date, a movie and dinner, made my spirits soar. She was charming. She was self-effacing, gentle, and so nice that my shyness melted away. As we continued dating, I could feel myself falling for her. I liked her a lot, but I was hesitant. The problem was that the more I got to know about Frankie's background, the scarier she seemed. Besides scuba diving, the only obvious thing we had in common was that we were both journalists. But saying that was like saying Renée Fleming and Dwight Yoakum are both singers. I wrote newspaper stories. She wrote nonfiction books and magazine articles. I was a water spider, skittering over the top of the events I reported. Frankie was a mermaid, plunging deep into the social and political currents she wrote about. We both "typed" for a living, and each of us knew what the other was going through constructing sentences and paragraphs. What was scary to me was that we came to our craft from different places, different worlds. Actually, what I thought was that we came from different planets. What I wondered was whether those planets revolved around the same sun.

I was born in Detroit and grew up on a farm in Michigan so unproductive that my surrogate father kept his factory job while my mother and I did the work. I called it our so-called farm, a sub-subsistence farm. I didn't know it at the time, but we were poor. I attended public schools and, with the aid of scholarships, went on to what started as an agricultural college, Michigan State University, one of 42,000 students. My class I called the Class of Bubba Smith because, as a star football player who went into the movies, he was its best-known member. At MSU, I discovered that I could earn money, which I sorely needed, writing articles for the school newspaper. From MSU, I went to a $96-a-week job taking dictation in the newsroom of the *Evening Star* in Washington.

My grandmother was the oldest of nine children born to immigrant parents from eastern Europe. Her father, Julian Jokajtys, was a German carpenter. He and her mother, Justina, were living as exiles in Prussia when he was conscripted into the Russian army. Sent to Finland, he went AWOL and fled to America in 1898. She followed him. At Ellis Island, immigration officers shortened his surname to Jokat. My grandmother, Emily Jokat, was born in Westfield, Massachusetts, in 1903. The Jokats moved to where jobs were, first to Detroit and then to Saginaw. They lost their first two houses to creditors and wound up on a subsistence farm near Hemlock, Michigan. On the farm next door lived a Polish immigrant named Anthony Filipiak. My grandmother married him and they had two children, Gertrude, my mother, and Elmer, my uncle. Granny divorced Filipiak, remarried, and had three more children. I knew nothing of my father and his ancestors other than his name: Watts. My mother had all but banished him from memory.

Frankie was born in Manhattan and grew up in New York City and in England and in Barbados, in big houses with lots of servants. She was chauffeured to private day schools in Oxford and New York. She and her horse went to an exclusive boarding school, Foxcroft, in Virginia, together. She was a brilliant student. She went on to Radcliffe College, graduating with honors.

She had formidable roots. The Parkmans and Peabodys on her mother's side were two of New England's oldest families, among the founders of the Massachusetts Bay Colony. Her great-grandfather Endicott Peabody founded Groton School. Her grandfather Malcolm Peabody was an Episcopal bishop in New York State. He and his wife, Mary Parkman, had five children, one girl and four boys—Frankie's mother and uncles. Frankie's mother, Mary (Marietta) Endicott Peabody, became a prominent and glamorous New Yorker, a delegate to the United Nations and socialite who knew all the important people in the city and had friends around the world.

Frankie's father, Desmond FitzGerald, was a descendant of Anglo-Irish aristocrats; his great-grandfather came to America in the nineteenth century. After Harvard Law School, Desmond became an attorney. During World War II he trained black troops in the South and then led irregular Chinese forces fighting the Japanese in Burma. After the war, he joined the Central Intelligence Agency and rose to become its deputy director for operations. He and Marietta divorced in 1947. Marietta then married Ronald Tree, an heir to the Marshall Field fortune. Their daughter, Penelope Tree, Frankie's half sister, became an internationally famous model. Frankie's father remarried and had two more children, Desmond and Joan.

Frankie's background and famous relatives were an awful lot for a shy Michigan farm kid to get his mind around. I had never met anyone with so much family baggage. Frankie helped by acting like a person without it. She never mentioned it. I asked her questions about her family, of course, but not about their fame and fortune. I told myself that if she thought such things were important to her she would tell me. She never did.

Likewise, she never flaunted her prodigious intellect. She exercised it, devouring books as though they were party canapés, and reading everything else she could lay her hands on. She could have easily made me feel stupid. But she never did, even when I was.

The Frankie I was getting to know was warm and friendly but she was stubborn in her habits and routines. She was fun to be around but she could be a stick-in-the-mud about change. I moved her furniture around once and she had a fit. Underneath her worldliness was a woman with needs and desires, and a child-like innocence about the realms of human experience that had escaped her. Things mechanical flummoxed her, and I took comfort in her terrible spelling. I took more comfort when I sensed she was interested in me. I did my best to play the role of dashing foreign correspondent.

Being a newspaperman had helped me overcome shyness. Being a foreign correspondent built self-confidence. I saw myself as a member of a unique fraternity that chased wars, coups, and other calamities around the globe with insouciance. We moved with a singular purpose: to get the story and then get it to our editors. We owed our jobs not to our fathers, our connections, or our wealth but to our abilities alone. We were Rust Belt escapees and former officers in the Coldstream Guards, Florentine adventurers and small-town southerners, graduates of the Ivy League, the lycée, and redbrick universities, refugees from the Outback and South Island. We typed on the same Olivetti Lettera 32 portables, wore the same clothes, stayed in the same crummy hotels, drank the same whiskey, bribed the same Telex operators, ate the same dust, told the same lies, and shared the same hours of boredom and seconds of terror that came with the job. This was a fraternity in which a boy from the Midwest could learn much about the world, and about himself. This was the side of me I wanted Frankie to see.

I hid the farm kid as best I could. But he found his way out of the closet often enough. One winter morning in Manhattan, I walked to her place over icy sidewalks.

"How is it out there?" she asked. For the farm kid, this was a setup line too good to resist.

"Slicker than deer guts on a doorknob," I said.

Too often, the farm kid wouldn't stay concealed under the foreign correspondent's trench coat. Good thing. As it turned out, she liked the farm kid.

The first time I asked her what impressed her most about me, she said it was something that happened in a downpour one evening in Barbados. On the way to a dinner, our rental car had a flat tire. I got out in the rain and changed it.

"You mean that impressed you more than my sense of humor or my shrewd analysis of foreign policy?"

"You got it."

We had a few more things in common. We liked to cook, go to movies, walk around New York, talk about the news, and take diving trips to the far corners of the equatorial ocean. But I had my doubts that we would ever become a couple.

I popped the question to Frankie one summer beside a car-sized boulder of pink granite that sits near Pemetic's south ridge trail a quarter mile from the mountain's summit. It took me years to get up the nerve to ask it. I thought about it for days. All the way up the mountain, I marshaled my courage. By the time we got to the summit, I was a nervous wreck. On the way down, I was ready to concede a lack of nerve. Then we stopped at the boulder, I held her hand, and said in a small, high-pitched voice, "So, do you think we ought to get married? Will you marry me?"

"I think so."

It took several more years to get an unequivocal answer. Neither of us had been married before. We had both been involved in relationships that hadn't worked out. But neither of us tried very hard to get married. If anything, I tried to avoid marriage. I wanted to be a good correspondent, able to go anywhere anytime my paper sent me. In my mind, marriage compromised that aim. Frankie's career as a writer gave her an independence that many women envied. The longer she remained unmarried the more independent she became. The more I traveled, the more distant the idea of marriage became. The older we got, the more particular and set in our ways we became.

Ours was a marathon courtship. When it began, I was tired of constant travel and eager to stay in one place for a while. I no longer felt a need to sublimate my personal life to my job. Getting married no longer seemed out of the question. Indeed, the more I got to know Frankie, the more the idea of marriage appealed to me. Marrying her took seven years.

Marriage turned out to be easy. Living together was the hard part. Affordable apartments in Manhattan were hard to come by. Finding a good one took time. Once you got one you hung on to it. Many New Yorkers said they had longer and more meaningful relationships with their apartments than with their lovers. Giving up a lover was a lot easier than giving up an apartment. If Rainer Maria Rilke had lived in Manhattan, his line about love in *Letters to a Young Poet* would have come out like this: "Love consists in this, that two solitudes protect and touch, and greet each other, and be willing to give up their apartments for one another." Giving up an apartment was an act of true love.

Frankie's apartment was in a landmark building on the East River in the Seventies. The offices of the *Paris Review* and the apartment of its editor, George Plimpton, were there too. My apartment was a ground-floor loft in Turtle Bay, across the street from Katharine Hepburn's brownstone and minutes from midtown Manhattan. Both were one-person flats. Each had a bedroom, kitchen, sitting room, and small office. Moving into either one on a permanent basis would have made for a tight fit for two writers.

We were married for two years before we moved in together. We lived separately during the week, then got together on weekends and over summers in Maine. It wasn't a bad combination. We each had our "space," we were married, and we were still "shacking up" on weekends. But the question nagged: If we lived together, where?

One day Frankie went off looking at apartments, as she did from time to time, and called me at my office to tell me she had found one she liked very much and suggested that I see it, too. I looked and liked it. We bought. All of a sudden, we were catapulted into domesticity, and it was bliss. We had an apartment with enough space for two writers to work in without feeling cramped. It had a maid's room that Frankie converted into an office and a second bedroom I turned into a study and workplace.

One problem remained: we now owned three apartments; or, rather, we and various banks owned them in contractual combinations that required us to send the banks monthly chests of gold. One apartment would have to go, perhaps two. Since my apartment was the most expensive to maintain, it was the logical one to sell first. But it didn't sell quickly, and we were hemorrhaging mortgage money.

Twenty minutes up Pemetic, as Frankie praised Herb Watson's tree-trimming skills for about the fifth time, I suddenly remembered a phone call I'd gotten before lunch.

"I almost forgot some big news," I interrupted. "I sold my apartment. My lawyer called and told me she has a signed contract."

"I'm thrilled," Frankie said. "How does it make you feel?"

"Nice, but a little scary," I said. "It's my old be-happy-but-hang-on-to-your wallet problem. I like it when nice things happen to me. But I've always felt that if I let on how happy I am, I'll get punished. Somebody will come along and take my happiness away."

Frankie said she had acted in much the same way, not letting on, even to herself, when something nice happened to her. She said that in 1972 she got a phone call from someone telling her that she had won the Pulitzer Prize for *Fire in the Lake*.

"I said, 'Thank you,' hung up the phone, and went back to work."

"So, after we got married, have you ever seen me really, really happy?" I asked her. She thought for a moment.

"Remember the phone call you got from Bob Gottlieb about the New Zealand piece," she said. "That had you dancing around the porch."

Gottlieb was the editor of *The New Yorker* at the time. I had written a profile of the prime minister of New Zealand, David

Lange. He had made an international name for himself and his country by protesting French underground nuclear bomb testing in the South Pacific and barring visits to New Zealand ports by American or any other warships carrying nuclear weapons.

The article was my first for *The New Yorker*. It was long and difficult. I finished it on August 8, 1989, drove straight to the Somesville Post Office, and sent it by overnight mail to Bob in New York.

I drove back to Frankie's place elated. Then I called Barry Kramer at the *Wall Street Journal* foreign desk to ask about the news.

"That guy in New Zealand quit," he said. "You know, your pal, that anti-nukes guy, Lange. He resigned."

"What? Come on, Barry, you've got to be joking."

"No, really. I saw something on the wires. He resigned."

Barry read me a wire service story. My subject had quit his job—the job that had made him, his policies, and his country interesting and significant enough to warrant a 40,000-word profile in *The New Yorker*! And he had quit on the very day I had finished the story!

I called Bob Gottlieb in New York and told him what had happened.

"Oh, I wouldn't necessarily worry about that," he said. "When I get the piece, I'll read it and we'll see."

Three days later, Gottlieb called back.

"I like the piece and I think it is a very *New Yorker* kind of piece," he said. "I want to run it. Of course you'll have to go back to New Zealand and update it."

I was euphoric.

"You were whooping, jumping up and down," Frankie said.

The story never appeared. By the time I got back to New Zealand to finish it, the communist regimes of eastern Europe were collapsing like dominoes. The saga of New Zealand and its anti-nuclear former prime minister got stale very quickly.

We walked across Pemetic's bald granite crown to its summit. We looked out over a horizon of ocean and islands to the south, green valleys and distant mountain summits to the north. We sat and gazed and held hands.

On the way down we stopped at the boulder where I had popped the question. It was a scene out of a dime novel. We hugged. We kissed.

"We're so lucky," she said.

I floated down the mountain.

Like the osprey and the eagle, people sometimes showed up at Frankie's place unannounced. The next afternoon, Frankie's impulsive and gregarious friend Richard gave us three hours' notice. He and his wife, Saskia, were en route to Mount Desert from New York to spend a couple of days. Come to dinner, he said. He already had a reservation. Frankie segued effortlessly into a counteroffer. No sense trudging down to a restaurant when they could come out here earlier, join us for drinks at sunset, then dinner. Besides, she said, we'd already invited two of their friends, Caroline and Tom, to our house. Richard said yes, and our first dinner party of the summer fell into place.

Richard and Saskia, both sociology professors, arrived first, and we ushered them onto the front porch for views and wine.

"What have you been up to?" I asked Richard, who was admiring my porch crops.

"We just got back from Prague," he said, moving his left hand close to his right arm then slapping it. "Amazing things going on all over eastern Europe these days."

Frankie brought out some tuna pâté and crackers and we all sat down and watched the sun turn red and sink on the horizon. I felt something on my forehead.

Slap.

"George Soros is funding this new university for eastern Europeans where the teaching is in English," Saskia said. "The idea is to connect the students to England and America."

Slap. Saskia swatted her ankle, but she didn't stop talking. The university was having start-up problems.

Just then Caroline and Tom arrived. Caroline, an author, had spent most of the day playing tennis. Tom, a university attorney, was up for the weekend.

Slap. I whacked the back of my left hand.

In declining their invitations to go out and insisting that everyone come to Frankie's place for sunset drinks and dinner, we had neglected to mention that guests had to endure one of the rituals of porch-bending in the woods: they would have to be fed upon before being fed.

It takes a certain agility to swat, spread tuna pâté onto crackers, sip wine, and conduct a conversation while being eaten alive by mosquitoes. Keeping up a spirited conversation while these flying hypodermics are relieving you of the contents of your circulatory system is essentially what sophisticated porch-bending is all about, at least at Frankie's place.

"I was just telling Jim and Frankie about this new university in Prague that George Soros is involved in," said Richard. "The problem is that it isn't really working. The students aren't terribly interested in learning much at the moment."

Slap. Frankie squashed a mosquito on her cheek.

We talked about the importance of sending students out to Western universities, the way China did after the death of Mao Tse-tung.

Slap. I got two with one swat to my thigh.

"Any blackflies around?" Richard asked. "Aren't they awful?"

"Knock on wood," said Frankie.

"They're usually gone by early July, but let's not malign one of Maine's great assets," I said, launching into a lecture on the virtues of Maine's fog and its hardy insect populations. Insects didn't have easy lives in Maine with its long, freezing winters and short summers. But two species, the blackfly and the mosquito, have contributed greatly to the task of keeping Maine unfashionable. Through the spring and early summer blackflies pounce on people and inflict fierce bites that draw blood in some victims and produce serious reactions in others. Without blackflies, Mount Desert would have long ago gone the way of the Hamptons,

Martha's Vineyard, and Cape Cod, overrun by well-heeled summer people. I could think of no higher tribute to the blackfly, except, perhaps, that the members of the women's soccer team at the College of the Atlantic, over in Bar Harbor, called themselves the Lady Black Flies.

Not until late June do blackfly populations diminish, and sometimes not even then. Cool, damp weather can keep them around well into July. By then, the mosquito population reaches sufficient strength to carry on the burden of menacing vacationers.

At Frankie's place, we tried all sorts of repellants over the years to make porch-bending at sunset more tolerable. We would bring out our Bug-O-Bucket citronella candles. These candles didn't promise much except to "reduce annoyance" from mosquitoes "in still air." They smelled nice, however. We tried Pic 5 Mosquito Repellent Sticks, which were giant green joss sticks made in Malaysia. They contained .25 percent D-Cis/Trans Allethrin, whatever that is, and 99.75 percent "inert ingredients." Directions on the box said that one stick repelled mosquitoes for a hundred square feet. The mosquitoes on our porch seemed to breathe in the Pic 5 smoke with pleasure.

With everyone swatting at mosquitoes more or less continuously by now, I decided to unveil a whole new concept in mosquito control—or so said the catalog in which I found them. I brought two little black boxes out of the tool room.

"What's that?" Saskia asked.

"I'm glad you asked. These are secret weapons—a battery-operated mosquito-repelling system!" I said proudly. "I'm going to put the batteries in, turn these things on, and voilà! Everybody stand back and watch the mosquitoes flee in horror."

I inserted the batteries then turned on the switches. I held one of the boxes up to Saskia's ear. She heard a thwapping sound.

"These babies work on the mosquito mind," I said. "That sound is the sound of a dragonfly. Dragonflies eat mosquitoes. You see, the mosquitoes hear the sound of dragonflies and skedaddle."

I positioned these menacing thwappers on the porch railing about ten feet apart, and waited. And waited. Our guests continued to talk and swat. The mosquitoes continued their attacks, not intimidated by my thwappers. The mosquitoes were so thick and so unintimidated by my magic thwappers that Caroline burst into giggles.

Slap! Slap! Slap! Slap slap slap slap.

In the interest of preventing further loss of blood we beat a hasty retreat from the porch.

Inside, Frankie and I offered a very traditional summer meal: baked salmon, basmati rice, and fresh snap peas. We tried to spruce up the salmon, but to my mind salmon is salmon. (It was good but—let's put it this way—it didn't detract from the conversation.) With it we served a green salad.

BAKED SALMON STUFFED WITH HERBS SERVED WITH RICE AND SNAP PEAS

On a broiler pan, lay a sheet of aluminum foil and, using a brush, paint the top of it with olive oil. With a filet knife, cut back the skin of the salmon so that it's almost off, then between the skin and flesh place a thick bed of chopped herbs; Frankie used chives, oregano, and basil. Place the salmon skin-side down on the foil. Paint the top, or flesh side, of the fish with olive oil and dust with freshly ground pepper. Preheat oven to 375 degrees and bake fish for 20 minutes, eyeballing the dish often to avoid overbaking.

We served this with basmati rice: 2 cups of uncooked rice; 1¼ cups of water; 1 can of chicken broth; 1 teaspoon of salt; 2 tablespoons of butter. Bring rice to a boil covered, then turn heat way down until the liquid is absorbed. Making too much is always our policy because leftover rice is the key ingredient for another favorite: fried rice.

Steam snap peas: the key is not to overcook.

Long before the table conversation began to wind down, I had spotted movement in a dim corner beyond the fireplace. Then a tiny ball of fur bolted from the shadows behind the couch, streaked across the floor by the table just behind me, veered left, and shot for the back bedroom. Saskia noticed, too, but pretended not to.

What came next brought conversation to a standstill. *Zip!* A fur ball charged out of the back bedroom, then in again, as if to come out on stage and take a bow. Everyone noticed. The table erupted in giggles. Another mouse darted from the back bedroom, turned right under the Buddha, and streaked under the couch. More giggles.

"I guess we have to do something about the mice," Frankie said after our guests were gone and we went about cleaning up.

Frankie and I had a generally harmonious relationship with the wildlife around the house. The seagulls and cormorants on the water out front didn't bother us. The loons announced their presence somewhere out on the water with their haunting calls, usually in the still evening twilight. Various wrens, thrushes, and chickadees came by, eschewing our offerings of seeds. When woodpeckers commenced their knock, knock, knocking, we would glance up from our desks to the tree trunks to watch them at work. The cheeping of our local osprey likewise got our attention, and we'd run for the binoculars if it perched on one of the dead tree branches out front. The neighborhood bald eagle was always a wonderful sight, whether he was gliding by at treetop level, circling high over the Somes Sound, or resting atop a big pine out by the water. Hummingbirds flitted around the house and we courted them with red sugar water in a feeder attached to a pine limb that drapes over the porch. My discovery of a brightly colored beetle on the porch was cause for a brief nature assembly, with magnifying glass. And watching spiders do their web work was fascinating.

We drew the line, however, at cohabitation. And this summer, as usual, it didn't take long for us to discover that we weren't the only mammals in the house. The evidence was telltale at first: strategic caraway-sized droppings beside the dryer in the utility room, the contents of a drawer in my desk trashed.

We, of course, were the interlopers, or, as replacements for combat units in Vietnam were called, FNGs (fucking new guys). The mice had an unmolested run of the place until we turned up. They moved in, we assumed, in the late fall or early spring, and went about the business of reproduction. I imagined loud orgies. In any case, they were relentlessly procreative.

"I guess we have to do something," Frankie repeated, rinsing a final plate.

Translation: I had to do something. But what? Get a cat? No, a cat might do the trick inside and out, ridding the premises not only of mice but squirrels, chipmunks, and birds as well. Getting some of those humane Hav-a-Heart traps and capturing our rodents live was an option. But I didn't recall seeing any of these traps in the local hardware stores, and besides, if I caught our mice live, where would I resettle them? Exiling house mice into the island wilderness didn't seem very humane.

One day on the bookshelf I found two volumes that seemed to frame my options. The first, entitled *Common-Sense Pest Control: Least-toxic Solutions for Your Home, Pets and Community,* was a 715-page tome written by Sheila Daar and William and Helga Olkowski. The authors ran the Bio-Integral Resource Center in Berkeley, California, an outfit that published information on environmentally sound methods of keeping pests at bay. This book came out in 1991, and I had come across it while researching a story on "integrated pest management"—using good bugs to control bad bugs—in Indonesian rice production. Perhaps *Common-Sense Pest Control* could tell me how to deal with our mice. Before I pulled it off the shelf, however, I spotted a much thinner volume that tweaked my interest even more. It was called *The Art of War,* written by Sun Tzu more than two thousand years ago.

Three

BAM! BOOM. POP POP POP POP. WHAAAAM!
What a dream! Was I hearing incoming mortars? Were those
AK-47s popping? Was I stumbling into a firefight? Was this another Vietnam dream? The noise filled my head, which was deep
into a soft pillow. I'm a sound sleeper. The action in my dreams
usually unfolds without waking me up. I toss and turn but stay
asleep. This was different. This was loud enough to jolt me to
consciousness. I opened my eyes and glanced at my watch. Five
minutes to eight. I localized the sound and realized it was coming from a half-opened window next to Frankie's desk. I threw
off my blankets, roused myself, and stumbled over to the rattan
shades as Frankie stirred.

"What . . . what the . . . what's going on?" I stammered, as I
pulled the roll-up cord on the front shade.

"Whatever it is, I've been listening to it for an hour," Frankie
said.

The banging was coming from just beyond a thick grove of
cedars, literally a stone's throw away—hammers hitting nails and
wood.

"Frankie, up, time for a recon," I said, rolling up the blinds.

We slipped into shorts, T-shirts, and running shoes, limbered
up, and padded up the lane toward the noise. We had to go a

hundred yards up a rise and then turn sharply back down a drive-way toward the shore to what had been a clearing in the forest. The clearing was an "improvement" on a six-acre lot. The previous owner had bought the lot in the late eighties with the intention of building a house. He had removed dozens of trees. Then he changed his mind and put the land up for sale.

Nobody seemed to want it. Years passed. We thought we were free of a new neighbor. Over the summers we had dreamed up schemes for keeping the lot and the rest of the peninsula undeveloped. One idea was to bring in some old tires, a couple of rusting car bodies, and an old refrigerator or two and arrange them artfully around Frankie's place, creating a motif. To animate it, we could add some chickens, perhaps a pig or two, and call the lane Tobacco Road. Another idea was to give Frankie's place a name like some of the fancy places around Northeast Harbor. But instead of calling it Water's Edge, Burnt Cove, or Seal Ledge, we'd call it Radon Point. That would make people stop and think.

Now it was too late. What we saw as we approached the clearing looked at first like an open pit mine, with great piles of dirt and gravel and rocks, and big holes where trees and ferns and pine needles used to be. As we moved closer, the place took on the appearance of a landing zone for the 101st Airborne. LZs and artillery fire support bases in Vietnam were usually muddy gashes in the jungle disconnected from everything around them. This looked like one of those. Here was a construction site that as the crow flies and, more important, as sound travels was fewer than a hundred yards from Frankie's place.

Four pickup trucks were parked at the end of the driveway. Just beyond them, carpenters were pounding nails into plywood. They were erecting plywood forms for pouring concrete for what appeared to be the beginnings of an enormous foundation. The carpenters waved and went about their noisy business as we walked by them. Frankie grimaced as she walked around the outline of the foundation, which appeared to face south and southwest down Somes Sound. A thick stand of cedar and spruce stood between Frankie's place and whatever this was going to be. But the original clearing had been expanded. Many more trees had been re-moved to create a large open space.

"You suppose this is going to be the lawn?" I said. "Maybe a giant New Jersey lawn in the middle of the woods."

As I looked around, a very old feeling came over me. It was a feeling that came from a long-buried memory of a field of deep grass and chest-high alfalfa next to a little house in a small town in Michigan where I had lived with an uncle and aunt when I was four years old. In the field yellow and black garden spiders clung to the center of huge bull's-eye-like webs. My young friends and I were scared of the spiders and we picked careful paths through the field to avoid them. Gradually, we overcame our fears and learned to catch the spiders by putting a jar on one side of the web and its lid on the other with a spider in between. Other kids less familiar with the field stayed out of it. So it was our secret field, mysterious and frightening, with our spiders. We showed off our captured spiders as though they were big-game trophies.

Then one day I came back from a summer visit with my grand-parents and found the field had been mowed; the grass and alfalfa lay drying in the sun, the spiders nowhere to be seen. In the next days, trucks and shovels came in to dig a big hole in the middle of the lot for a basement. A house was being built and our won-derful field was gone.

When Frankie and I got back to her place, I could tell she was distressed. She was quiet over breakfast and I heard none of the usual popcorn-making eruptions from her old Remington dur-ing the day, only a few pecks now and then. Then things went from bad to worse.

When we got back from our afternoon foray to town, Frankie stepped onto the front porch and screamed. As I rushed up be-hind, I could see her looking through the clearing down Somes Sound. There, in the middle of the view that Herb Watson had restored, sat a huge yellow construction barge with a giant crane attached.

"What is this? What in the world is going on *now!*" she shouted. I grabbed the binoculars and we went out to the far end of the porch for a better look. The barge was facing down the Sound, its stern toward us. Across the back of its cab something was written. I twirled the focusing knob on the binoculars until the lettering became clear: "Art Tibbetts, Marine Contractor, 1-800-OWN-DOCK."

"You're not going to believe this," I said, passing Frankie the binoculars.

The banging next door was one thing. We heard it but we didn't have to look at it. Now, every time Frankie looked up from her work and gazed out the window, she would see this barge and think the worst: that a dock was under construction in the middle of her view, a dock she might have to look at forever.

A dock! We just stood there letting the full force of what we were looking at sink in. A dock? Right there? If the size of the barge was any indication, this wasn't going to be some little canoe-launching pad. This was going to be a humongous bridge out over the water. And given the size of the tides and the strength of the wind and waves in Somes Sound, it had to be both sizable and solid—like the big, long docks in front of the huge shore houses farther down the sound near Northeast Harbor. Those docks had walkways that rested on giant slabs of granite and thick wooden piles and they extended hundreds of feet out over the water, towering twenty or thirty feet above sea level at low tide. They had long, hinged ramps, and at the end of each ramp was a big, wooden float where boats tied up.

The only docks near us weren't visible. The Bar Harbor Boating Company's dock was tucked into a cove around a bend of shoreline. Abel's boatyard and lobster pound dock was a mile up the sound. The dock at John M. Williams Co., another boatyard, was two-thirds of a mile directly across the sound and obscured by the trees in our front yard.

We imagined a veritable Brooklyn Bridge spanning Frankie's view. And a big dock meant there had to be a big boat. What if it was one of those giant, diesel-burning tubs from Florida that were so despised in these waters? A giant tub smack in the middle of our newly restored view! Frankie marched straight to the phone and called 1-800-OWN-DOCK. She got a recording and left a message. At sunset the phone rang. It was Mr. Tibbetts. He invited Frankie to come over for a visit any time she wanted.

"I'll be there first thing in the morning," she said.

The next morning, Frankie peered through her binoculars at the barge and then set off to find Mr. Tibbetts. I went about my usual routine. When Frankie returned, she said Mr. Tibbetts told her he was building a big dock, although not as big as some of the monsters near Northeast Harbor. He told her that it would be situated farther down the shore from where his barge was anchored and, therefore, might not be visible from our front porch. He also told her that several moorings would be set in the waters around the dock and that at least one of them would be visible from the porch.

While we were eating breakfast, Linn, a photographer, called. She lived just across the cove. She got out and about a lot and she always heard a lot more about local doings than we did. She had been to town already and she also had been working the telephone, and she had some things to report of the "you're not going to believe this" variety. Those things turned out to be about "that thing" next door.

"Weeell," Linn said, what she'd heard was that "this guy," an American who worked for a company in Europe, had paid an arm and a leg for that lot next to us and was building this enormous house and—get this—a big swimming pool beside the house.

A swimming pool? In Maine? People in Maine don't have swimming pools. People in Palm Beach have swimming pools. The only swimming pool in Northeast Harbor I knew of belonged to the swimming club. A swimming pool? In the middle of the woods?

We spent the day feeling low. Around three o'clock, some new monster began to roar next door. It clanked, too.

"We might as well take a look on our way to town," I said. When we drove over the rise, we saw it and stopped. A big orange bulldozer was pushing dirt around foundation footings.

"It's like Jurassic Park around here," she fumed. "You never know what monster will turn up next."

The day didn't take a turn for the better until Sam Peabody, Frankie's uncle, called and invited us to dinner that very night.

To understand what happened next, it is important to know that we were not allowed to eat lobsters outside of Maine. It was Frankie's rule and, while it was always tempting to violate, I reluctantly came to believe in it. Various foods, in her view, had places and seasons, and the lobster's place was Maine in the summer. Eating lobster year-round, here and there, wherever it turned up as an exotic offering, would spoil its special appeal in Maine. Eating it out of context—without fog and fireplace, seaweed and seagulls— would dilute the experience. This meant that the Maine lobsters we came across in saltwater tanks in New York City fish markets were off-limits. This meant that when we opened restaurant menus and scanned the seafood selections to Maine lobster, I had to avert my eyes or start feeling sorry for myself. Clawless tropical lobsters didn't count. If we were somewhere near the equator and a spiny lobster turned up on the menu, we didn't turn it down. It was, of course, a very different creature, a species apart, a creature that lived a cushy life in warm waters, inhabiting crevasses in colorful coral reefs. *Homarus americanus,* by contrast, was a stoic, a product of the icy brine, muscular and tastier, in my opinion.

The problem with this Maine lobster rule was that it had a cloudy corollary that reached deeply, if mysteriously, into Frankie's history in Maine. I say mysteriously because, when interrogated directly about the subject, she would offer murky explanations. If you listened carefully, you could hear vague references to the history of both the FitzGerald and Peabody sides of her family. Then she trailed off into dangling participles, mumbles, and bouts of silence before feebly changing the subject. In any case, the corollary was this: Lobsters were for special occasions. They were not to be devoured willy-nilly just because we were in Maine.

Imagine how it feels to arrive in Maine after an arduous journey and many months of lobster deprivation and hear this corollary. This was a rationale rooted in ancestral parsimony and handed down the generations like a family Bible, I decided: gluttony must be faced squarely, stared down and resisted in all its forms. The lobster, of course, is Maine's principal offering to gluttons and non-gluttons alike. It is an offering millions of people came to the state each year to devour. My argument—that we were not doing our share to help the state's economy—had no effect on Frankie's view. She also insisted that lobsters were a reward for good works and achievements big and small, but tending toward big. Besides, she reasoned, as soon as we broke down and indulged ourselves—say, just the two of us at home alone with a couple of two-pounders—we would be invited to dinner at somebody else's house and, sure enough, they'd serve lobster. Okay, it happened. But over years of monitoring our lobster intake, I noticed that it was an extremely rare summer in which we ate lobsters more than three times. I reported these findings to Frankie on a regular basis, to no effect. Precious weeks would pass in our Lobster-Free Zone.

Not this year. Frankie's Uncle Sam had called to invite us to dinner and Frankie had agreed to meet him and Susan Mary Alsop at seven-thirty at Abel's Lobster Pound. This was a genuine lobster loophole in the making!

Sam Peabody, an elegant New York philanthropist and former headmaster, came to Northeast Harbor each summer to see friends and relatives and take vigorous mountain walks. He stayed for a few days at a time, sometimes for as long as a week, and he usually stayed with Susan Mary Alsop, a journalist and author who came up early each year from Washington. She and her late husband, the journalist Joseph Alsop, were fixtures of the old Georgetown establishment. Susan Mary's house was situated high above the water overlooking Bear Island at the entrance to Northeast Harbor.

Sam's dinner invitation lifted our spirits. I could already envision a big chunk of succulent white lobster tail plunging into a bowl of melted butter. Frankie could temporarily push the yellow barge out of mind.

But when we arrived at Abel's and looked over the menu, I could see that Frankie had a problem. She could opt for a big plate of steamer clams, of course. But before she could place her order, both Sam and Susan Mary ordered lobster, and I quickly followed suit. Frankie hesitated, then caved. We all had lobsters. They were delicious and, in Abel's grand tradition, they cost an arm and a leg. I was momentarily sated, but I realized that this lack of lobster discipline so early in the summer might have its consequences.

"Well, that's it for lobsters until Labor Day," I laughed.

Frankie said nothing.

Fortunately there was yet another corollary to Frankie's lobster-rationing logic, a gaping loophole that could present itself at any time and at a moment's notice: houseguests. Houseguests had to be treated right. Houseguests from far away who rarely if ever ate lobster had to be treated to lobster. Houseguests forced to endure the rigors of the FitzGerald Survival School absolutely had to have lobster as a reward for all the aches and pains and muscle spasms. Houseguests fooled into taking "a little swim," only to find themselves practically flash-frozen in Somes Sound, were entitled to lobster.

Houseguests automatically deserved lobster for another reason. Whenever they arrived, rain and fog inevitably arrived with them. It was the Houseguest Weather Rule, and we weren't the only ones who believed in it. It was part of the local religion: houseguests beget fog and foul weather; houseguests get wet and cold; houseguest spirits need lifting. How? Lobsters, no question. There was no better way to make houseguests feel that they weren't absolute fools for coming in the first place. Imagine them driving for hours only to wind up in pea-soup fog and rain, then sitting down to a plate of steaming lobster and roasted corn on the cob while flames roar in the fireplace.

It was this vision that sprang to my mind when Frankie's friend Ron called the next afternoon to announce that he was in Skowhegan, just a couple of hours inland from us. An author and political science professor, he had come east to attend a conference in New Hampshire and was now headed our way. He would be our first houseguest and, I thought cunningly, the second genuine Lobster Loophole of the summer.

Ron arrived and presented us with an enormous cache of bagels and a problem. He announced that he was on an extremely restricted no-fat or cholesterol diet, meaning absolutely no lobster, no lemon butter, and no buttery corn.

Worse, it started to rain. Fortunately, after a light sprinkle the rain turned to mist, the sky lightened, and we decided that visibility had improved enough to take a walk up Cedar Swamp Mountain. We would traverse one of the lightly traveled trails in the park, but one that offered interesting terrain and a great variety of views: south to the smaller islands and open ocean, east to Upper Hadlock Pond, Somes Sound, and Blue Hill off on the horizon. From the top of the mountain, we could go down the other side and end up at a wonderful waterfall where Hadlock Brook descended under a great stone bridge on a carriage road. It was one of our favorite walks.

As we started up the South Ridge Trail, we quickly entered a low bank of fog that seemed to get thicker and thicker as we ascended. Soon, Frankie and I were making what came to be known over the years as "the fog spiel."

"This is normally a spectacular view," Frankie said. "Down over there, if you could only see it, is Upper Hadlock Pond . . . the ocean is over there . . . and a whole bunch of beautiful little islands stretch out there to the right. In back of us are Sargent and Penobscot mountains and behind them is Cadillac Mountain, the tallest peak on the island at 1,530 feet above sea level." And then, brimming with pride as our guest stared into nothing but fog, I said, "Cadillac is the highest point along the coast of the Atlantic Ocean north of Brazil. You can look it up!"

Back home, I switched culinary gears to accommodate Ron's dietary regimen with a fat-free yogurt soup and beans.

Over the years, I'd experimented with a cold soup of cucumbers, yogurt, chicken broth, and fresh herbs and spices in varying combinations and strength. It was simple, always delicious, and it got better overnight in the refrigerator.

COLD SOUP

Into a blender or whatever moosher is handy, plop a fistful (say 2 cups) of fresh dill (or cilantro, chives, mint, basil, chervil) and 2 or 3 medium-size kirby cucumbers. Moosh until liquefied. Add a pint of yogurt (fat-free for Ron's dinner). Then squeeze in the juice of half a lemon or lime, grind in some fresh pepper or shake in lemon pepper, add one can of chicken broth, and moosh some more, until it is soup. Refrigerate, for days if need be, but remove to serve at a little cooler than room temperature.

I'd developed something of a bean-cooking fetish over the summers. Whenever I ate some really good beans, I'd pester their creators for recipes. I had the best luck with white navy beans, but any beans would do—pintos, northerns, limas. I tried one of those bags containing ten or twenty different kinds of beans and lentils (tricky to cook to get the big ones done without the little ones turning to mush). I tried brown lentils, too, with a no-dill, tarragon-laced marinade. Terrible!

I had stored in memory a recipe for a wonderful bean salad served at the wedding of some friends one June in Connecticut. The caterer, Vanessa Cortesi, was the daughter of a friend of ours. After much pleading and three helpings, she relinquished the recipe.

VANESSA'S BEANS

Soak a standard 16-ounce bag of small white navy beans over-night, using twice as much water as beans, and changing the water two or three times (to reduce gas generation).

Into a crock pot, or a large kettle on a burner set to low heat, place a square of fatback, a couple strips of bacon, or (in this case for Ron's sake) 2 tablespoons of olive oil. Add whatever basic flavorings you want: a quartered onion, two or three cloves of garlic, four or five slices of fresh ginger, one or two bay leaves. Whatever. In this case, I chose two 4-inch sprigs of rosemary and ½ cup of thyme branches. Add just enough chicken broth to cover the beans and simmer on the lowest heat possible until they are done but still firm.

(*In my crock pot, this takes about 2 hours.*) *Drain* (*saving the liquid*) *and remove everything but the beans—that is, chunks of stuff and stems, everything but the rosemary and thyme leaves, which will have detached from their stems.* (*I suppose you could put all these spices into a bouquet garni in cheesecloth, but I never did.*)

In a small bowl, combine 2 tablespoons of red wine vinegar, the juice of ½ lemon, and ¼ cup of olive oil to make a vinaigrette. Finely chop 1 cup of any fresh herbs you have handy: chives, tarragon, basil, chervil, oregano, cilantro, dill, and/or mint. Add to vinaigrette. Add some of the bean-cooking liquid, say ½ cup. Let this mixture sit at room temperature, stirring occasionally so the flavors infuse the liquid. Then mix the beans and the vinaigrette. You can put this combination in the oven to warm at low heat, say 200 edges, or serve at room temperature—NOT COLD. Cold masks flavor. If you cook the beans in advance and refrigerate them, take them out well before serving.

Ron was a stimulating houseguest, intellectually, if not gastronomically. He had written a biography of journalist Walter Lippmann some years before, and during his stay he told us lots of stories about Lippmann, who had lived on and written about Mount Desert for many summers. Ron left on Monday morning, and the clouds parted as if on cue. The day became warm and sunny. I did two things. I took Ron's biography of Lippmann off the shelf and started reading, and I placed a call to our friends David and Katherine. They were July people from Houston, and they had two houseguests arriving from Texas that afternoon— making them a certified, eight-legged Lobster Loophole. I begged them to come to dinner that night. They agreed.

Although I had managed to take over various cooking chores, lobster preparation was strictly Frankie's department. After years of practice, she had her timing and technique finely honed, and I felt no need to muscle in. Indeed, I came to see my role as offering color commentary to dinner guests and to herd any I thought were faint of heart out of range of the sights and sounds of what was about to begin. I took upon myself the additional role of keeping an eye peeled for any representatives of animal-rights organizations.

One such group demonstrated each summer at the Rockland Lobster Festival on the other side of Penobscot Bay. They wanted lobsters liberated, not eaten. They thought that dispatching live lobsters in boiling water and steam was no way for man to treat crustaceans. What if they were on patrol? What better place to gather evidence than here, where lobster mayhem was about to begin.

Over the years, Frankie and I listened to a lot of debate among friends and read articles advancing ideas for cooking live lobsters quickly and humanely. Whatever effects these conversations and articles had on Frankie's thinking weren't apparent. Indeed, just how Frankie transformed herself in a matter of minutes from the gentle friend of nature into no-nonsense lobster chef I do not know. It is best left not fully understood, like the transformation of werewolves.

What can be said for sure is that what went on in a kitchen that contained both Frankie and lobsters wasn't for the squeamish. It involved lots of banging and crunching, which, I noticed, sent guests retreating to the far side of the fireplace. Sometimes when it was over and Frankie yelled, "Time to sit," it was difficult for me to glance at the kitchen, let alone set foot in it. It had been turned into a battlefield of dripping and greasy countertops, with tiny flecks of red lobster shells sticking to the wall or the refrigerator or the kitchen window.

STEAMED LOBSTERS

Frankie assembled six lobsters (Frankie prefers them to be 1¼ to 1½ pounds), a big metal lobster pot filled with 2 inches of water (seawater is the preferred liquid of the Peabody clan, but I couldn't tell the difference from tap water), and some lemon and butter. She brought the water to a violent boil, removed the lobsters from their paper sack in the fridge, and plopped them all in headfirst to dispatch them quickly. Noncarnivores were advised at this point to cover their ears for the next few seconds while the lobsters thrashed and scraped around inside the pot en route to the Great Lobster Beyond. (While the lobster libbers claim this to be the crucial time frame, experts marshaled by the Maine Lobster Promotion Coun-cil argue that as water insects, essentially, lobsters have nervous systems that aren't very complex and, thus, boiling or steaming was probably the way to go.) They were done in twelve minutes, their shells turned bright reddish-orange. Frankie poured off the water, placed the steaming lobsters one at a time on the wooden cutting board and went at them with a hammer from the tool shelf in the back room. She whacked the claws and arms, breaking their shells, then turned each lobster over and sliced up the inside of their tails with a sharp knife. She served them, rubber claw bands still attached, in big Vietnamese soup bowls. (Bowls are required be-cause lobsters contain all sorts of strange gooey liquids that reveal themselves during the stages of dismemberment that follow.)

Eating lobsters is a messy business. Hands and fingers are re-quired. Nutcrackers and picks help a lot. Paper towels are ex-tremely welcome.

In the Peabody households to which I was invited, improper lobster-eating etiquette, if observed, wasn't discussed at the table. Experienced lobster eaters differ as to which of the creature's vari-ous parts should be consumed and in what order. In general, I think I can say from observation that the real pros always start small; that is, with the legs. They pull off a leg, crack its exoskel-eton, and suck out the tiny morsels of flesh inside. Only the boor-ish go straight for the claws or tail. Skilled veterans like Frankie's uncles knew every little secret crevice where a choice morsel could hide. To leave these crevasses unopened, to leave spindly legs not sucked and the creature's huge carapace unexplored, its inner green tomalley unplumbed, is the mark of an amateur, and could raise a Peabody eyebrow.

Lobsters were so common on Mount Desert in the nineteenth century that they sold for two or three cents apiece, and it was said that indentured servants had it written in their contracts that they were not to be fed lobster more than twice a week. Pre-sumably, much leftover lobster littered servant plates. That was then. Now, leaving various limbs and body parts unexplored betrayed little understanding of the Lord's wrath toward wast-rels. I studied the Peabody technique with the concentration of a reverential apprentice. I envied the indentured servants who ate lobster twice a week. I ate lobster two or three times a sum-mer, and that meant only two or three times a year. I wanted to savor every little hidden morsel I could find. I learned well. After a while, no Peabody eyebrows were raised at me.

FRANKIE'S CORN ON THE COB

In contrast to her lobster preparation, Frankie's corn-roasting technique was elegant and simple: she roasted ears of corn in the oven, husks and all.

The key is fresh, young, local corn, although we've made do with young corn from a distance and even adult corn. If you can get it the day it's picked, you are blessed.

Don't remove the husks! Simply remove any loose husk leaves and hair from the ears and then run water over them. Preheat oven to 375 degrees. Put in corn and roast for 20 to 30 minutes. You can tell by the smell when it's done. Serve with butter, salt, and a pepper grinder.

Our Texas friends were as practiced at devouring lobsters as we were. They could disassemble a lobster and tell stories at the same time.

As the candles flickered, we sat in silence and near darkness with great piles of husks and lobster shells filling big bowls on the table and greasy paper towels scattered in between. We didn't bother with bread, salad and cheese, or dessert. We just sat sated and inert, feeling the effects of the wine.

After these lobsterfests, we usually consigned great piles of lobster leavings to a plastic bag in a garbage can on the back porch, and frequently a local masked marauder paid a visit in the night. For reasons I didn't understand Frankie was very fond of this back-porch dilettante. He was smart and picky. He didn't bother when we ate steak or chicken or fish. Only lobster guaranteed his ar-rival and that night he was right on schedule.

Four

The porch was a mess in the morning. The garbage can had been toppled, the plastic bag inside ripped open, its contents strewn across the deck, steps, and yard, the orange lobster carapaces shredded. We policed up the masked marauder's handiwork, hosed down the porch, and then went about our morning routine. The air was crisp and clear.

"It's a spahk-lah," Frankie said as we finished stretching and set off up the lane. Red squirrels chattered out alarms as we jogged by. A wood thrush sang its flutelike song. Up a little hill we ran, breathing in scents of spruce and pine and the deep earthiness of the damp morning woods. A power saw whined from the construction zone as we passed by and trotted down a long slope where the lane curved gently through a dense stand of cedar.

Around the curve we spotted a large black lump of trouble, its ears perked in our direction. Eyeing us, it jerked its head up, leaped to its feet, erupted in a snarling fit, and charged straight at us, teeth first. Instinctively, we lurched to the edge of the lane and grabbed sticks to fend off the assault. Thus began the summer's reunion with our neighborhood Darth Vadar in curls—a big black poodle I called "Fifi of the North."

Fending off Fifi had become a ritual over the summers. I don't know why she disliked us, but I had no doubt that she would sink her teeth into us if given the chance. I had sprained an ankle, bruised a knee, and fallen down several times in defense of my anatomy. I imagined Fifi's anger had to do with her surroundings. Here was a pampered Boston poodle who found herself having to endure her masters' bizarre summer habits of exile in the Maine woods instead of, say, Provence.

I'd mentioned Fifi's aggression to her owner over the summers.

"Oh, that dog wouldn't hurt a flea," came the reply. "Try dog biscuits. You'll be friends fast."

I said I'd try dog biscuits. I preferred a trusty stick.

"Maybe I'll try dog biscuits this summer," I told Frankie when we were safely beyond Fifi's incisors.

"If you could spend the money from your apartment on anything you wanted, what would it be?" Frankie asked the next afternoon on a walk.

"Anything I want?" I said, "You mean like a new Jaguar?"

"Something like that. Do you want things? Toys?"

"I don't know. I used to. Now, not so much."

We walked in silence for several minutes.

"I think if I could buy anything," I said, "I'd buy time."

"That's interesting," Frankie said, "You want to live longer?"

"No, not that kind of time. I mean time to myself, time off work."

"Why?"

I reminded Frankie about getting my first newspaper job and how I noticed quickly that the best reporters in the newsroom worked all the time. Whenever I got there, they were already there—days, nights, weekends—working the phones, writing stories. I wanted to be like them, so I worked all the time too. Putting in the hours wasn't hard to adjust to. I'd done it before, on the farm. Doing it as an aspiring reporter was far more exciting.

My first job, at the *Evening Star* in Washington in 1966, was called "dictationist." It was a coveted position. We dictationists sat around a "dictation bank" wearing headphones and typing stories dictated to us by reporters around Washington and beyond. When we weren't taking dictation, we wrote obituaries or turned press releases into one- or two-paragraph "shorts." To show how enterprising we were, we could report and write Saturday "church features" or other feature stories in our spare time. We were competing to get on the *Star*'s training program. One trainee at a time worked with an assistant city editor for six months learning to report and write stories the *Star*'s way. Being a good trainee meant being fast, accurate, concise, and enterprising. Working all the time helped demonstrate to editors how badly you wanted to be a reporter. I rushed to the scenes of bank robberies, covered boring school board meetings, and worked for the paper's "Action Line" column, tracking down lost pension checks and badgering unscrupulous TV repairmen to refund bloated bills. I went undercover and infiltrated the Georgetown marijuana and LSD hippie drug scene. After a year, I was offered a job as a reporter.

James Reston intervened.

"Hello, Sterba?"

"Yes," I said curtly.

It was six-thirty in the morning. I was working early obits in the empty *Star* newsroom, compiling information on what the cops called "cheap murders" in poor black neighborhoods. And I had talked to a woman who had learned hours before that her husband had been killed in Vietnam. She had burst into tears as I questioned her. Milking street addresses and middle initials out of grieving young widows at six in the morning could make you cynical about your chosen career fast. Getting street addresses and middle initials wrong in an obituary could end that career fast.

"This is Scotty Reston."

I jerked my head around to see who the clown was in the newsroom pulling my leg. Nobody there.

"Right," I said dubiously.

"I've got this job over here and a friend passed on your name and said you might be interested in it. Why don't you come over and have a little talk."

James Barrett "Scotty" Reston was the most famous newspaperman in Washington. Born in Clydebank, Scotland, to strict Scottish Presbyterian parents, he moved with his family to Dayton, Ohio, when he was eleven. He was a champion golfer at the University of Illinois and a publicist for the Cincinnati Reds before taking a job with the Associated Press. He joined *The New York Times* in 1938, covered World War II from London, and went to Washington in 1941. During the next forty-eight years he got many scoops, won two Pulitzer Prizes, turned the Washington Bureau into the most powerful reporting team in Washington, and wrote the most influential column in the nation.

When I arrived at Reston's office the next day on my lunch hour, Iver Peterson introduced himself as Reston's clerk and told me that Scotty had been called to an urgent meeting. We grabbed sandwiches and talked. Peterson told me how Reston had gotten the idea of hiring clerks, as Supreme Court justices did, from justice Felix Frankfurter. Each June, Scotty hired a college graduate who wanted to be a journalist to work for him for a year as a personal assistant and researcher. He usually hired Ivy Leaguers like Peterson, a Harvard grad who had gotten the job the previous June. But Peterson was leaving four months early to take a job in Vietnam with the U.S. Agency for International Development, and Reston needed a fill-in before a June graduate would be available. He had offered the job to Sam Smith, my first friend in Washington. I had roomed with Sam during the previous summer, when I worked as a summer intern at the U.S. Commission on Civil Rights. Sam was publisher of the *Idler,* an iconoclastic magazine of politics and culture, and the *Capitol East Gazette,* a weekly newspaper. He was deeply committed to community journalism and he liked what he was doing enough to turn down the job and recommend me.

After an hour talking with Iver, I returned to the *Star.*

The following Friday, Scotty and I were on a flight together to Michigan. I had taken the day off. He had invited me along to talk on the plane, where we wouldn't be interrupted. He was on his way to see Governor George Romney, and he proposed that

I try out for the clerk job by handling the column on Romney he was about to write. My task was to read it for factual errors, misspellings, dropped words, and the like, bring these to his attention, and then dictate the final version from Lansing to the Washington Bureau. This I did. We parted company. He went back to Washington and I went to Owosso, to see my mother and my hometown girlfriend, for the weekend.

Reaction to the column came instantly. Phone calls and telegrams poured in. The Detroit papers reported an embarrassing Reston blunder. Scotty had written that Governor Romney poured himself a cup of coffee during the interview. Romney was a Mormon. Mormons don't drink coffee. He had poured beef broth. The primary responsibility of a Reston clerk was to catch such mistakes. I had failed miserably.

Scotty hired me anyway. He said he liked the idea that I was from the Midwest, that I hadn't gone to Harvard, and, most important, that I had a hometown girl. In truth, he believed in the power of forgiveness, and it worked. From that day on I would have done anything for him and for the *Times.* Soon I was in the bosom of the Gray Lady, ensconced in an office next to his in the Washington Bureau of the *Times,* researching, proofreading, answering mail, and buying Walnut pipe tobacco.

Scotty was an arresting figure. He was fireplug short, muscular, and jaunty in his usual bow ties and vested suits. He had a kind of moral dignity. He sympathized with the powerful men he wrote about, but when he sat with his reading glasses perched low on his nose and his pipe was belching smoke in front of his battered typewriter on deadline, you knew he was telling them to do the right thing. There was no one he couldn't get on the phone.

Scotty was a Washington insider. He cared about his country and its values, he worried about it and its leaders. He wasn't the least bit cynical. Working for him was exciting. I worked all the time. From the bottom of Washington's journalism ladder, writing about "cheap murders," I found myself now at the top, viewing Washington through his eyes. I was a privileged gofer.

"Sterba, I left my golf clubs at Williamsburg over the weekend," he announced one day. "They're over at the White House.
Go get them for me, will you?"

Scotty had gone to Colonial Williamsburg to play golf with
President Lyndon Johnson and had forgotten to bring his clubs
home. The clubs came back to Washington on the president's
helicopter. So, on my first visit to the White House, I came out
past the security guards and onto Pennsylvania Avenue with a
bag of golf clubs over my shoulder.

"Sterba," he said, leaning into my office from his office one
afternoon. "The president is on the line. Take some notes."
Johnson chewed Scotty up and down for fifty minutes, accus-
ing him of joining critics who were disloyal to America, who
wanted the communists to win, people out to destroy our country.
Scotty had written a tough column criticizing the president's
Vietnam War policies. Johnson rattled on, spewing profanities,
not stopping to catch his breath. Scotty couldn't get a word in
edgewise. I scribbled seventeen pages of notes on a yellow legal
pad. When the president hung up, I could read only brief snatches
of what I'd written. I rushed into Scotty's office and confessed
what happened.

"Oh, that's all right," he said gently. Then his frown turned
to a big grin.

"I think I got the drift," he laughed.

"Sterba," Scotty said months later, coming out of his office
with Hubert Humphrey after a closed-door heart-to-heart ses-
sion about the president, the war, and the forthcoming election,
lubricated by a couple of belts of whiskey, "have you got the key
to the men's room? The vice president has to take a piss."

When Scotty traveled, the news editors in the Washington
Bureau, Robert Phelps and Alvin Shuster, found reporting as-
signments for me all over town. There was plenty to do and I
was eager to do it. I substituted for reporters on vacations. Russell
Baker, another *Times* columnist, was just down the hall and he
suggested stories and offered reporting tips. Tom Wicker, the
Bureau Chief, went to bat for me once when a story I wrote about

drug policy was going to lead the front page of the *Times* the next day. The kid deserves a byline, he argued to New York. No way, said New York. Clerks don't get bylines.

What I got instead was reporting experience. In October of 1967 I helped cover a march on the Pentagon in which about one hundred thousand people protested United States involvement in the Vietnam War. I spent the night dodging tear gas, watching police carry off demonstrators, and phoning in urgent updates. Some six hundred and fifty people were arrested during the demonstration, which Norman Mailer immortalized in *Armies of the Night*. In April of 1968 I spent days covering the riots in Washington following the assassination of the Dr. Martin Luther King, Jr. By the time my apprenticeships at the *Evening Star* and with Scotty were over, I was ready to become a *Times* reporter.

But first I took a brief detour. Harrison Salisbury, another great journalist, was the editor in charge of the paper's coverage of 1968 national political conventions, the Republicans in Miami and Democrats in Chicago, and he took me on as his assistant. I became another glorified gofer in charge of logistics. I rented hotel rooms and cars and made sure they were assigned to the right reporters and editors. I checked up on phone installations, credentials, copyboys, watercoolers, and workspace. During the conventions themselves, we worked almost around the clock, especially when Mayor Richard Daley's police set upon antiwar demonstrators in Chicago.

In the fall of 1968, I became a reporter in New York. I spent weeks covering a city teachers' strike and the quest by black leaders for community control of local school boards. The next spring I was asked to go to Vietnam as a war correspondent and I jumped at the chance. The war was the most important event of my generation.

At that moment Eugene L. Roberts took me briefly under his wing. He had covered the civil rights struggles in the South and had just returned from two difficult years in Vietnam to become National Editor of the *Times*. I was due in Saigon in May. In the meantime, I'd work for him.

"Why don't you wander around the country for a couple of months, see what's going on, and write about it," he told me. That's all he told me. I started wandering around the Midwest. I took buses and talked to all sorts of ordinary people. I wrote features about small towns and interesting characters. Unlike the city editors in New York who wanted to know what I was doing every few hours, Gene never asked. Weeks passed. I got nervous, so I called him to explain my plans. He listened briefly.

"Well, you just keep those cards and letters coming," he said. It was my first insight into why everybody wanted to work for Gene. He trusted his people. He treated them as adults. He gave them time and space, and he went to bat for their stories.

I spent a year and a half as a war correspondent in Vietnam in 1969 and 1970. American troop withdrawals were beginning when I arrived but a lot of fighting went on, too. During those two years, 13,635 American soldiers were killed and 80,225 were wounded. The American deaths were dwarfed by Vietnamese combat deaths on both sides, estimated at 722 per day, not including civilians. I spent a lot of time in the field, writing about grunts in combat units. I left the war shaken, exhausted, depressed, and delighted to be getting out of it.

From Saigon I moved to Jakarta, Indonesia, and roamed around Asia covering all sorts of stories from coups to textile disputes, Third World poverty to "miracle" rice. I wrote about communist insurgents in Thailand and Malaysia, Muslim insurgents in the Philippines, and Tamil insurgents in Sri Lanka. I covered the 1971 war between India and Pakistan from the eye of the conflict, Dacca, which became the capital of the new nation of Bangladesh. I spent much of the next year covering turmoil in what was left of Pakistan, famine in Afghanistan, and peace talks between Pakistan and India. After five years of racing around Asia, I was worn out. I asked Gene Roberts for a reporting job on his staff. He said he'd find one.

Before becoming a national correspondent, though, I wanted to take thirteen weeks vacation, drawing on a bank account of vacation time that I had not used. I planned a long, slow trip home from Indonesia to Australia and then across the islands of the South Pacific, stopping off in places like Fiji and French Polynesia. Gene thought it was a great idea. But long before I set out on my dream trip, he quit the *Times* to become editor of the *Philadelphia Inquirer*.

When the time came, I quietly set out. I flew to Sydney, and started decompressing. I had no wars, no deadlines, no worries. I went to see Robert Trumbull, the great World War II war correspondent for the *Times*. He lived in Sydney in semiretirement and wrote about the South Pacific islands I was headed for. My excitement grew.

Around midnight of my third day in Sydney, my hotel phone rang. It was David Jones, Gene Roberts's replacement as National Editor of the *Times*. We exchanged pleasantries. Jones told me how much he was looking forward to having me on his staff, the sooner the better. He said he hadn't been aware of my plans for thirteen weeks off. He said he had lots of national news and a shortage of national reporters. A couple of bureaus were unmanned, one reporter was sick, and some important stories were bubbling in the Rocky Mountain region where I was headed. Could I possibly cut my vacation short to cover them?

Instead of saying absolutely not, I stupidly tried to explain to Jones how long I'd been looking forward to my trip, how much it meant to me, and why. But I was sleepy, the phone line was filled with static, and Jones interrupted often, saying, "Hold on a minute." He said he understood my dilemma. He said he wouldn't be asking me for "this favor" if he didn't think it was important for me to fly back from Sydney, settle into Denver, and get in some "good, solid reporting" to make an "impressive start" on my new assignment. Then, once his staffing problems were ironed out, he said, I could resume my South Pacific vacation right where I left off.

I said okay. It was the beginning of the end of my career at the *Times*.

I rushed to Denver, landing in a spring snowstorm with a sense of urgency. I covered a story about a private company detonating small nuclear bombs to melt oil out of shale deep under western slopes of the Continental Divide. After that, I found myself in a sleepy region.

Months passed. When I raised the vacation issue, Jones said the timing wasn't right. When I raised it again, Jones said I was "too valuable" to go off for the twelve weeks I had coming. When I raised it yet again, he pulled a fast one. He said that since I had accumulated the vacation time working for the foreign desk, the national desk, a different section of the news department, had no real obligation to give it to me. He said he'd try to pay me for some of it and dole out the rest by adding a week to my normal vacation annually. Twelve weeks off was out of the question.

How could I have acted like such a hayseed, a newsroom friend chided. Didn't I know this was no longer the *Times* of Scotty Reston, Russell Baker, and Tom Wicker. This was the *Times* of A. M. Rosenthal, he said, and I had betrayed a pitiful ignorance of the everyday manipulation, back stabbing, battles between fiefdoms, and overall feudal atmosphere that pervaded Abe's *Times*.

Five

Most of the summer people we knew came to Mount Desert to play. They came for a vacation from work and a change of scenery. They came for a week or two, or for a month or more. Some of them were fairly relaxed about their holidays. Others appeared to fill every waking moment with play, relentlessly walking, lunching, hiking, biking, fishing, boating, sailing, picnicking, kayaking, golfing, tennis playing, cocktail partying, and dining out.

The main difference between most summer people and us was that while they played we typed. We weren't the only writers by any means. A fair number of writers spent their summers on Mount Desert, and they were a productive bunch, too. Their books lined the shelves of local bookstores. They gave readings and autographed copies. Like us, they sat at their desks through lovely days fending off friends who beckoned them to come out and play. Or so they told us. Thinking of them holed up in their houses figuring out plots or characters or chronologies was enough to keep Frankie typing. Frankie had the willpower to resist the temptations of a lovely day or a good offer. Not me. I was better at resisting the demands of willpower. For example, our friend Walter came to Mount Desert for only two weeks each summer, and he liked to play golf. So when he called proposing a game, my reasoning, while not up to Mother Teresa standards, went like this: It would be selfish of me to let Walter suffer by himself out on the golf course while I sat at home in front of my laptop merely composing paragraphs.

"I'll be there in fifteen minutes," I'd say.

Early rusticators went on walks. Modern rusticators go on walks, drives, treks, expeditions, and back-and-forth commutes to the world. The operative word was "go." They made "going" high art. They sat around dinner tables and gabbed on the phone endlessly plotting, planning, and committing themselves to going on various forays. Some people thought nothing of driving for hours to visit an antique shop they'd heard about on the other side of Camden, or to some specialty gadget place up near Bangor, or that wonderful restaurant halfway to Machias. People who owned or chartered roomy sailing and cruising boats planned expeditions. They enlisted crew and companions for passages of two or three days or more to Roque Island, forty miles Down East on the other side of Jonesport. They gathered enough friends to fill a lobster boat, packed a lunch, and left in the late morning for Mount Desert Rock to look for whales and seabirds and have a picnic at sea. They set off for Isle Au Haut, one of the big outer islands that is part of Acadia Park, to walk its isolated trails, watch its birds and cruise its shoreline. Or they embarked on intricately plotted itineraries to a combination of islands and harbors that would keep them busy sailing and otherwise camping out on their vessels for days. I had no problem with this type of going as long as I didn't have to go very often.

The kind of going I disliked was leaving Maine for a job, a meeting, or a doctor's appointment that couldn't be put off. Some people had to pop down to Boston for a meeting, or wing to Washington because something had come up that needed personal attention. The kind of going I couldn't stand was commuting. We had friends who commuted most of the summer, and I felt sorry for them. They'd leave early Monday mornings and return late Thursday nights. I did it one summer and felt sorry for myself. I got up at four in the morning to catch a sunrise flight from Bangor to Newark. After work on Thursdays, I'd catch an eight o'clock flight back to Bangor and be home at Frankie's place around eleven.

I didn't much like going anywhere. By the time I started spending summers at Frankie's place, I figured I had already spent too much of my life on the go. The adventure part of travel had lost its appeal. I didn't mind being in exotic places, however inhospitable or uncomfortable, but getting there was no longer fun.

The idea of recreational going didn't interest me much either, except when it involved high adventure or enormous comfort, or both. Once I was invited to write the closing essay for a special travel section in the *Wall Street Journal*. I began it this way: "Do yourself a favor, don't go." It was published, but the editors never asked me to write travel essays again.

We tried to do five or six hours of work each day before going out to play. That meant we were ready to get some exercise in late afternoon. Most people knew we didn't budge before four o'clock, and they didn't bother to roust us beforehand. But when someone called proposing a morning walk, we'd counter by suggesting an afternoon walk. The counteroffer was our standard operating procedure for handling drinks and meals as well. Our philosophy was that over here was better than over there. A porchbender in town? Why not come out to our porch in the woods and face some real mosquitoes?

Dinners? Going to dinner at friends' places was fine, as long as we didn't have to do it more than once or twice a week. Most of their houses were only ten or fifteen minutes away. If we came home from a walk at six, we had an hour and a half to type before piling into the car at seven-thirty. And we were usually back by ten-thirty.

We rarely went to restaurants. One restaurant dinner a summer was a lot. In my first ten summers at Frankie's place, I could count the number of restaurant dinners we ate on two hands.

What we liked to do most for dinner was stay home and cook. More often than not, we prepared a meal for ourselves and sat down to a candlelit dinner for two. Less often we invited a few friends or relatives over. Occasionally, a dinner party materialized out of our deft counteroffers. These offers did not stop with the simple truth that we'd rather cook over here than eat over there. Sometimes we lied.

Before going for a walk that afternoon I had filled a ten-quart pail with mussels from the rocks out front and tossed in a few dozen thimble-sized sea snails called periwinkles as well. I had cleaned and sorted the mussels into two groups. Three dozen small, clean mussels went into the first group, which I washed and stored in the refrigerator along with the periwinkles. The remaining mussels I cleaned, steamed, and shelled. We were having four friends over for dinner that evening, and I was making mussel stew.

I don't have anything against cookbooks. I like reading recipes. I thumb through Julia Child for key ingredients, oven temperatures, and general ideological guidance. We kept a thick file of recipes from newspapers and magazines. I'd ruffle through them from time to time, but I hated to cook with a cookbook open in front of me. I had an editor once who felt about the thesaurus the way I felt about the cookbook. One day I asked him if he had a thesaurus I could borrow to find a better word.

"That's so chicken shit," he said. Editors said such things among themselves to poke fun at writers. In their view, a thesaurus was a crutch unworthy of a truly professional wordsmith. I have peeked into the thesaurus sheepishly ever since. Still, peeking into a thesaurus while writing seems more natural to me than peeking into a cookbook while cooking.

When I made something entirely new, I'd find a recipe, read it and follow instructions. The next time I made it, I might glance at the recipe but I didn't let its instructions deter me from experimenting. A dish cooked experimentally can turn out differently every time. For dinner guests, this has its pleasures and perils.

I had experimented with mussel stew over many summers, carrying the recipe around in my head like a melody. I never strayed far from the basic formula, but I tried different herbs and ingredients.

MUSSEL STEW

Fill a standard 10-quart pail with mussels and clean, scraping off limpets and beards. Set aside 3 dozen of the smallest, cleanest mussels.

In a lobster pot, bring an inch of water to a vigorous boil, dump in the rest of the mussels, and cover. Steam the mussels until the water foams up and the mussel shells open—usually about 7 minutes.

Dump mussels and water into a sink and let drain. Spray cold water over mussels and let them cool. Remove steamed mussel meats from their shells, pull off any beards, and clean off any shell fragments and other matter, then rinse. Yield: 2 to 3 cups of mussel meat.

Chop 2 medium-sized onions, 4 cloves of garlic, and 2 large baking potatoes (into ice cube-sized chunks), and sauté them in the bottom of a kettle in a slather of olive oil and butter—onions first, then garlic and potatoes. Add a cup of chopped celery and/or leeks and some chopped chili pepper or flakes (if you want some bite).

Pour in 2 bottles of clam broth, a can of chicken broth, and a cup or two of white wine. Add a handful of chopped cilantro stems, and let simmer for 20 minutes. If you want color, add chopped red bell pepper. (I've tossed in a chopped zucchini once in a while, just to get it out of the fridge.) Add a dried bay leaf or a cup of bayberry tea. Make this tea by boiling a couple of branches from a bayberry bush in water until it turns light brown.

Add cleaned mussel meat, mussels in shells, and periwinkles. The periwinkles give the stew a nice sound effect. They sound like marbles when the stew is stirred.

Bring all this to a middling boil, toss in a cup of chopped cilantro, parsley, and/or such herbs as oregano, chives, thyme, basil, even tarragon (but not rosemary). Add one cup of freshly shucked peas (half a box of frozen ones will do) and a cup of milk.

Just before serving, squeeze in the juice of half a lemon. Add salt, pepper, and butter to taste, if necessary.

Our friends arrived at seven-thirty and we ushered them straight indoors to deprive the porch mosquitoes of liquid refreshment.

Walter came with the latest news about the World Cup, which he delivered with the enthusiasm of a fourteen-year-old Brazilian. Walter was editor of a university press and knew a great deal about a lot of things, but I had never met anyone who was as excited and erudite a fan of international soccer as Walter. He was just as enthusiastic and learned about opera and baseball too. He could segue in minutes from the status of an Italian goalie's shin injury to an assessment of Cecilia Bartoli's last five performances of *La Cenerentola* to the history of Roger Clemens's earned run average.

Jamie arrived with news from his lobster boat, on which he had spent most of the day dealing with an engine repair and studying the instruction manual for his new global satellite positioning system. Jamie, an investment adviser, knew a lot about making money and the gadgets money could buy, especially those having to do with boats, and I counted on him to keep me informed on what was new.

Susanna, Jamie's wife, was a book editor in New York commuting to Mount Desert over long weekends. She had just gotten off the plane and reported that New York was hot and clammy. It was music to our ears on a chilly evening sitting in front of a blazing fire.

Linn came with local gossip. The latest: an affair between a local wife and a summer person's son, and that's not all!

It was a relaxed and cozy group, and the mussel stew was a hit. Eventually, after second helpings, salad, and cheese, we moved back around the fireplace for coffee. Walter noticed a thick unbound manuscript on the coffee table and picked it up. It was a biography, and with it was a letter from Frankie's publisher with a request for a blurb to be delivered in two weeks.

"So Frankie, are you going to do it?" Walter asked.

"I doubt it," Frankie said. "I'm trying to write my own book and I don't really want to stop and read this one."

"I didn't ask you if you were going to read it," said Walter, grinning.

"In all honesty, I don't want to take the time," Frankie said.

"Publishers don't want honesty," Susanna said, laughing. "They want blurbs."

"Actually reading the book is going a bit far," said Walter, laughing.

"So why don't we make up a blurb right now?" I said.

"What if it's an awful book?" asked Jamie.

"Better not read it, just blurb it," I said.

What if the author and publisher were Frankie's good friends and were counting on a blurb from her? Walter asked. What if Frankie agreed to write a blurb for it, then actually read the manuscript and hated it? This was a delicate position. Could Frankie renege? Should she drop a note to the publisher saying, "This thing stinks!" Should she be dishonest and write a blurb heaping praise on the book?

The real talent, we decided, was in writing a blurb that seemed fine and fulfilled the obligation but was ultimately unusable.

"You mean you write a couple of sentences that look good but in a language so innocuous that the publisher can't use them," I asked.

"Right," said Walter. "Okay, think of one."

As we drained our coffee cups, we fell into a deep silence.

"See, it's not easy," said Walter.

"How about the truth?" I asked. Everyone laughed.

An honest assessment of a terrible book you had agreed to blurb would offend your friends, the author, and the publisher, said Susanna. I went on:

"How about this. Why anyone would pay twenty-five dollars to buy and then actually expend vital energy to read yet another biography of . . . boggles the imagination."

Nope, said Walter. That was an illustration of how a damning blurb can be turned into praise.

"I can see it now, right on the front cover," he went on. "Boggles the imagination . . . raves the *Wall Street Journal*."

Long after the guests departed and the dishes were cleaned up I retreated to the bookshelf, retrieved *Common-Sense Pest Control,* and looked up mice. In the index, just after the entry for "Mexican chicken bedbugs," which I felt darned lucky not to be up against, came "Mice." I turned to a subsection entitled "combating," and read:

> Summary: Least-Toxic House Mouse Control:
> 1. Mouseproof your house as you would weatherproof it by repairing all small holes through which mice might enter. [Since Frankie's place wasn't even winterized, mice had almost as much access to it as did the cold. Stopping both mice and cold was a very expensive proposition.]
> 2. Store grain and other foodstuffs in tight-fitting glass or metal containers.
> 3. *Trap mice that have already entered the house.* (Emphasis mine.)

There it was. *Common-Sense Pest Control* was saying it was all right to trap mice, to wage war against these invaders. Now, all I needed was weapons and a war strategy. And there was no better war strategist than Sun Tzu. I was struck by two passages: "Supreme excellence consists in breaking the enemy's resistance without fighting." And: "The skillful leader subdues the enemy's troops without any fighting."

But wait a minute! How could I do that? According to *Common-Sense Pest Control,* our situation was beyond winning without fighting. The mice had already won. They were all over the house, acting as though they owned it. We couldn't "mouseproof" the house by covering up all the holes the mice might use to invade. Their invasion was over.

I couldn't win without fighting. I had to root out an occupation force. Yet I knew I needed a rationale for doing so. Without one I risked rousing antiwar sentiment from the other end of the house.

As luck would have it, my rationale arrived the next morning as we were sitting down to berries and newspapers. A panel truck from Brown's Appliance in Ellsworth pulled into our driveway and a man came to the front door and introduced himself as Roger Sprague. He said he was responding to our call for someone to come and see why the clothes dryer wasn't working. We pointed him in the direction of the utility room and went back to our breakfast and papers.

Roger went about his work. The utility room was a tight fit for washer, dryer, hot water heater, water pump, fishing tackle, tools, anti-mosquito devices, porch-farming gear, and lots of plain junk. We heard grunts and squeaks. Roger sounded like he was doing some heavy lifting, or at least heavy pushing and pulling. We were just getting to our coffee when he emerged.

"So, you got mice," he said solemnly, as if he were announcing we had some sexually transmitted disease. His implication was clear: people like us weren't supposed to have mice; indeed, no one with a modicum of self-respect in these parts "had mice." We sheepishly dropped our heads. He led us into the utility room to confront what he called "evidence." There, on the floor behind the dryer, which he had pulled out from the wall, were enough clumps of shredded rags and droppings to suggest we were looking at a headquarters, what Vietnam vets might refer to as a kind of mouse COSVN. (These were the initials for the Central Office of South Vietnam, the jungle headquarters of the Viet Cong.)

Roger also showed us a burned-out thermostat, and while he didn't directly accuse the mice of causing it, he did say, "I've seen it happen." He replaced the thermostat and changed the dryer's worn fan belt.

The bill came to $114, I immediately seized upon this as evidence that the mice were engaged in economic sabotage. They were assaulting our economic well-being. This was no longer a simple problem of four-legged squatters. This was a pocketbook issue. And it wasn't the first time. A few summers back, we had discovered that mice had eaten through the electrical wiring under the house and shorted it out. This short had caused all sorts of calamity, including the cancellation of a dinner for eight. An electrician had to be summoned to patch things up, and a large check was written. Another July, when we turned the oven switch on the electric stove, the stove erupted into sparks and smoke, blew a fuse, and filled the house with acrid fumes that smelled like exploding white phosphorous rockets. We found that our furry friends had built a cozy nest inside the stove's control panel. It took another large check to the electrician to undo what that nest had done. The smell lingered for weeks.

Now this. I thanked Roger in a solemn tone that masked my inner glee.

The next afternoon, around four o'clock, I heard Frankie shouting across the house.

"Let's do boat," she yelled. I couldn't believe my ears, but she got no argument out of me. I'd go for a boat ride anytime at a moment's notice. We grabbed slickers and charts and were out the door in ten minutes.

"Let's go to Southwest Harbor and get some gas then go for a walk on Great Cranberry," I said.

Our boat was registered as a "motor vessel." Fortunately it was too small as motor vessels go to be labeled "stinkpot," which is what bigger boats with built-in engines were called by sailors. That was an important distinction in these waters because this was serious sailing territory. Here, sailors, whose aesthetic required them to acquire and maintain, sometimes at enormous cost, vessels whose primary means of propulsion was the wind, had no use for motor yachts. Motor yachts blew diesel smoke out of their exhausts. Sailboats, of course, had auxiliary engines, but using an engine for more than pushing through doldrums or maneuvering in a snug harbor was the mark of an amateur. Most offensive were the metal-hulled, motor yachts that looked for all the world like bloated sardine cans.

Frankie's Uncle Chub was a terrific yachtsman who often sailed his ketch, *Long Haul,* from Boston to Northeast Harbor, alone across the open ocean. Once when we were sailing with him and one of these belching tubs roared by he said, "There's all this free energy out here, and they're burning up a thousand dollars worth of fuel."

Sailboats greatly outnumbered recreational motorboats in these waters, and they came in every description and shape and size, from great tall ships, restored to full glory, to low and sleek new ketches and yawls and schooners made by local boat makers, to modest barks and tiny, tipsy, two-person Mercury racers. On good-wind days, in Somes Sound and the waters beyond, white canvas triangles were everywhere. In these waters, if you didn't know how to set a jib or loft a spinnaker, you were advised to keep it to yourself.

The Maine coast was also the home to lobster boats, both working and recreational. Technically, these were stinkpots, too, but they were "local" stinkpots; that is, an indigenous part of the waterscape and local economy and, therefore, perfectly okay. They came in two varieties: lobstermen's work boats and work boats built or restored for use as recreational runabouts by summer people. It was impossible to mix them up. The working-boats lacked mufflers and their hulls were grimy. Seagulls followed them from one lobster buoy to another in hopes of getting handouts of discarded bait. Radios aboard lobster boats were likely tuned to country music stations.

The recreational lobster boats were built the same as working lobster boats but they were polished and varnished and quiet, their decks adorned with director's chairs instead of lobster traps, their forward cabins converted from gear-storage dens into sleeping quarters and kitchenettes.

In this floating hierarchy, our boat ranked a step above "putt-putt." It was a utility runabout, and a preowned runabout at that. We'd talked about buying a boat for years but never got around to doing it. Friends with boats invited us on theirs almost enough to satisfy our boating desires. I lacked the motivation to plunge into boatdom. Then one summer I got it—in Tiananmen, Beijing's central square.

One morning in May 1989, I was in the New York office of the *Wall Street Journal* working on a story about relations between man and cockroach when Norman Pearlstine, the managing editor, stopped by my desk and asked if I had any interest in going to Beijing. The Chinese capital was in turmoil. Students were camped out in Tiananmen. Reporters and television crews from around the world had been invited to China to cover the visit of Mikhail Gorbachav, the Soviet Union's Communist Party general secretary. But the reporters and cameras quickly focused on the unprecedented student demonstrations for democracy in the square that had erupted after the April 15 death of Hu Yaobang, the former secretary general of the Chinese Communist Party.

"I'm on my way," I told Pearlstine.

I had been reporting from China, off and on, for a decade, and I spoke a little college Mandarin. My first visit was in 1979, just after President Jimmy Carter officially normalized relations with the Beijing government. I was based in Hong Kong for the *New York Times,* and I went in to cover Vice President Walter Mondale's visit. After that, I went in a lot. I moved to Beijing in 1981 and lived there for more than a year. During the 1980s, I went back often for the *Wall Street Journal.*

The day after I told Norm I'd go, I had a tourist visa and was on a Japan Airlines flight to Tokyo. It was the evening after Beijing authorities had declared martial law. On the Tokyo-Beijing leg I found Graham Earnshaw, a Reuters correspondent I had worked with in Hong Kong and Beijing. At the Beijing airport we found no taxis. But Graham, a fluent Mandarin speaker, found a student with a car who was taking supplies to his colleagues in the square and persuaded him to give us a lift to the Great Wall Hotel. There, we dropped our bags and went straight to Tiananmen. We spent the night in the square, walking from encampment to encampment, watching caravans of cars and trucks loaded with young people waving banners calling for democracy and calling China's leaders fascist pigs and hopeless incompetents. As dawn broke, we hired a cyclo-bicycle to pedal us back to the Great Wall Hotel, where I took a shower and wrote a story.

All hell broke loose in the days and weeks that followed. Several army divisions were called into Beijing. On the evening of

June 4, soldiers attacked the demonstrators with bullets, bayonets, and tanks, killing hundreds of them and driving the rest from the square. The streets came alive with gunfire and clanking tank treads. From a balcony of the Beijing Hotel I watched a man walk in front of the column of tanks, stop, and raise his arms. The column stopped. The man refused to move. He taunted the soldiers in the tanks, daring them to run him over or shoot him. Tears rolled down my cheeks as I watched. It was the bravest act I had ever seen. Then another man came out and led him to the side of the street. He melted into the crowd.

Getting around town to report was difficult and dicey. The authorities imposed a dusk-to-dawn curfew. Day and night, bullets flew. Shooting erupted in unexpected places as soldiers patrolled the streets of the capital confronting angry residents. I rode around on a Flying Pigeon bicycle. The residents were friendly, even helpful. They would tell me what streets were dangerous and point me away from alleys where soldiers were stationed or on patrol.

For two months I lived on adrenaline and hotel buffet food, sleeping very little, writing through the nightly curfew, venturing out to report the story during the day. It was draining emotionally, and thinking about Maine helped. I thought about Maine a great deal. One day I vowed to buy a boat.

I left Beijing in early July and arrived at Frankie's place ready to go boat shopping.

One of the first people we asked for advice about boat owning was George Peabody, Frankie's uncle. George was genial, warm, and funny, and the three of us had gone sailing and had gone on picnics together over the summers. I learned a lot about sailing from George. He had attended the University of North Carolina and had been an officer in the Coast Guard during World War II. He was an officer aboard troop carriers and supply ships in the Pacific, ferrying Marines and their gear to island battlegrounds, including Iwo Jima. After the war he entered a seminary and became an ordained minister in the Episcopal Church. He eventually left the church and started a leadership training company and began conducting seminars on innovation, power, and leadership for major corporations and government agencies.

Asking Uncle George about boat buying was a stroke of luck because he said he, too, was looking for a boat. If we found one, he said, he'd buy in as a partner, sight unseen. We were thrilled. We would own one-third shares. Frankie and I felt like swabbies teaming up with an admiral.

We quickly found what we were looking for and on July 15, 1989, we bought our boat for $8,000. It was eleven years old but it was sleek and sat low in the water. Its 70-horse Johnson outboard had a battered cowling and looked like it had hit its share of rocks, but the engine was easy to start, and ran fine.

Our days of depending on other people's boats to get out to sea were over. As a first-time boat owner I had the same feeling of independence I'd felt when I got my first car. We could go out to little islands and explore, take walks, and have picnics. We could go look for dolphins and seals and sea birds. We could go fishing or simply idle up to the head of Somes Sound and visit a rocky ledge near a bald eagle's nest.

We had one problem: our boat needed a name. Every boat, from the sleekest Hinckley sloop to the tiniest fiberglass dinghy, had a name. But our boat didn't come with a name. We had to think of one. Our tripartite ownership arrangement necessitated a consensus. We sought the counsel of Uncle George. We figured that since he had been both an officer in the Coast Guard and minister in the church he had expertise in both boats and inspiration and would give this issue some serious thought. He didn't let us down.

"How about calling her the *Constitution*," he said. "No sense thinking small."

A wonderful idea, I thought. Then I began to wonder what it might be like to have to call the Coast Guard and report that the *Constitution*, a seventeen-foot Boston Whaler, was adrift in Somes Sound.

Frankie was thinking small. She was partial to names like "Chanterelle" or "Gwendylyne," the latter being the name of one of the three sheep that her friend Mary McCarthy, the writer, kept at her place in Castine, over in East Penobscot Bay. I said if she could spell Gwendylyne, I'd consider it. Meanwhile, I was thinking smaller. I remembered a boat named *Frog,* a junk some friends owned in Hong Kong named *Low Profile,* and Sam Smith's tiny sailboat in Washington named *One Iota.* Frankie, George, and I talked about boat names each time we were together. We mulled and mulled. No consensus emerged. This was going to take time. It took years. *Scoop,* the title of Evelyn Waugh's classic novel about foreign correspondents, became an interim name. I adopted it as a marine radio call sign, since call-sign rules required stating the name and number of your vessel when calling. Then, one summer, in a lightning lobbying blitz, I ordered yellow shirts and black hats monogrammed with "Scoop, Northeast Harbor" for all three of us from the Sporty's Tool Shop catalog. *Scoop* stuck, but it wasn't her full name. The name I stuck to her stern was "HMS Scoop." It sounded regal, I thought, and authentic, since Waugh was an Englishman.

It didn't take very long to discover that *Scoop* had what George called "a personality." That is, the old Johnson 70 outboard was hard to start and it stalled a lot. Minor tune-ups were of no avail.

"Got no compress'n in one cylinda," one mechanic told us. The outboard's other drawback was that it lacked a hydraulic lift. It had to be tilted in and out of the water by hand, and that took a great deal of exertion and back straining. This wasn't easy for me, and was even less so for Uncle George. After three summers of back pain we decided to buy a new Mariner 60-horsepower engine with hydraulic lift for $3,900. With this marvel of modern engineering, we simply pushed a button on the control lever to tilt its propeller up and down. The Mariner started reliably and never stalled unless we let it run out of gas. When I asked if we might get some trade-in allowance for the old Johnson, the salesman at the boat store laughed.

"Ya want my advice," he said, "you might wanta drop 'er in the sound, tie a line to 'er, and try use'n 'er fer ya mooring."

That Johnson sat in a shed at the Manset Boat House for more than a year. Then a man phoned and offered us $500. We quickly took the money. But I retained its spare propeller as a piece of memorabilia. I thought it would make a great dining table centerpiece. Frankie didn't.

When we got home from our boat trip that afternoon, I took a look at my porch crop and noticed that the sorrel had grown like topsy.

"Let's have sorrel soup," I said.

"Great idea."

Sorrel was a great porch crop. I could pick it now and it would grow fast enough to pick again in a couple of weeks.

SORREL SOUP

In a lobster pot, heat a quarter cup of olive oil and add 2 medium-sized chopped yellow onions and 2 golf-ball-sized (or slightly larger) red potatoes (skins and all), chopped. Sizzle onions and potatoes until the onions are translucent then add a loosely filled pail of sorrel leaves, stems and all, plus 3 or 4 sprigs of fresh peppermint. Cover and steam until the sorrel wilts. Pour this into a blender and moosh until it becomes a thick, gelatinous goo. Add a can of chicken broth and moosh some more. Strain through a sieve with big holes into a pot (you have to work the gooey liquid through until what's left is tough fiber, which you discard). Heat slowly, adding milk—half a cup or more, as necessary. Grind in fresh pepper and melt in a couple of tablespoons of butter.

After that we had what at Frankie's place was called kitchen-sink pasta. We threw in leftovers, freeing up space in the refrigerator. It produced an easy and, if the leftovers were good, a delicious main course.

KITCHEN SINK PASTA

Remove whatever leftover meat or fish you can find in the refrigerator. (I found one grilled chicken breast, five slices of crisp bacon, and three hot Italian sausages.) Cut into bite-size pieces. Into a heated wok, put 2 tablespoons of chili oil and 3 chopped scallions.

*Stir-fry a minute or so, then add the meat and whatever you want
in the way of veggies and herbs: chopped zucchini, snow peas,
cilantro, basil, dill, even leftover cooked carrots or potatoes, chopped.
Boil whatever kind of pasta you desire and drain.*

*When all the stuff in the wok gets nice and sizzling, add some
olive oil, shake in a couple of tablespoons of soy sauce, squeeze in
the juice of half a lemon or lime, and quickly dump it on top of the
hot, steaming pasta.*

*Serve in bowls with freshly grated Parmesan cheese. Follow with
salad and warmed bread.*

Fortunately, the mice let us eat most of our dinner in peace.
Their floorshow began with the salad course. Our four-legged
Rockettes pranced and cavorted, performing every maneuver
short of a chorus line.

I helped Frankie clear the table, then retired to the couch and
again opened *Common-Sense Pest Control*. I already had an economic justification for war. But, as any Pentagon major would
advise, I had to demonize my foe before I attacked, and positioning myself as the good guy. This is what the military called
"perception control"—a propaganda offensive. I needed demonizing data, and on page 208 I found it:

Mice damage food, clothing, documents and other human
artifacts and structures through gnawing, urination and def-
ecation. The damage to food stores from mice waste is probably 10 times the damage attributed to direct feeding. Many
fires of "unknown cause" undoubtedly occur when mice
or rats chew through electrical wires. Although the complete role and extent of mice involvement in human dis-
eases is not yet known, Table 16.3 on the facing page points
out some of the connections that have come to light.

On Table 16.3 I found bubonic plague, salmonellosis, lym-
phocytic choriomeningitis, rickettsial pox and leptospirosis, ratbite
fever, tapeworms, and dermatitis. This was a fairly awesome little

list, and I made a mental note to refer to it if Frankie protested. Frankie could be shamelessly two-faced when it came to animal-rights issues, one minute dispatching the noble lobster without the slightest twinge of guilt, siding with potential carriers of bubonic plague the next.

Bubonic plague! I could see the headline in the *Ellsworth American:* "Bubonic Plague Outbreak on Island Linked to Mice Appeasers."

Demonizing works. I was ready for war.

Six

We assumed that the construction workers, who arrived next door before seven in the morning six days a week, spent their Sunday mornings in the pews at a local house of worship, or else recovering at home from a festive Saturday night at one of the local taverns. We didn't know. We frequented neither church nor saloon. All we knew was that on the Sabbath the silence was golden on our little peninsula, and we slept late.

On the morning of the third Sunday in July we slept later than usual. It was a good thing, too, because when we finally rousted ourselves up and out to the porch we discovered that Somes Sound was full of sailboats. They were sleek International One Design sloops, thirty-three feet long with four-person crews. These were the greyhounds of sailing and they were preparing to race.

"This sort of thing wouldn't have happened in Bishop Peabody's days," Frankie said. The Reverend Malcolm Endicott Peabody, her grandfather, summered in Northeast Harbor and was a keen sailing racer. But he did his best to keep Sunday mornings sacred, even for rusticators and sailors. In fact, the Internationals didn't race on Sunday. Their competitions were usually scheduled for Saturdays and Mondays.

But here they were right out front. A glance down the sound explained why. A second day of pea-soup fog was down where the Fleet usually raced.

As we watched, the boats sailed back and forth, jockeying toward their starting positions and almost colliding as they tacked near an invisible starting line. One boat came about and turned straight toward another boat, which itself had to turn sharply to get out of the way. This maneuvering was a tactic. Racers used right-of-way to their advantage. The rule was that if your boat was on a starboard tack you had the right-of-way over boats on a port tack, and so had to get out of the way.

Suddenly a loud *ka-boom*! came from the starter's gun. They were off, the biggest, most beautiful racing boats in the Fleet, streaming for their first mark across and down the sound toward Acadia Mountain.

I had no sailing experience before coming to Frankie's place. Her uncles George and Chub and her sister's husband, George Denny, gently showed me the ropes, or, rather, the lines and sheets. When friends with sailboats invited us out on the water, I'd learn a bit more.

Frankie was an old salt. She started sailing early. She sailed with her grandparents and with her uncles. Her father didn't like to sail but he sent his children to the Fleet for rowing and sailing classes, and for racing. The classes were like boot camp and turned kids, Frankie among them, off sailing. But watching the International Ones streak down the Sound, she thought out loud about racing again.

"You thinking about . . ."

"Just thinking," she said.

As the Internationals glided down the sound, Frankie stretched and bent and crunched on her pink mat on the porch. Finishing a set of sit-ups, she said, "I finally feel good, no aches. It's taken three weeks."

"That just goes to show you that the FitzGerald Survival School isn't what it used to be," I said. It certainly wasn't the paratrooper training I remembered from my first visit. But it did its magic summer after summer. The morning exercise, afternoon walks, and spurts of metabolic overdrive triggered by flops into the sound took pounds off. I'd be able to take a pair of well-rested trousers with a thirty-four-inch waist out of the closet in mid-August and try them on. They'd fit perfectly. I'd exile my size thirty-sixes but only to the back of the closet, knowing they were just a few cheeseburgers away from full employment once again. The weight I lost each summer found its way home, Lassie-like, through the calorie-filled canyons of Manhattan over the winter. This happened in spite of trips to the gym, where I replicated my Maine roadwork, even doubling and tripling the distance. This wasn't easy on an indoor track where not a single squirrel or mushroom broke the monotony.

While the Internationals raced, we trotted up the lane and back and jumped into the water, wearing swimsuits so we wouldn't distract any racers. We showered and sat down to breakfast. Before long, the boats had tacked for a run to the finish line. With the wind behind them, they lofted bright-colored sails called spinnakers and surged up the sound. As they neared, a bald eagle flapped across our view along the shore.

Frankie finished her coffee and retreated to her Remington. I was on my way to my Toshiba when I was waylaid by the bookshelf. I was thinking about sailing and the coast of Maine.

Sailors raved about the Maine coast. Southwest winds of fifteen to twenty knots were predictable on most afternoons, but other coasts had ample winds. What made Maine so special were its islands and its jagged coastline of rocky headlands, peninsulas, and bays. These features offered great scenery, ever-changing sailing conditions, and protection if the sea got rough.

I grabbed a couple of familiar books and settled into the couch. If I knew how many islands the Maine coast had, I'd forgotten. I opened *Islands in Time: A Natural and Human History of the Islands of Maine,* written by Philip W. Conkling and published in 1981. Conkling was president of the Island Institute, a nonprofit group dedicated to helping Maine island communities and their ecosystems. Surely, he'd know. He didn't. Maine had more islands than all other East Coast states combined, he wrote. But:

How many islands are there out there? Maybe we should know, but we don't. Can't even count them. The number changes too often with storms, history, and the tides—but mostly with the tides—to make the effort seem worthwhile. If you count them at high water, for instance, you end up with a lot of islands that are actually attached to the mainland or to other islands at low tide; if you count at low water, you count hundreds that disappear ten to twenty feet under at high tide. In most places in this world you might be able to accept Webster's definition of an island as a piece of land smaller than a continent surrounded by water, but not here. Not in Maine. These islands are, like their inhabitants, hard to pin down.

In other books, I found estimates as high as sixty-two hundred. The United States Geological Survey, using satellite imaging technology, counted around three thousand islands and ledges that are more than one acre in size at high tide. The College of the Atlantic reported that fifteen hundred islands are both larger than one acre and have names.

Maine's islands are spread along a coastline that is only 228 miles long. But that coastline threads in and out and around so much that if you were to pull the thread into a straight line, it would stretch from New York to Los Angeles. If you pulled the thread hard, it might stretch to Hawaii and beyond.

From any summit on the island we could look over some interesting geology, and geology was a subject I knew something about. I had tried to impress Frankie over the summers with my knowledge of rocks and minerals, geological formations and how they got that way. Once, she asked me why Mount Desert's pink granite was pink.

"Nonferromagnesian feldspars," I said, matter-of-factly, picking up a piece of granite. "Have a look. Orthoclase here, and over here, plagioclase. See the striations?"

That would impress her, I thought.

"How do you know that?" she asked. The story of how I knew was more interesting to her than what I knew, because it started with Sputnik. I was a teenager when the Soviet Union, on October 4, 1957, launched the world's first earth-orbiting satellite and threw the United States into a Cold War tizzy. Alarmists said the communists were ahead in science. To close the science gap, the Eisenhower administration created the National Science Foundation. One of its missions was to interest kids in science careers. It set up scholarships for high school students to study at colleges and universities during the summer. I got two of them, in successive years, one to study physical and historical geology under a legendary professor named Charles C. Bradley at Montana State College in Bozeman. We traipsed over the mountains all summer, learning as we hiked. It was the most fascinating learning experience I'd had, so fascinating, in fact, that I later found science courses taught in lecture halls and labs at Michigan State so boring I switched to journalism.

Mount Desert's natural beauty was the result of geological and climatic trauma.

Between four hundred and fifty and five hundred million years ago the region was covered by sea, which laid down a blanket of mud and silt that gradually metamorphosed into fine-grained and gloomy layers of gray rock called Ellsworth schist. Erosion and volcanic eruptions piled sedimentary layers of gravel, silt, and volcanic ash over the schist. Then, a hundred million years later, give or take fifty million years, huge bodies of molten rock pushed from deep within the earth disrupting the layers above it. One of these bodies was a giant glob of molten lava. In some places, the glob melted the layers above it and eventually reached the earth's surface. In other places it stopped under the sedimentary layers. There the glob slowly cooled, allowing minerals to form into crystals of quartz and feldspar and hornblende that solidified into pink granite.

Hundreds of millions of years passed. Dinosaurs came and went. The rock layers above the granite were gradually eroded away by rain and wind. The granite, harder and more resistant to ero-

sion than the schist, emerged as a huge mountain ridge with
V-shaped valleys cut into its face.

Ice was a latecomer in this geological history. Glaciers began
to arrive about a million years ago. They advanced southward
from Canada, covering New England with massive sheets of glacial
ice thousands of feet thick. The glaciers advanced and retreated
at least nine times in cycles that lasted about one hundred thousand years. The last glacier arrived eighteen thousand years ago,
covering New England as far south as Long Island in New York.
The weight of that ice sculpted the granite ridges of Mount Desert,
smoothing and rounding them. That glacier receded about ten
thousand years ago and left behind a series of U-shaped valleys
strewn with giant boulders, the fjord that came to be named Somes
Sound, and a range of magnificent bald mountains.

These mountains, arising from the sea, as they do, are an arresting sight. In 1930, William Warren Vaughan, a summer resident,
wrote:

> Few persons realize what an extraordinary creation Mount
> Desert is. I mean literally extraordinary. For almost all of
> the Atlantic Coast of the United States is painfully "ordi-
> nary"—one of the most uninteresting coasts in the world.
> From Cape Ann to Mexico the shores are deadly dull and
> flat, with miles on miles of sand and marsh, worthless to
> mankind save as it meets the sea and becomes a beach for
> the people to play on. But this island is the exception.

The people who settled Mount Desert were just as fascinating
to me as the geology. I was interested in who they were and where
they came from, in part because a descendant of Mount Desert's
early summer people was pounding away on a typewriter at the
other end of the house.

Over the years I had read about the Native Americans who
came to the island in the summer, about the Europeans who discovered and settled it, and about the creation of Acadia National
Park. One bookshelf at Frankie's place held a dozen volumes

devoted to Mount Desert. They ranged from a history by Samuel Eliot Morison to a Golden Guide.

In these volumes, I'd read about the early summer visitors who came to "rusticate," and about the arrival of landscape painters. Thomas Cole came to the island in 1844. He led a small invasion of landscape painters from the Hudson River School. Their depictions of the natural beauty of Mount Desert's untrammeled wilderness were seen in exhibitions and galleries in New York, Boston, Philadelphia, and other places. The paintings put Mount Desert on the map. People who saw them wanted to see the island for themselves. As Pamela J. Ballenger describes this phenomenon in her book *Inventing Acadia: Artists and Tourists at Mount Desert,* the painters became shills for a budding new business called excursionism. They were rewarded, in turn, by a growing interest in wilderness. Their renderings of wilderness became enormously popular.

Rusticators, painters and excursionists arrived on Mount Desert by boat in the early days. Weekly steamship service was established along the coast in 1824. The steamboats traveled from Boston to Bangor, with stops along the way. Passengers bound for Mount Desert disembarked at Belfast, Castine, or Rockland, and transferred to fishing schooners for the final passage to the island. Steamship service between Portland and the island in the 1850s made the passage easier. Visitors could also come by stage-coach from Bangor, a trip that took eight hours. Rail service wasn't available until 1884. Rail passengers took the train to the coast, then boarded a ferry for the final eight miles.

Early landscape artists and rusticators lived simply among the local population of farmers and fishermen, renting rooms from them. But as more visitors arrived, guesthouses and hotels were built to accommodate them. Then wealthy visitors to the island bought land and built their own houses, which were called cottages but were, in fact, mansions. They were concentrated on the eastern side of the island in a village then called Eden, and subsequently renamed Bar Harbor. Eden was gradually transformed from a rustic retreat into one of the most fashionable resorts of the Gilded Age. On hand to observe this was E. L. Godkin, a British expatriate and the founding editor of the *Nation* magazine. He came to Eden as a summer boarder whose diet was, exclusively, fish. Godkin's description of the transformation was passed down the generations and embellished. In *Lost Bar Harbor,* a collection of photographs of Eden's grand cottages published in 1982, G. W. Helfrich and Gladys O'Neil wrote this version:

> The first summer visitors are artists and naturalists, well-to-do clergymen and their families, college professors and students—in short, people with leisure time. They board with the natives, accept the plain and homely fare, and find their pleasure in the open air, in sketching, fishing, hiking, boating, or in simply admiring the scenery. At the end of the summer, they depart, and their hosts, counting their money, conclude that taking in boarders is an excellent thing. Boarders return year after year, become old boarders, and get the best rooms. The proprietor soon finds it necessary to enlarge his dining room, perhaps add a wing, and offer his guests fried mutton and potatoes to supplement the usual diet of herring and beans. He begins to advertise, and he solicits testimonials from ministers and editors. His success, of course, does not go unnoticed by his neighbors, who are quick to follow his example. New boarding houses spring up. Small boarding houses grow into big boarding houses, then into hotels with added refinement such as guest registers. Then the hotels grow larger and larger, until the day arrives when Bar Harbor (Eden) has become famous—and crowded.

But long before this stage, the first cottagers appeared. They were, in most cases, especially in the early years, former boarders who, impressed by the tonic air and the grandeur of the scenery, decided to buy a lot and build on it. The first cottages were simple single-story structures, often referred to as huts or shanties, and their owners continued to take their meals in the hotels. Inevitably, more and grander "cottages" and "Italian villas" were built, with carefully manicured lawns, private tennis courts, footmen in livery, and other plutocratic excrescences. The now lowly boarder soon found himself a trespasser on every desirable site from the Ovens to Great Head.

Access to Mount Desert Island got a lot easier after the Civil War, when surplus troop-carrying ships were turned into ferries. Hotel construction on the island boomed. *Harper's* magazine in 1872 called Eden *the* place to vacation, and more and more vacationers came. Wealthy summer people built "cottages" with fifty or sixty rooms in which to "rusticate." These enormous mansions had electricity, running water, and lots of servants. The owners held elaborate lawn parties and picnics. They gave Eden a reputation for summer extravagance, with Old Money and nouveau riche mixing in a stew of excess. There was no shortage of New Money. Between 1861 and 1897, according to historians Charles and Mary Beard, the number of millionaires in the United States went from three to thirty-eight hundred. The new rich wanted to spend their summers where the old rich spent their summers. They pushed into Newport. Many people in Newport decamped for Eden. The social whirl in Eden became so hectic that some of the occupants of the cottages built "camps" on the other side of the island in which to recuperate from rusticating.

In his 1948 book *The Last Resorts: A Portrait of American Society at Play,* Cleveland Amory noted that the 1909 edition of *Baedeker's United States* rated Bar Harbor as the only resort "vying in importance" with Newport. He wrote, "Certainly in the salad days of resorts, it was, after Newport, the recognized second stop on the socially popular Grand Tour of resorts—one which also included the Berkshires in early fall, Hot Springs or White Sulphur in the late fall, and perhaps spring also, and Palm Beach in the winter."

A Boston clipper-ship trade magnate named Alpheus Hardy built the first cottage, a rather modest structure, on Birch Point in 1868. Joseph Pulitzer, the publisher, arrived in 1895. The summer directory for Bar Harbor in 1916 listed 217 cottagers, 115 of them from New York, 28 from Boston, 23 from Philadelphia, 12 from Washington, and the rest, note Helfrich and O'Neil, "came from remote outposts in the hinterland (e.g., Chicago)."

In the 1920s, following the deaths of some of the island's pioneering rusticators, Bar Harbor became stuffier and snootier as a sea change took place in cottage ownership. In 1922, the sale of George Vanderbilt's cottage was the first big piece of Bar Harbor real estate to change hands in fifteen years. In the next three years, forty-seven cottages were sold. Leading the move in were enormously rich Philadelphians such as E. T. Stotesbury, the banker-financier who in 1929 bragged that he was worth one hundred million dollars, and A. Atwater Kent, the electronics and radio pioneer. The Stotesburys bought a cottage in 1925, spent $1.3 million remodeling it, and ended up with Wingwood House. It had eighty rooms—including a new thirty-room wing for servants—fifty-six electric wall heaters, five hot air furnaces, twenty-eight bathrooms, fifty-two telephones, and twenty-six fireplaces made of hand-carved imported marble.

Bar Harbor, wrote Amory, "passed into a white tie era, which if it did not actually mean white tie at least meant that the age-old virtues of Bar Harbor—walking and talking—were all but forgotten." He says the summer people let their three principal social commodities—walking, talking, and flirting—"fall into disrepair." The arrival of the automobile on Mount Desert in 1915 did in walking, he says. The growing habit of drinking cocktails ruined conversation and flirting because when men drank they stopped talking to women.

Bar Harbor gradually lost its opulence. The imposition of the federal income tax in 1913, the crash of 1929, the Depression and then World War II eroded the riches of some summer residents. Rising wage levels increased the cost of servants. During the war, money was tight and the men were away fighting the Germans and Japanese. Then, in 1947, the Great Fire swept the island. It burned eighteen thousand acres, ten thousand of them in Acadia

National Park. In Bar Harbor, the fire destroyed five hotels, sixty-seven cottages, and a hundred and seventy homes. Mount Desert Island, still a scenic gem, faded. Bar Harbor became a has-been resort, falling into disrepair and a sleepy postwar existence.

Twelve miles away, in Northeast Harbor, a very different summer community began to take shape in 1880. In the winter of that year, Charles W. Eliot, the president of Harvard, William Croswell Doane, the Episcopal Bishop of Albany, and Joseph Henry Curtis, a landscape architect from Boston, built houses and founded a summer community of relatives and friends from Philadelphia, Boston, Albany, and New York. They were educators and church people for the most part, and all of them wanted to live simply, quietly, spiritually, and in harmony with both nature and the local population.

Northeast Harbor was unpretentious, discreet, and slow to grow. From there Eliot saw trends and commercial developments elsewhere on Mount Desert that he didn't like. One was the land boom around Eden. Speculators were buying up land and promoting it. More and more mansions were going up on the shoreline of Frenchman Bay. Hotels were built on top of Green Mountain (now Cadillac). A developer had bought the peak of the highest mountain on the island, erected hotels there, and built a cog railway to carry guests up and down in scenic comfort. Still another ominous trend was the advancing technology of timbering, specifically the advent of the gasoline-fueled power saw. Previously, sawmills were powered by water wheels or steam engines, and they had to be in low-lying areas close to the source of their power. Bringing trees to them from far away wasn't economical. Gasoline-powered saws were mobile. They could get close to the last good timber, up on the sides of Mount Desert's beautiful mountains. Lumber companies owned huge tracts of land on the eastern side of the island. With the new technology, they could denude the mountains.

Eliot, George Dorr, and others sought donations of land and money to acquire land, specifically the scenic highlands on the southeastern side of the island. Their efforts led to the acquisition of more than six thousand acres and in 1916 this acreage was turned into the Sieur de Monts National Monument. It was named after the French patron of explorer Samuel de Champlain, who had discovered the *l'île des Monts-deserts*—isle of bare mountains—in 1604. (Actually, a Portuguese explorer, Esteban Gomes, was the first European to see Mount Desert, in 1525, but he didn't know he'd "discovered" it.) In 1919, the national monument was renamed Lafayette National Park and Eden was renamed Bar Harbor. By 1929 the park had grown to forty-six thousand acres, encompassing nearly half of the island and including parts of the outlying Isle au Haut and the Schoodic Peninsula, on the eastern side of Frenchman Bay. In that year, its name was changed again to Acadia National Park, after the former French colony in the region. The commonplace names of its mountains were changed by park authorities to reflect the park's ties to its early explorers and settlers.

The mountains of Mount Desert had old names that were both simple and logical: Green, Black, Brown's, Little Brown's, Robinson, Dog, and so on. But as Acadia National Park came into being, these names were no longer thought to be grand or historic enough. And in one case they were no longer proper enough. That case was a pair of rounded domes between Jordan Pond and Eagle Lake long called "The Boobies" or "Bubbies," because that's what they looked like: a woman lying on her back with her breasts reaching for the sky. The Boobies were renamed The Bubbles.

Green Mountain became Cadillac Mountain. Brown Mountain, named after the Brown family farm just north of it, was renamed Norumbega, after a fabled mythical city walled in gold on the Penobscot River. Robinson Mountain, also named for a nearby farm family, became Acadia, the French name for the region. Black Mountain became Pemetic, a Native American word for the entire mountainous island. Dog Mountain was changed to St. Sauveur, after the missionary settlement established by French Jesuits nearby in 1613. Dry Mountain, near Bar Harbor and so named because it lacked a spring, was renamed Dorr

Mountain, after George Dorr, who became Acadia National Park's first superintendent.

Although the mountains' new names appeared on new maps, the old names continued to be used on trail signs into the 1960s and '70s, and in some cases longer.

The twenty-six mountains on Mount Desert Island are relatively small as mountains go. Cadillac Mountain is the highest at 1,530 feet above sea level. Flying Mountain is the lowest at 284 feet. In contrast, Katahdin, the highest peak in Maine, rises to a 5,267-foot summit. Alaska's Mount McKinley, the tallest mountain in the United States, peaks at 20,320 feet. Nonetheless, Mount Desert's mountains are arresting because of their proximity to the ocean. From an approaching boat, they appear to rise straight out of the sea. From several of their peaks, the vista of waterscape and islands is unique.

An enormous thunderstorm arrived in the night. Lightning crackled, winds howled, and rain fell in sheets. By midnight the electricity had gone out.

We awoke in fog. The air was damp and cold—the first sweater weather of the summer. The fog wrapped itself around Frankie's place like a wall of cotton. It closed in so tight the trees just outside our bedroom window looked like apparitions. Somes Sound was not visible. Only a ship's foghorn hinted of the world beyond.

The electric power was restored just as I was firing up the charcoal grill to boil water for coffee. We were soon back to work. But as I turned on my computer, I couldn't help but wonder how much humidity it would take to short it out. I wondered how long it would take to grow mildew on my diskettes, how long it would take for Frankie to make some smart aleck remark about the perils of progress and the virtues of her old Remington. The workday passed without electrical shorts. The mildew held off.

The fog held. The next morning Frankie's place felt like a cold steam room. Every cranny of the house was soggy. Towels stayed wet. Humidity incapacitated the salt shaker. Envelopes glued themselves shut.

The fog was so thick I could make out only the outline of the 1-800-OWN-DOCK barge from the porch. We padded up the lane and back and down slippery rocks to the sound. The tide was very low. We had to climb down into the barnacle belt to get to the water's edge. At high tide, the walk from the front porch to the water's edge took ninety steps and it was an easy trek over smooth, clean granite. At low tide the water's edge was one hundred and twenty steps, the last thirty of them over rocks encrusted with sharp white barnacle shells. We had to pad carefully. One misstep barefooted and we could bleed. Mats of olive-green seaweed, mostly rockweed, covered the lower rocks and crevasses where mussels and starfish lived. At the water's edge we could see crabs, urchins, and more mussels just below the surface. Baby lobsters, looking like inch-long mosquito larvae, hovered in the water above them.

We had a favorite low-tide ledge where we could undress and plunge in. From this ledge we could also see four dark-red anemones attached to the tops of granite about five feet below the water's surface at this low tidal mark. Anemones are filter feeders, and when their fine white tentacles were extended they looked like waving flower arrangements. Watching them, of course, extended the time before we actually jumped.

"You go first."

"No, you go first."

"Come on, by now your skin is thick, this is nothing but a brisk dip."

"Speak for yourself."

The water was surprisingly warm. We had no instant urge to scramble for shore. This was novel. The water was actually warm enough for real swimming.

"Bet you can't make it to that lobster buoy," said Frankie.

"No way."

It was only thirty yards and we made it easily, laughing and splashing.

"Wow, I don't think I've ever been out this far before," she said.

"You can see the house," I said, pointing up over the rocks and through the trees and fog. We swam and swam. It was the first real swimming of the summer.

The fog stuck with us all day.

Mount Desert Island is laced with trails. The Native Americans who came to the island in the summer months built many of them. Europeans connected their early settlements with them before roads were built. Rusticators built trails and paths that allowed them access to mountaintops and scenic vistas. By 1915, the year cars were allowed onto the island, Mount Desert had more than two hundred miles of walking trails. Road construction picked up after that. Upkeep on the remaining trails declined. Over the years since then, about seventy-five miles of trails had been turned into roads or reclaimed by nature.

In addition to the trails, fifty-seven miles of roadways for the use of horse-drawn carriages snaked around the mountains. They were built between 1913 and 1940 by John D. Rockefeller, Jr., a summer resident of Seal Harbor. Rockefeller, who first visited the island as a college student in 1893, rented a Bar Harbor cottage in 1908 (son Nelson was born there on August 8), and liked it so much that he came back with his family the next year. In 1910 he stayed in Seal Harbor and found the summer people there and in neighboring Northeast Harbor to be more intellectually stimulating than the socialites of Bar Harbor. He bought one hundred and fifty acres above the village on Barr Hill, expanded a big stone house on it, and called the estate The Eyrie. The Rockefeller family has been in Seal Harbor ever since. Over the years, John D. Rockefeller, Jr., bought up land discreetly and eventually he donated much of it to the park.

The carriage roads that he wanted to build in the park were controversial—they were going to either despoil the wilderness or open it up to the public, or both. Rockefeller Jr. learned road building from his father, John D. Rockefeller, Sr., who had built landscaped carriage roads on his estates in Ohio and New York. The son designed and supervised the construction of the carriage roads. He hired architects, stone cutters, and construction crews. The workers cut and installed huge granite stones along the outer edges of the roadways to serve as guardrails and filled the road-bed with crushed rock. They built sixteen stone bridges across brooks and ravines and two stone gate lodges.

Over the years, plants and bushes grew right up to the edges of the carriage roads. Trees grew tall, their branches arching over-head, their leaves shading the roadbed at regular intervals and creating patterns of dappled sunlight. Small trees and bayberry bushes flanked the road. Moss, lichens, bunchberry dogwoods, and ferns lined the road's edges. This greenery gave the road an intimate, closed-in feel.

The carriage roads were landscaped to fit into the natural set-ting. I'd been walking them for a dozen years and I didn't find them any worse for wear.

Then the park authorities began tearing them up. The Bar Harbor Times called it the carriage road "upgrading" program, a task that would take many years and cost millions of dollars.

We had read that "upgrading" work had begun on the car-riage roads around Parkman Mountain and we decided to have a look in the fog that afternoon. We had been up Parkman more than any other mountain in the park. Frankie first went up it when she was six years old and she knew every stone and turn on the trail to the top of its 941-foot summit and down the other side.

The Bar Harbor Times reported that one section of the Parkman carriage roads upgrade would cost $1.6 million and involve bring-ing in a hundred and sixty thousand tons of crushed rock. As soon as we pulled into the Parkman parking lot, we could see what that meant.

A big orange sign announcing "construction site" greeted us. Behind it sat a backhoe, a small bulldozer, and a mechanized roller used to flatten roadbeds. Another, smaller sign announced that the carriage roads were being "improved." The road heading north from the parking lot was a mess. The bed of the road had been raised and widened with crushed rock topped with fine gravel and then rolled flat. The raised and flattened bed looked more like an actual road than a carriage road.

The roadside vegetation was gone. Overhanging tree branches had been cut down. Small trees and bushes had been removed from a ten-foot swath on each side of the road. With its canopy gone and its green fringe removed, the road was open and the effect was startling. There was no shade left. Sun could blanket it. Even in the fog, the roadbed and its edges seemed dried out. The moss, ferns, and lichens that helped form great roadside swaths of damp, padded habitat so perfect for mushrooms were gone. We found a few mushrooms poking bravely from the edge of the maw of "improvement" gravel, all but buried alive.

"Welcome to Route 66," I said. "It's perfect for speeding mountain bikers but it looks like wanton destruction of mushroom habitat to me."

Seven

We put people who came by boat in a special category. If they called ahead, fine. If they didn't, we'd see what we could do. Some called on arrival to announce, "We're here." Mount Desert was, after all, a destination. And if you came by boat, it was the last Down East destination of any note. Beyond it were Roque Island, Cutler, Quoddy Head, and the Canadian border.

Our friend Chris liked to arrive unannounced. A lawyer, he liked to sail up from Connecticut. Chances were good he'd turn up in bad weather, as though he'd heard about houseguest weather over our way and decided to come and experience it for himself. Sure enough, as the late-afternoon fog gave way to an early evening rain, we returned from our walk and found a message from Chris.

"We got to the mooring at four," Chris said. "I've made a reservation at a very fancy restaurant and we're all going to go out to dinner and eat wonderful food, drink way too much wine, tell lots of stories, stay up late, sing songs, and . . ."

Frankie tracked Chris down by phone at a friend's house and fielded his offer with aplomb. Hanging up, she turned to me and announced proudly that Chris, his wife, Hillary, a painter, her friend Katrina, and Chris's dog, Aengus, were due for dinner at seven-thirty.

★ ★ ★

Grilling with charcoal was one of the treats of summer for us. Living in Manhattan, we did no grilling. So by the time July rolled around, we were suffering from carbon envy and were starved for grilled chicken, lamb chops, steaks, fish, and vegetables.

While Frankie monopolized lobsters, I lorded over grilling. I used an ancient little Weber that spent winters in a crawl space under the house near the canoe, firewood, and porch-farming implements.

At first, I grilled on the front porch. Then one summer I nearly burned the house down. I had bought a chimney charcoal starter, a handy device I had not used before. I set it on the porch on top of a sheet of aluminum foil, loaded it with charcoal, and lit some newspaper at the bottom to get the charcoal started. The coals were glowing in no time. Then I smelled burning cedar. By the time I realized what was happening, the heat of the coals had burned a black circle into the deck under the foil. Later, I sanded off the blackened deck cedar as best I could but a scar remained for all to see. My Weber and I were exiled to a place near the garbage cans on the back porch. I set the Weber on a sheet of galvanized tin and placed the chimney starter on a piece of flat granite.

GRILLED CHICKEN

Cut a whole fryer into 8 pieces (better: have your butcher do it) and lay them out flat on a large serving plate. Drizzle on hot chili oil or olive oil, then soy sauce, and squeeze on the juice of ½ fresh lime (or lemon). (Sometimes I chopped up porch herbs such as rosemary, oregano, or basil and sprinkled them on top. Other times I made a marinade of ½ cup of red wine and herbs and let the chicken soak in it in a plastic bag for several hours or overnight in the fridge.)

Fire up a chimney full of charcoal. This usually takes 15 to 20 minutes. Dump the glowing coals into the grill and place the grate on top. The hot coals should be about an inch below the grate. Wait a couple of minutes for the grate to heat.

Baste the chicken with marinade and place on the grill skinless side down. Brush marinade on top and grill uncovered until bottom of chicken reaches the level of carbonization you want. If you get a flame-up, put the grill cover on briefly to smother the flames. Grill 10 to 12 minutes. Baste with marinade again and turn chicken over. Grill uncovered for about 5 minutes. Cover, leaving vent holes open about halfway, and grill for about 8 minutes more.

Move chicken from grill to plate, squeeze on juice of ½ lime, and serve immediately.

FRANKIE'S OVEN–ROASTED HERB POTATOES

Cut 4–6 tennis ball–sized potatoes w/skins into halves or quarters and place in a Pyrex oven dish cut-side up. Drizzle on olive oil and then a handful of chopped thyme, rosemary, or sage, or all three. Roast in a 400-degree oven 30 to 45 minutes, until brown and crisp on top.

We served fresh steamed green beans with the chicken and potatoes, followed by salad, cheese, and warm bread. We told lots of stories and laughed ourselves silly. Then, instead of singing, we just sat at the table in a kind of food and wine coma. It was a one-helping-too-much feeling, with the wine supply dwindling and candle wax dripping. None of us was in much of a condition to notice what was happening in the shadows. But Aengus, a big, gray weimaraner, was all eyes and ears as he sat beside the table with a "let me at 'em" vigilance that he expressed in a half-suppressed whine. Only his good manners kept him from pouncing on the impudent little beasts marauding in the corners.

It was nearly midnight when our guests and their well-mannered dog completed their three-curtain departure. Then, while Frankie washed dishes, I took three new Victor snap traps out of their cellophane, baited them with bacon, and positioned them along known infiltration routes.

In the morning I proudly announced my overnight success in

my best imitation of the old Five O'Clock Follies briefers in Saigon: "Results: 2 KIA. Outstanding."

Frankie grimaced.

At noon, the fog began to lift and from the window where I typed I could see birds flitting between the trees, maybe a dozen of them. What signal had they gotten from the weather to come out and feed? They seemed to arrive outside my window on cue. I didn't know what the cue was. First came little bark-probing brown creepers that flitted vertically up and down the spruce and pine trunks outside my window. Then came chickadees, chasing one another from branch to branch.

As I watched, a major transformation of the weather unfolded. At twelve-thirty a bright sun pierced the haze. A light breeze began to stir the surface of the sound from its mirrorlike flatness. Suddenly, it was a beautiful day. Within an hour, I thought, real estate prices probably jumped twenty percent.

The change in weather stirred me. Time to defer typing, I thought, and do chores. I took the salt shaker from the kitchen countertop into the warm sunshine on the porch and opened it. I yanked down the damp towels from the bathrooms and spread them out on the porch railing. I went to the back porch to inspect our garbage.

Although our neighborhood raccoon rarely ransacked the garbage cans unless we ate lobster, we tried not to tempt him or other creatures by letting the cans overflow. With the sun out, this was as good a time as any to police up, so I carried plastic bags of garbage, paper bags full of bottles and cans, and piles of old newspapers and magazines out to the Volvo and loaded them.

When I arrived at the Town Garage, I discovered that both its entrances were blocked, one by a taut cable stretched between two posts, the other by a new swinging gate that was padlocked shut. How could the Town Garage be closed? The Town Garage never closed. There was no explanation and I was miffed. I had a car full of garbage and I couldn't get it anywhere near the garbage truck or the recycling bins. I began carrying garbage bags, two at a time, around the cable and up the driveway to a garbage truck, fifty yards away. I made four trips, fuming all the way. Then I dropped two bags full of bottles and cans beside the Dumpster unsorted. Take that, I thought.

Just then our friend Walter pulled up, took two small paper bags of wine bottles from his trunk, and stacked them next to the Boy Scouts redemption box, which was full. I unloaded six bags of our wine bottles and stacked them next to Walter's.

"Have you considered checking in for rehab?" he said, eyeing my stack.

The next day started routinely enough. The fog was gone. We exercised, worked, then went into town for food and newspapers. We drove along Somes Sound, admiring the sailboats, past the tennis courts and the library, parking in front of Brown's Hardware. Frankie picked up the newspapers at McGrath's and bought a few odds and ends at the Pine Tree while I headed in the opposite direction, to Provisions, for protein. Our Northeast Harbor foraging took less than fifteen minutes. We stopped at the tennis courts on the way back and banged balls for an hour, then drove home.

The light was blinking on the answering machine. I pushed the PLAY button. A man's voice came on: "Please call Officer Griffith at the Mount Desert Police Department! 276-5111."

I looked at Frankie. She looked at me.

"What could that be about?" she said.

"I don't have a clue," I said. I really didn't have a clue, but I found my mind going off on its own. It was shifting, as if against my will, into a guilt mode. Surely, you've done something illegal, it was thinking. You're guilty of something, that's for sure. You always are! But what this time? It began cataloging my recent actions.

"What have you done?" Frankie chimed in like a homicide detective.

"How about trespassing," I thought out loud. We had been sneaking into Jurassic Park next door on recon missions with some regularity. Maybe one of the workers ratted on us!

"I bet it has something to do with your driving," Frankie said. "That U-turn you made up the hill in Northeast this afternoon. That must be it."

"That couldn't have been it," I told Frankie.

"I've got it," I said. "Skinny-dipping in Somes Sound! In broad daylight!" I envisioned complaints piling up at police headquarters from "observers" across the sound, observers with high-powered binoculars.

"They told the cops they were innocently observing the bird life when, all of a sudden, their binoculars came across us in our birthday suits rudely polluting their view!"

"That must be it," Frankie laughed.

What was it? Had we forgotten to get new license tags for the car? Or the boat? Nope. Had a check bounced? Had evidence been found at a crime scene that implicated . . .

Suddenly, I remembered the Town Garage.

"You're not going to believe this," I said, telling Frankie the story of how I had slipped around the closed gate and dumped our garbage in the garbage truck after official working hours. How I had piled our bottles and cans beside the recycling bins, unsorted, to protest government red tape.

How did they know the dumpee was me? Surely Walter hadn't squealed. Lots of people could have recognized the Volvo. But nobody else was around. The place was shut tight. Had they found evidence in my bags of leavings that pointed the finger at me?

I thought about "Alice's Restaurant," Arlo Guthrie's antiwar song, and imagined calling Officer Griffith and hearing him say, "We found your name on an envelope underneath seven bags of bottles and cans deposited illegally at the Town Garage and we wondered if you had anything to say about it." Arlo's alibi, of course, was, "I cannot tell a lie. I put that envelope under that garbage." What could I say?

I dialed the Mount Desert Police Department and listened nervously as the phone rang. The dispatcher answered, identified herself, and said Officer Griffith was on his way to find us. Whoa! I thought. He's coming after us! This must be even more serious than I thought! Then the dispatcher said that Officer Griffith was on his way to Smallidge Point to inspect our "vehicle."

"Why?" I asked.

She explained that the police department had gotten a report that someone had run into our "vehicle" while it was parked in front of Brown's Hardware store that afternoon. She said that Officer Griffith had been dispatched to the scene to check it out, but that by the time he had arrived we'd driven off. I told the dispatcher that we hadn't noticed anything wrong with our car, and that, in any case, it wasn't at Smallidge Point, which is in town and where the Peabody family place was located. I told her where our car was, not far from the Town Garage. (Perhaps, my criminal mind thought, I shouldn't have mentioned the Town Garage to her. It was evidence that I was familiar with its location.)

The dispatcher said she would relay this information to Officer Griffith and perhaps he would drive out to see us and perhaps not. His decision, I assumed, depended on how much trouble the local criminal element was causing in Mount Desert that evening.

Then I remembered that I was a likely member of the criminal element myself, and I had just given the dispatcher directions to my location. What if Officer Griffith arrived and discovered other suspicious activity? Was it illegal, I wondered, to gather mussels without a permit? Did we need some sort of authorization to grill on the back porch?

Frankie would deny everything. She'd finger me and say, "Not me Officer, that man is solely responsible for any grilling that may or may not have gone on on the back porch or anywhere else on the premises. I have absolutely nothing to do with it."

Then I thought about Bentley, the car-humbling canine up the lane. By now, Bentley was a grizzled veteran of vehicular chicken. He had built a reputation that had spread across the island and even spilled onto the mainland. This summer he had halted not just cars but some of the biggest construction equipment in Maine. Dump trucks, backhoes, even bulldozers. Bentley would leap fearlessly in front of them and their startled drivers would jam on their brakes. In many cases the drivers would have to open the cab door on their vehicle, climb out and try to shoo Bentley off. It didn't work, of course. Bentley would stand there, just beyond the truck's hood ornament, daring the driver to press on. And when the driver did, Bentley would race out front or run alongside, snarling at the tires, inches from death. It was the kind of canine courage, or stupidity, around which legends are born. Bentley was a four-legged David battling ten-wheeled Goliaths. Soon all the workers and drivers at Jurassic Park had their own name for Bentley: Lugnut.

Now what? What if Bentley was on patrol near Kevit and Gail Cooks' house when Officer Griffith showed up in his police cruiser? Surely, he would set off on a jubilant front-end chase, and who could blame him. It wasn't often that a police cruiser came down our lane. Officer Griffith would nab Bentley and discover that the plucky terrier had a long rap sheet. He'd been apprehended running around loose several times. When that happened, Bentley's owner, Gail Cook, would find her name listed in the crime section of the *Bar Harbor Times*. Bentley had even been nabbed once by the feds. One summer Bentley and his pal, Rollo the elkhound, decided to climb Sargent Mountain with some tourists they happened upon. They wound up at Eagle Lake, hot and sweaty, and jumped in. National Park rangers caught them and hauled them in, and Gail made the crime page again.

If I was Lugnut, I thought, chalking up a law enforcement vehicle to my long string of triumphs would be something I wouldn't be able to resist. Bringing a dump truck to a grunting halt was old hat by now. Trucks were a dime a dozen all summer. But a bubble-topped police cruiser? Well, in Lugnut's terms, that would be like finding and stopping an extraterrestrial's spaceship.

We had dinner and waited. Officer Griffith never showed up.

The next morning I dragged myself out of bed, padded to the front door, and poked my head outside. The air was cool and the sky was overcast. The fog on the sound was a wispy haze, as though someone had watered down the pea soup.

My morning battlefield inspection came first. I opened the utility room door, flicked on the light, and found a dead mouse, eyes bulging, in Trap No. 1. I stepped into the back bedroom where I had set Trap 2 along a known infiltration route. Bingo! Dead mouse number two. I checked Trap No. 3 near my desk in the other bedroom. Another furry rodent, belly up! I collected the traps and carried them out to the front porch rail. There I removed the mice and tossed them by their tails into the bushes. Three for three. Not bad, I thought. My body count stood at five KIA.

My next stop was the small room in back where I spent the first part of each morning communing with my toothbrush, contemplating the day, and undertaking my morning ablutions. The room was special. The rest of the house had been repainted some years before, its walls lightened to the color of cream to make it feel brighter inside. The back bathroom had been spared. Its walls were the color of walnut, giving it a dark, cavelike coziness. On cool, foggy days, it felt so warm and comfortable that I was reluctant to leave it for the front porch and exercise. On those days, I stayed longer than usual, devoting the extra time to *The New Yorker* magazine. I was a devoted but sporadic reader. I had a pile of unread *New Yorkers* going back years. I didn't thumb through them just for the cartoons. I gave each issue a thorough read and this paid off over the years. Sometimes I happened upon a sentence or a paragraph that made me marvel. It would stop me, back me up, and make me read it again. Sometimes I'd find a passage so interesting that I would cut it out and save it, like a recipe. In one 1989 issue, I came upon an article by Janet Malcolm containing a paragraph about journalists and their interviewing techniques. I clipped it out and passed it around the office.

Every journalist who is not too stupid or too full of himself to notice what is going on knows that what he does is morally indefensible. He is a kind of confidence man, preying on people's vanity, ignorance or loneliness, gaining their trust and betraying them without remorse.

I thought "morally indefensible" was a bit strong, but I had to admit that I knew journalists who acted like confidence men. I had to admit, too, that in my career I had preyed on the ignorance of people to gain their trust so that they would spill the beans and I would get my story. I kept Malcolm's quote handy in case I was tempted to do it again.

After that I searched out Malcolm's articles. This summer I found a little diamond in a piece about a popular postmodernist painter named David Salle. She referred to him over and over as "the artist David Salle," as if to mock the very notion. Then came this: "The ritual celebrations of artistic achievement—the book parties, the opening-night parties, the artists' dinners—give outward form to, and briefly make real, the writer's or performer's or painter's fantasy that he is living in a world that wishes him well and wants to reward him for his work."

It was enough to make a person think about a mid-career veer into plumbing.

In my pile of old *New Yorkers* were issues from Tina Brown's stint as editor, which I savored. Under her the magazine had taken on a new flavor. Instead of a three-part series on the history of wheat, which I used to read avidly as well, there were now more articles about Hollywood and show business. The old *New Yorker* had articles profiling people who were brilliant, talented, or both. Tina's *New Yorker* contained articles about people who weren't brilliant or talented or even admirable. Ms. Brown liked to create what she called "buzz" for the *New Yorker,* and I guessed that unpredictability and shock effect were tools she used to keep the right people "buzzing." There was no telling what unsavory person, goofy idea, or shocking art might turn up in the *New Yorker* of Tina Brown. A pedophile priest one week, a doctor who murdered his patients the next. The magazine had a lot more sex and four-letter words in it than ever before, just the kind of stuff to keep me glued to its pages. I kept my stack of unread *New Yorkers* from Tina's era in the water closet because that's where I read them. I began to refer to what I read as "toi-lit."

You never knew when something worth buzzing about would turn up. This morning, I turned a page and came to a review by John Updike of a dreadful-sounding biography of F. Scott Fitzgerald (no relation to the FitzGerald on these premises), by Jeffrey Meyers. Updike perfunctorily recounts Fitzgerald's life as chronciled by Meyers: his drinking; his early success writing novels and short stories; his failed efforts to become a screenwriter; his last years turning out skimpy little pieces for *Esquire* for a few hundred dollars each; his death at forty-four; his normal enough penis . . . *his what?* Why did Meyers write about Fitzgerald's penis? Why did Updike mention it in his review? What in the world is F. Scott Fitzgerald's penis doing in the *New Yorker?*

Suddenly an ant at least an inch long appeared near the bathtub. It was big enough to be a queen ant, or perhaps a wingless termite. Perhaps it was a gentle forest ant that had ambled into the house and couldn't find a way out. In any case, my policy toward cute indoor insects was catch-and-release. So, using a page of Updike's review, I scooped the ant up and carried it out the front door and sat the magazine on the porch rail so the ant could crawl off the page. But the ant wouldn't move. It sat there gripping the page. Just as I was about to flick it away, I noticed that it was clinging to the top of a paragraph of Updike's review in which he was describing Sheilah Graham, Fitzgerald's Hollywood mistress: "Well informed about all shapes and sizes of male sexual organs, she found the tubercular, drug-addicted and often alcoholic Fitzgerald a credible performer . . ."

Eight

I found myself playing with a paragraph on my computer screen most of the morning thinking about Officer Griffith's call. I couldn't concentrate on paragraph construction when my mind was focused on crime, law enforcement, and our motor vehicle. I wondered why Officer Griffith never showed up. I wondered if, perhaps, Officer Griffith was, at this very moment, on his way to Frankie's place to inspect our "motor vehicle." I decided to beat him to the punch. I'd do an inspection myself.

Our car was a 1966 Volvo 122S station wagon. Named Ahuan by its previous owner. In Persian, "Ahuan" means caravan, or caravanserai, an inn for caravans.

When I first arrived on the scene in 1983, Frankie stored Ahuan outdoors in winter in the parking lot behind Fernald's garage and general store in Somesville. Its body was pocked with rust, the bottom of its front and rear fenders rusted through. Its bumpers were pitted and corroded. Its padded dash was dried and cracked. But with a little tuning each spring at Fernald's garage, Ahuan started up and ran all summer.

One summer Bill Fernald mentioned that since Ahuan's engine and transmission seemed to be in good shape perhaps a little body work and a new paint job would be a good idea. He suggested that I drive over to Manset Point to see a man named Nibby, the proprietor of Nibby's Auto Body Shop. Bill said Nibby did good work and didn't charge an arm and a leg. I drove Ahuan over to see Nibby. His face covered with epoxy dust, Nibby came out and paced around Ahuan a few times, pushing his thumb through some fender rust.

"Fenders is shot," he said.

If I got new front fenders, he said, he could patch up the other holes, rebuild the rocker panels and paint Ahuan for $1,700. I told Nibby I'd talk it over with Frankie and get back to him. Nibby's estimate seemed high to us. That was a lot of money for a little body work and a paint job. It was more than I'd ever paid for a whole car.

We mulled. Another season came and went. Nibby passed away.

The next summer we vowed to get Ahuan a face-lift if we could find a reasonable body man. Bill Fernald told us that with Nibby gone the odds of finding such a fellow on Mount Desert Island weren't great. Quite a few summer people kept old and antique cars on the island; they drove them around in July and August and stored them the rest of the year. Some of the places they used for repairs, Bill said, had taken to calling themselves "auto restoration facilities" and charging an arm and a leg. Frankie told me about the time she took Ahuan to one of these places for winter storage. The proprietor took one look at Ahuan and said he wouldn't be able to take her. He didn't say why but Frankie always suspected that he thought Ahuan was too decrepit to be stored in the same garage with restored antiques. It was like being blackballed at the country club.

One day, in what I assumed would be a futile exercise, I called up Dick's Body Shop in Northeast Harbor and asked if I could bring Ahuan by for an estimate. A lot of people in town referred to Dick's Body Shop as "Mrs. Astor's Body Shop," because it is situated on Neighborhood Road across the street from the summer house of Mrs. Vincent Astor, the New York philanthropist. I assumed that any body shop across the street from Mrs. Astor charged plenty.

Dick's had a sign painted on a shiny car door hanging from a frame made of pipe just up the street from Mrs. Astor's driveway. I pulled in and found Dick inside with three cars and the strong smell of epoxy. Dick came out into the sun and paced around Ahuan, poking his finger through rust holes. After a few minutes, he said I'd have to buy new front fenders. If I did that, he said, he'd patch up the other holes and paint Ahuan for $1,700. Suddenly, $1,700 seemed cheap. I agreed on the spot.

The next summer we arrived to find Ahuan looking like new with a shiny forest-green paint job that made her other flaws less easy to ignore: pitted bumpers, a missing front bumperette, and a missing "L" from its hood's name (the name, thus, read "VO VO"). No matter. Ahuan was beautiful! Strangers would walk or drive by and say "great car" or give us a thumbs-up.

One afternoon in the next summer white smoke began pouring out of Ahuan's tailpipe. I drove her to Fernald's garage. Joe the mechanic shook his head ominously.

"I'll take a look, but don't get ya hopes up," he said. "I'll tell ya, it looks bad."

The following afternoon, Joe phoned and told me he had removed a couple of spark plugs and found that they were caked with carbon.

"It's all carboned up," he said with a tone of finality. "Look's like the engine's shot. I'll be honest with ya, I don't wanta mess with it."

Sadly I explained the situation to Frankie. We should have checked out Ahuan's vital organs before spending $1,700 on cosmetic surgery. Should we give Ahuan a decent burial, cut our losses, and move into the modern motor vehicle world?

The next morning I ruffled through the Greater Ellsworth Yellow Pages and came across an ad for a place that specialized in Volvo, Saab, and Honda service and advertised itself as "The Car Dealership That Cares." I thought that this was probably a code phrase for arm-and-a-leg prices but I phoned anyway and spoke to the proprietor. He offered to take a look at Ahuan if we had her towed to his shop. We arranged the tow and two days later he phoned.

"You've got a great little car here," he said. I expected him to say next that all we needed to do was rebuild the engine for a couple of thousand dollars and Ahuan would run like new.

"But what about all that white smoke?" I asked.

"Oh, that's a minor problem," he said. He explained that a line from the brake system's master cylinder had sprung a leak. Brake fluid spewed out over the engine each time the brake pedal was pushed. Some of the brake fluid got into the carburetor and into the engine where it combusted with the gasoline and caused the carbon buildup. This problem, he said, could be fixed in little time and at little cost.

Ahuan had a new lease on life!

I began my inspection by giving Ahuan a bath. I usually soaped her up once a summer whether she needed it or not. This summer she needed it badly. The summer wasn't any drier or dustier than other summers, but there was more dust on our peninsula. That was because part of the lane had been "improved." From the main road to Jurassic Park the lane had been smoothed over and widened with a layer of rolled sand. It had been transformed from two tire tracks of pine needle–covered hard pack, with grass growing in the middle, to a flat surface of sand that looked just like one of those "improved" carriage roads. The old grassy lane had been full of bumps and potholes that caused drivers to slow down. The new lane was flat and smooth, allowing cars and trucks to go faster and kick up dust.

The more I thought about the lane "improvement," the more it reminded me of Begajah, a village on the island of Java in Indonesia that I first visited in 1971 for a *New York Times Magazine* article. Begajah was a very poor village then. Its farmers grew only one crop of rice a year because its fields were not irrigated. Villagers walked everywhere in bare feet. Women washed clothes and bathed in a stream while children played in the water. Homes had dirt floors, woven reed walls, and palm-frond roofs. Only a few families owned bicycles. The village was poor but it was very beautiful. It looked like a tropical Asian paradise. It was quiet and serene. Its trees were laden with fruit. Chickens and goats wandered here and there. The fruit trees and animals made the village seem wealthy, but this was deceptive. Villagers could rarely afford to eat much of the food they grew. They sold their papayas, mangoes, bananas, eggs, chickens, and goats in the market and used the money to buy such less expensive essentials as manioc, soybean cakes, dried minnows, and, when they could afford it, rice.

What this village didn't have was garbage. There was not a speck of litter anywhere to be found. I stayed in the village for many days before it dawned on me why it had no garbage. People were simply too poor to throw anything away. Hair combings were saved. The long black strands of women's hair could be sold to a man who came around now and then and bought them for wig factories in Singapore. Everything the villagers used had a second and a third use. An empty coconut shell became a water scoop. Banana leaves were turned into umbrellas and wrapping materials. Nothing the villagers could afford to buy in the local market came in disposable containers or wrapping paper. Paper was rare. Village officials kept statistics on a chalkboard.

The other commodity missing in Begajah was dust. There was no dust in the rainy season or the dry season. It didn't dawn on me until I sat down to write my story about this village that the reason Begajah had no dust was because nothing moved fast enough in it to kick up dust. Villagers walked, for the most part. Only a few rode bicycles.

When I returned to the village in 1986, I found that Begajah had grown rich in the course of fifteen years. An irrigation system had been built and farmers now harvested three rice crops a year. Many homes were made of brick and had tile floors. Wires connected to the tops of concrete poles had been put up along the main road, and villagers in Begajah were just getting access to what those wires carried: electricity. But this magical source of power was relatively expensive and considered to be a luxury, so only the wealthiest families in the village applied to have it hooked up to their houses. They weren't modest about it. They had their electric meters installed on their porches beside their front doors as status symbols.

The first new enterprise I noticed was a hairdressing salon. Instead of selling their hair, women now had it cut. Hair had gone from a cash crop to a commodity you paid someone else to remove. Village women could now afford fashion. The village could now afford litter, too. Villagers had turned into litterbugs. Litter was everywhere. Dead batteries dotted roadsides. Foil packets that shampoo came in and other wrappings littered the ground. Clear plastic bags that cold drinks came in clung to the bushes.

The village buzzed with motorbikes. Walking paths and bicycle lanes had been widened into narrow roads to accommodate them. Transportation had gotten noisy and fast. The motorbikes went fast enough to kick up dust, and that dust now covered the leaves on bushes and trees beside the roads and trails. Villagers seemed to take the noise and dust for granted. If they were considered to be irritants at all, the irritation was a small price to pay for getting places quickly. The village no longer looked like paradise. It had been "improved" and, at the same time, sullied.

Now I felt the same way about the lane to Frankie's place. The lane was now dangerous. Cars and trucks could go faster, their drivers no longer leery of hitting an unseen chunk of granite or gnarled root. They didn't have to worry about running into a jarring rut or scraping their undercarriages on a protruding rock. The faster the cars and trucks went, the more fun Lugnut had ruining their brakes and the more dust these vehicles kicked up. Dust covered the raspberry and blueberry bushes along the lane. Dust covered the moss. Dust clung to oak, maple, and birch leaves and even coated the needles of pine and fir trees. Dust coated everything, including Ahuan.

After her bath, Ahuan looked beautiful, except for her pitted and peeling chrome bumpers. As she dried off in the sun, I gave her an inspection, starting up front and moving around the driver's side to the back. There I saw it: a round, basketball-sized dent below the rear license plate. It didn't indent very far, but it certainly looked new. I felt it and rubbed my finger on a spot in the middle where some paint had chipped off. That spot looked like an impact point.

Looking closer at the rear end, something besides the dent didn't look right to me. I looked from one angle, then another. Finally I saw that the rear bumper was tilted several degrees upward. It looked as though someone with a big crowbar had tried to twist it off or something heavy had smacked into it from behind! Whatever it was, Ahuan must have taken a serious hit.

I went inside and called the Mount Desert Police Department. I told Carol, the dispatcher, what had happened on the previous day and how, after giving Ahuan a bath, I had discovered the fresh dent. Carol said she would call back. Two hours later, she phoned and said Officer Griffith had asked her to relay to me a name and two telephone numbers belonging to the alleged perpetrator, a female. Carol suggested that I give her a call, talk over the situation, and swap insurance information. I wrote down the phone numbers.

The alleged perp's name was vaguely familiar but I didn't know her. So I called an old friend who might. He told me that she was one of the most prominent citizens of Northeast Harbor. She had been a summer person with powerful connections in Washington who had retired to live in the village year-round. She did volunteer work and served on all sorts of boards and committees. She'd once held the prestigious post of chairman of the library's board of trustees.

Having never telephoned an alleged perpetrator before, let alone one of such eminence, I had to build up my courage, and that took most of the afternoon. When I dialed one of the numbers, I got a female voice on an answering machine. I left a simple message asking the voice to return my call. I didn't say why I called.

When we returned from our afternoon pilgrimage to town, I noticed that the message light on the answering machine was blinking. It was the alleged perp.

I picked up the phone and dialed her number. She answered. I identified myself and said I was sorry to bother her. I explained that the police dispatcher had called and told me that an accident had occurred and that Officer Griffith had suggested I call her and swap insurance information for future reference. She interrupted.

"It couldn't have been me," she said abruptly. "It wasn't my car and I'm the only one who drives it. I didn't do it. I don't go bumping into people. I didn't do it, I don't know how in the world all this came up."

I was taken aback. Her denial was so emphatic that I apologized. I told her that somebody probably made a mistake. Goodness knows, I said, how mistakes like this can be made. Then she hung up on me. I immediately called the police department, got the dispatcher, and reported. She put Officer Griffith on the line. I explained what the alleged perp had just told me. He listened silently. Then, in a "now let me tell you the way it really is" voice, Officer Griffith told me what his investigation had uncovered.

As our "motor vehicle" sat in front of Brown's Hardware that afternoon, another vehicle pulled up from behind and rammed it, with a loud bang. Two employees at Brown's Hardware saw and heard it happen. One of them, the cashier, a female, called the police department and reported the ramming. Another employee, male, saw it from Brown's front window. This male had pretty good credibility because when he wasn't working at Brown's he was working as a policeman in Bar Harbor! Officer Griffith said his department had a file of the incident that was pretty convincing. If the alleged perp won't cooperate, he said, my insurance company could go straight to her insurance company and pursue a claim.

Officer Griffith seemed so professional that I felt I had the law on my side and was relieved that he didn't have to come out in inspect Ahuan after all. Lugnut was safe.

★ ★ ★

The mouse war raged on. My results, statistically, were McNamarian. Morning after morning I checked my traps first thing—usually before Frankie woke up.

One morning, while Frankie was exercising on the porch, I carried the traps out, put them on the porch railing, de-trapped three little mouse corpses, and tossed them into the bushes.

"Oh no," Frankie shouted between hip flexes. "It must be a whole family."

"Eleven KIA," I said.

"Eleven!" Frankie shrieked. "You're a regular Julian Ewell."

In the Vietnam War, General Julian Ewell was notorious for commanding combat units that racked up suspiciously high body counts. When I first got to Vietnam, he commanded the Ninth Infantry Division in the densely populated Mekong Delta. When the Ninth was withdrawn, Ewell was promoted to three-star rank and given command of III Corps, an area that encompassed one-fourth of South Vietnam, including the capital, Saigon. Ewell was in charge of all the fighting units in the corps and he visited them regularly, popping in by helicopter for briefings and inspections. One morning he descended on the headquarters of a brigade of the First Infantry Division near the Michelin rubber plantation in the jungle northwest of Saigon. I happened to be in the brigade's tactical operations center at the time, and the briefing officers invited me to stay for their "dog and pony show" for the general. They asked me to take a seat in back.

As I lurked in the shadows, Ewell strode in with a retinue of subordinates and sat down. A major and a lieutenant colonel appeared, unfurled huge maps, pulled out their retractable pointers and briefing papers, and began a rundown of the week's actions in the brigade's area of operations. They detailed the number and location of combat assaults by brigade units, the hostile actions by enemy forces, the amount of artillery fire, the movements of maneuver battalions and companies, the number and location of air strikes, and the number of enemy defectors. Before they could get to pacification efforts and programs to win the "hearts and minds of the people," Ewell raised his hand slightly and asked, "How many did you kill?"

"One confirmed, sir."

The general rose and walked out of the room in disgust.

Nine

One day giant concrete mixing and pouring trucks began to arriving at Jurassic Park. One after another, these bulbous behemoths turned off the main road and onto our narrow lane, clanking and grinding and belching diesel fumes as they rolled toward the construction site. Lugnut was in heaven.

When Sunday morning rolled around, we were anxious to see what the cement mixers had wrought, so we limbered up quickly and jogged over to Jurassic Park in a light, warm rain. From the driveway, we gazed upon an enormous foundation of hardened gray concrete. As we got closer, it looked like a giant maze of right angles, with walls inside of walls rising up to the height of our shoulders. Actually, it looked like two foundations, one inside the other.

"Wow, this is going to be huuuugggge!" I said as Frankie peered over into a dirt hole.

"Yeah, some house all right."

"House. Shmouse. This could be an arena for a new NBA franchise! Mount Desert's own Madison Square Garden. Professional hoops on Somes Sound! This team needs a name." I thought for a moment.

"The Mount Desert Moose?" I said. "Too obvious. How about the Somes Sound Sonics? Or the Somes Sounds Perwinkles. I can see the headline: WINKLES WALLOP WARRIORS. You don't like that? How about Mount Desert Moules? MOULES MALL MAVERICKS."

In reality, the foundation wasn't so big. But it was big enough to suggest that the house to be built on it would be the size of some of the old cottages in Bar Harbor and new mansions in Northeast Harbor. Such a house would fit in either of those places. On our little peninsula alongside four much smaller houses, though, such a mansion was like a hundred-dollar chip tossed into a dollar-ante poker game.

Walking around to the back of the property we noticed another foundation under some tall pines.

"What do you suppose this is for?" asked Frankie.

"A garage, maybe, or a guest house," I said. "I don't know, but it looks major. I don't see any sign of a swimming pool, though."

We continued around to the front of the foundation and made our way to shore to inspect the handiwork of Mr. Tibbetts from the 1-800-OWN-DOCK barge. The tide was low. Huge beams bolted together in A-frames rose up out of the granite and the water. Thick chains held the beams to hooks that had been drilled into the granite. Lots of work remained to be done, but this dock looked huge.

"This is going to be another Mackinac Bridge!" I said. "This guy must own an ocean liner or something."

The good news was that we couldn't see the dock from Frankie's porch, so we wouldn't have to look at whatever ocean liner, stinkpot, or cigarette boat eventually tied up to it.

Instead of going back up the driveway, we decided to walk from this dock-in-progress along the shore over big granite rocks. We had to walk carefully for a hundred yards or so to reach the rocks in front of Frankie's place where we swam. From there we had a clear view of the dock next door, which meant that anyone standing on that dock would have a clear view of us. We stripped and plunged into the sound.

We lingered longer than usual over the breakfast table and the newspapers on Sunday, catching up on the local newspapers.

The *Ellsworth American* and the *Bar Harbor Times* were excellent weekly newspapers with solid local reporting of news in Hancock County and on Mount Desert Island. I picked up the *Ellsworth American,* the more sober-looking of the two papers with its old-fashioned layouts and typefaces. Its front-page headline read, "Steuben Pushes Tax Equity; State Valuation Rises, Federal Value Drops." The story concerned a dispute between federal and state authorities over property values.

The *American's* editorials were usually as sober as its layouts. They scolded the nincompoops in Washington and Augusta. They reminded readers of the virtues of the North Atlantic Treaty Organization. I, for one, was glad to be reminded. NATO wasn't something that sprang to mind very often at Frankie's place.

The *American's* opinion page always featured a photograph of a local natural scene or a pastoral setting. Under the photo there was always a poem by J. Russell Wiggins, the paper's editor. Often the subject of the photograph and of the poem were the same. Wiggins, a former editor of the *Washington Post,* wrote poems about local affairs. (I couldn't remember a single Wiggins poem devoted to the virtues of NATO.) When the Maine Department of Environmental Protection began closing down town dumps across the state, Wiggins for example, raised poetic concern about dump diners.

> *The Schoodic seagulls called a meeting*
> *To find out why they are not eating.*
> *The county's seagulls by the bunch*
> *Once came for dinner, breakfast, and lunch*
> *At city dumps about the state,*
> *Where they no longer congregate.*
> *The seagull's life is incomplete*
> *Without a place where he can eat.*
>
> *They used to find the finest fare*
> *In village dump grounds everywhere:*
> *The very best of meats and cake*

That Downeast cooks knew how to make.
The DEP has made life hard
For birds without a credit card;
They've made the country very neat;
But what are seagulls going to eat?

I always liked to read the *American*'s letters to the editor, especially those written by people who shared the paper's disdain for incompetent bureaucrats.

Frankie and I were compelled to write a letter ourselves one summer after Somes Sound was buzzed for several days by strange black helicopters. Not since a First Air Cavalry Division combat assault in Vietnam had I heard such relentless thwapping. The *American* reported that the helicopters were performing drug enforcement operations in Hancock County and that observers in the helicopters had spotted some marijuana plants growing on property belonging to J. Russell Wiggins himself. We couldn't help ourselves.

Dear Sir:

  As devoted readers of the American, *we turn eagerly each week to your inspired poetry on the front page of the editorial section under a usually blissful photograph of some facet of this beloved region.*

  Imagine our surprise this week, whilst hurrying through the news to get to the aforesaid inspired poetry, to come across on page 12— a spot more cynical readers might refer to as "buried" news—the story about the vigilant efforts of federal, state, national guard, county, and local law enforcement agencies, using the latest in helicopter surveillance techniques, to rid Hancock County of its infestation of noxious marijuana plants.

  We can think of no better way to spend the post–Cold War peace dividend, our tax dollars, and our military and law enforcement personnel's time than on the eradication of the aforesaid plants.

  As for the eight plants discovered on the Brooklin property owned until last week by the American's *esteemed editor, we absolutely deplore any miscreantial connections others might draw between the poetry and the aforesaid plants. We will, however, be monitoring the poetry in hopes that its inspirational levels remain high, so to speak.*

Our letter was printed under the headline, "Watching from on High."

After reading the editorial and the poem I turned to blueberry news.

Nowhere have I seen news coverage about blueberries that came anywhere near the consistent, unrelenting, and in-depth reporting and writing the *Ellsworth American* delivered summer after summer. Week after week, the *American* could be counted upon to report without fear or favor the annual saga of the growing and harvesting of one of Maine's most important crops. Reading the *American*'s stories about the blueberry crop was like watching an Indonesian shadow play with its ancient story line diverted by exciting twists and turns.

The *American* reported estimates by University of Maine researchers of a crop in the state that ranged in size from 40 million pounds to 72.3 million pounds. The gap between the low and high estimates was large because all sorts of factors such as temperature, humidity, rainfall, and disease go into the production of a blueberry. While forecasting the size of the crop was a specialized science, the scientists who did it tended toward broad and safe estimates before the harvest actually began. The range in this latest estimate encompassed the previous year's crop of 64.6 million pounds. But it fell short of the extraordinary 1992 crop of 84.2 million pounds. That crop helped North America set a record, with 314 million pounds picked. The harvest consisted of both wild and farmed blueberries. Maine and Canada's Maritime Provinces grow wild blueberries, which sell at a premium. Together, they brought in 114.4 million pounds of wild blueberries in 1992.

After a couple of summers of following the *Ellsworth American*'s blueberry news, I began to see a pattern. Early assessments each summer stressed an "iffy" crop with all sorts of too-early-to-tell variables fogging up the forecasts. Growers at this stage were usually cautious if not downright pessimistic—like farmers everywhere. Next, university blueberry experts weighed in. They were more positive than the growers. Their estimates were even rosy, or at least that's the way it looked until you read the fine print. They often forecast a bountiful crop and then larded their forecast with all sorts of ifs and buts to cover untoward eventualities without dampening their overall optimism.

What happened next in this pattern was a major dramatic twist. A story would appear on the *Ellsworth American's* front page, seemingly from out of the blue (so to speak), about deep trouble. Something had gone wrong. It had rained too much. It had been too hot or too dry. Insects were gnawing like locusts on the blueberry bushes. Disease was rampant. Experts were now forecasting a terrible crop. Growers were predicting a blueberry disaster. What would happen next?

This was nail-biting time for anyone who followed the blueberry news. Blueberry news took these dramatic twists and turns summer after summer. I had no evidence to suggest that the *Ellsworth American* was sensationalizing the blueberry drama to sell newspapers. Still, each summer the newspaper seemed to find an arresting development that threw all the rosy scenarios into question.

When the actual blueberry harvest began, lo and behold, the crop turned out to be good, bountiful, or even terrific. At this stage, the *American* would report that the crop had "exceeded expectations." Whew! I was relieved. During my first summers of following this saga, when I saw the phrase "exceeded expectations" I figured that that was good news. Everything was going to be okay in blueberryland. Little did I know of the perils to come.

Sure enough, as the harvest went on, the *American* found all sorts of harvesting troubles. A bumper crop meant there were lots of blueberries to harvest, and that meant a labor shortage. A bumper crop also meant a price drop. Blueberry buyers, citing a glut, started offering less money to growers. With a perishable crop on their hands, the growers had to take what they could get. The growers, in turn, offered less money to migrant harvesters. The harvesters threatened to stop harvesting or even walk off the job and go pick blueberries for someone else. They also grumbled to the *Ellsworth American*. The paper would run stories about their plight, sometimes with photographs of their poor working and living conditions.

Week after week, summer after summer, Maine's blueberry saga played itself out on the pages of the *Ellsworth American*. Sometimes, as it climaxed, I'd force myself to stop working and rush out to buy a copy of the newspaper, hot off the presses, and devour the latest blueberry news.

Not that the *Bar Harbor Times* lacked drama. The *Times* was the *Ellsworth American*'s chief competitor and it vigilantly kept track of the ever-growing numbers of people visiting the national park and the island. Its editorials tended to fear the worst. This week's offering, entitled "The Limit," began with a warning:

> Acadia National Park is in danger of being overrun. And it is not just the millions of private visitors who come each year who are guilty of loving the park to death.

The editorial went on to say that all sorts of commercial enterprises were multiplying to sell bicycle tours, bus tours, glider rides, sightseeing flights, mountain-climbing lessons, kayak instruction, whale watching and bird watching. Meanwhile tourist cars were overflowing parking lots, spilling on to roadsides all over the park. Reckless mountain bikers were turning carriage roads into danger zones. It concluded:

> With just a few tens of thousands of acres, the park cannot take it for long.

That night over dinner, we reminded ourselves that in a few days we were moving. Frankie's brother, Des, and his family were coming for a week and there was no room for us.

When Frankie and her brother Des and sister, Joan, built the place in the early seventies, the idea was to live in it together, spending time as a family over each summer. Then Des got married and Joan got married. Both started families. Soon, the place wasn't big enough to hold all the FitzGeralds at once, so an informal time-sharing arrangement developed. Eventually Joan, her husband, George, and their three children moved into their own place over near Pretty Marsh on the quiet side of the island. Des, who had four children and lived in Camden on the other side of Penobscot Bay, got busier and busier with his fish-smoking business, Ducktrap River Fish Farm, and spent less and less time on Somes Sound. Still, he liked to bring his family over for a change of scenery, for biking on the carriage roads, for camping and picnics.

This year, Des and his family were coming for just a week. So we would vacate temporarily to make room for two adults, a nanny, four children, and a very large Labrador retriever. We found temporary shelter at a house in town that friends had rented for August. It had plenty of spare bedrooms. We could take our pick.

We worked until four-thirty, then went to town. Northeast Harbor was swarming with people. Over the weekend an enormous, almost tidal, change had taken place all over the island. July people packed up and went home. August people flooded in. Overnight, rental houses were occupied by August people.

Augotrash! That's what I jokingly called them. I didn't call them that to their faces, of course. After all, some people who came to the island in August were close friends. Still, as a veteran of July, having piled up a month's seniority on the island, I felt somewhat superior to the August people. They were newcomers. No matter that they, like many of the July people who preceded them, had been coming to Mount Desert with the regularity of migrating birds since before I was born.

The banging next door began shortly after seven o'clock and, unlike the alarm clock, it had no turn-off button. I jerked upright. The Parade of the Cement Mixers began shortly thereafter. They moaned their way down the lane to Jurassic Park. Frankie rolled over, I noticed she was wearing ear plugs. I hustled through porch exercises, ran up and down the lane, and jumped into Somes Sound before Frankie stirred. We ate breakfast and left.

We drove into the village through morning fog, wound down past the library, turned right at the bank, drove along Main Street up and beyond Neighborhood House to St. Mary's-by-the-Sea Episcopal church, and found ourselves in the driveway of a giant turn-of-the-century wooden cottage with cedar-shingle siding.

Some friends, Tony and Roxana and Jamie and Susanna, had rented the cottage for the month of August. They offered us use of a spare bedroom on the third floor. Roxana, like us, typed in the summer. She wrote short stories, novels, and biographies. She came out to greet us.

Roxana told us that this was one of the first seaside cottages built in Northeast Harbor. We climbed steps to a massive, wrap-around porch. The front of the house and porch faced a land-scape that sloped to the shore. The view beyond was out the Western Way, the sea passage south between Greening Island and Great Cranberry that sailors took to go west into Blue Hill Bay and beyond. Roxana showed us inside, into a big dark living room with a massive fireplace and a high ceiling. To one side was a formal dining room and in back a restaurant-sized kitchen. A steep, narrow stairway wound up two stories to bedrooms and bath-rooms. The bathrooms were in the grand tradition of the old cottages, Roxana told us. They lacked certain "modern" features. They had plenty of bathtubs but no showers. As we moved our bags in and up the stairs to a third-floor bedroom, it dawned on me that we were no longer forest dwellers. We were going to spend the next week living in town. We were temporary townies!

We unpacked. Frankie brought along some books but left her Remington back home. I brought my computer and some re-search files.

"So what are we going to do now?" she asked. "Walk? Swim? Boat?"

"I don't know about you," I replied, self-righteously, "but I'm going to work."

She went for a walk with Roxana.

I unpacked my laptop, plugged it in, booted it up, and called up a blank screen. I was going to write a story I had done the reporting on before we got to Maine. About fog.

Ten

Eight years after the *Wall Street Journal* first offered me a job, I accepted. It was 1982 and I had been with the *Times* for nearly sixteen years. I was unhappy, but since most people at the *Times* seemed to be unhappy, I figured I was normal.

Quitting wasn't easy. I thought that since I already worked for the best newspaper in the world, going anywhere else would be a comedown. I may have been unhappy but at least I knew how the paper worked, which editors would reward good writing by editing it with a light hand, which ones attacked stories with their Cuisinarts. And while the *Times* seemed less like a family to me, it was the only home I had. I had job offers elsewhere. The truth was that I was afraid to leave.

Many years before, a friend had quit the *Times*. She was a good writer and she wanted to try going it alone, writing books and magazine articles as a freelancer. Unlike many *Times* reporters, she had the nerve to try it. She had traveled a great deal for the *Times* but she operated for many years out of the newspaper's busy newsroom on the third floor of the *Times* building at 229 West 43rd Street, off Times Square in Manhattan. The newsroom was a nerve center. Information streamed into it from *Times* reporters around the world, across the nation, and all over the city. The third floor bustled in the afternoons and evenings, when the next morning's edition was assembled, and she usually wrote her stories at a desk in the middle of it all. Then she resigned, and the day soon arrived when she no longer went to the newsroom.

I ran into her months later, and I asked her what it had been like to leave. Traumatic, she told me. She said it felt as if she had jumped off a giant cruise ship full of people and commotion and lights and sounds, and found herself alone in her own little rowboat. The giant *Times* ship was beside her, festive and busy. Its lights were bright and its people noisy. She felt comforted beside it, as if she was still a part of it. Then, slowly, the big ship and her rowboat began to drift apart, and the lights and the sounds of the larger vessel began to fade. Before long, the cruise ship was a distant glow of light on the horizon. Then it was gone. And she was sitting in her little boat in the middle of a big ocean feeling more alone than she had ever felt in her life.

Unhappiness may have been endemic and historic at the *Times,* but before I left, newsroom psychologists blamed the gloom on Abe Rosenthal, the executive editor. Many *Times* reporters eagerly awaited Abe's mandatory retirement at age sixty-five. They figured that when that day arrived, the clouds would part on a sunny new dawn of joy and good cheer at the *Times.* I had my doubts.

Abe had come to China when I was there and we spent a week touring the countryside. (I believe I hold the distinction of being the only person ever to have spent a night in a Mongolian yurt with A. M. Rosenthal.) Every day of our travels he told me he was not retiring. He said he had a "responsibility" to the paper not to. He said he needed more time to select and train a new generation of editors. He said "that sonofabitch [Ben] Bradlee," his rival at the *Washington Post,* wasn't retiring, so why should he? He said, in so many words, that since he'd been the best foreign correspondent, the best writer, the best editor, and the most loyal, dedicated, sacrificing, and caring *Times* journalist in the history of the newsroom, the publisher couldn't possibly enforce company retirement policy in his case. I figured that the odds of being happy at the *Times* were one in four. One: Abe doesn't retire, place stays unhappy; two: Abe retires, someone just like him takes over, place stays unhappy; three: Abe retires, a well-intentioned editor takes over, but finds it impossible to rid the newsroom of the poisons and gloom of the Rosenthal era, place stays unhappy; four: new editor takes over, sweeps out the gloom, place becomes happy.

Joining the *Journal* was, as it turned out, a blessing for me. Editors at the paper made me feel at home. They were refreshingly nonchalant about fiefdoms. They invited me to live in New York and commute to Asia, an arrangement impossible to contemplate at the *Times*, with its patchwork of fiercely guarded territories and turfs. The *Journal* editors didn't want the news covered as much as they wanted it found out. They wanted journalists who did original reporting, not journalists who filled orders or covered the same news events everyone else was covering. They cared about good writing and they rewarded it with minimal editing. The Journal had its share of tin-eared editors, to be sure. Designer-news types were lurking in the shadows as well, ever eager to have meetings, plan coverage, think up lists of stories, and assign them to order-filling field hands. But when I joined the Journal, these people were held at bay by experienced New York editors who believed that if they'd already heard about a story somewhere in the hinterland it probably wasn't news. They treasured good writing above all. These people became my new surrogate family.

"Without the *Journal,*" I reminded Frankie, "I would have never moved to New York and met you."

I didn't go to the *Journal* because I was interested in or knew anything about business, financial, and economic news. I did it because I had long envied *Journal* reporters and the way they went about their work. *Journal* reporters I had come across in Asia were unhurried and thorough. They didn't face daily deadlines or feel compelled to file a story every time some potentate held a press conference. In my early years in Asia, before long-distance phone service reached reliably into the Third World, a *New York Times* foreign correspondent was more or less expected to file a story if the wire services—the Associated Press, Reuters, and United Press International—were filing one. It wasn't a hard and fast rule. But if a *Times* correspondent was someplace where news was breaking, editors in New York expected their man to file the story. They would use a wire service story in such a situation, but only as a last resort. If the correspondent didn't file a story editors thought should be in the *Times,* he'd better explain why. If he consistently ignored breaking news, however unimportant he thought it to be, he might find himself reassigned to the *Times* bureau in, say, Trenton, New Jersey. This policy kept *Times* scribes busy both duplicating wire service stories and supplying the background, history, and analysis the newspaper also delivered to its readers. This policy made it impossible for *Times* reporters to venture off into the hinterland too far or for too long. To spend time away from the capital, or the center of the action, was to risk being scooped by the wire services or, even worse, by the *Washington Post* or the *Los Angeles Times.* This could lead the foreign editor to dash off an angry cable: WASHPOST FRONTS BHUTTO BLAST PENTAGONWARD STOP WHY YOU NOHAVE QUERY.

I enjoyed the *Times* reporting regimen but began to think that when I was reporting the news I was missing the story. I began to think the news got in the way of the story. Duplicating the wires took time—time I could have spent wandering off and looking for something new.

The *Wall Street Journal* foreign correspondents couldn't have cared less about the day's news. They were under no compulsion to file a story, no matter how important, that their editors could get from the wire services—services the *Journal,* like the *Times,* paid good money for. Journal correspondents never wrote stories that began, "President Bhutto today denounced." They never wrote a story from Vietnam as I often did for the *Times* that began: "B-52 bombers hit fresh suspected enemy strongholds south of the Demilitarized Zone today." *Journal* correspondents went looking for their own stories, often wandering serendipitously across the landscape, going wherever the thread of an idea took them. They seemed to take as much time as they needed. They were allowed to write in a way that made their stories accessible to their readers. They could be subtle. They could even fool their readers with an amusing opening and get them hooked into reading about an important issue—an issue readers thought they had no interest in. The *Times,* in contrast, didn't believe in making important points in subtle ways, or tucking them into amusing feature stories.

In 1972, I was in Pakistan covering every twist and turn in the government's efforts to keep the country from falling apart. In the wake of that nation's defeat by India in the war that turned East Pakistan into the new nation of Bangladesh in December 1971, the provinces of West Pakistan were threatening secession too. Separatists were threatening war and engaging in sabotage. Ethnic and regional groups were demonstrating and striking. The economy was a shambles. The big question was whether the government of Zulfikar Ali Bhutto could prevent West Pakistan from Balkanizing into warring ethnic enclaves. As international stories went, it was fairly important, and I was tied down for much of the time in the capital, Islamabad, with quick trips to Karachi and Lahore, and filing two or three stories a week.

That March, Peter Kann, a reporter for the *Wall Street Journal* based in Hong Kong, came to Pakistan on a reporting trip. Peter hung around Karachi for a leisurely couple of days and talked to diplomats and government officials to get a feel for the place. Then he ambled off into the countryside to attend some camel races. A week or so later, his story appeared in the *Journal.* It began:

> SIBI, Pakistan—*"You must go to Sibi. Great tourist spectacle, smashing good show,"* the diplomat in Islamabad says.
> *"You've been there, then?"*
> *"Not personally."*
> *"But you know people who have?"*
> *"Not personally."*

Still, it's a strong recommendation: a visit to the annual horse and cattle show (and camel races) at Sibi, a mud-walled dot of a town in the deserts of Baluchistan Province, 22 hours from Karachi by an "express" train called the Bolan Mail.
But an expedition to Sibi offers an introduction to more than bulls and camels. Sibi, during this particular week, plays host to many of Baluchistan's tribal sardars (leaders) and its nawabs, khans and mirs (titular nobility) and serves as a center for their sundry political intrigues.

Nowhere in the headline or first seven paragraphs was there any mention that the story was really about the centrifugal forces threatening to pull Pakistan apart. Mentioned early, they would have caused the average *Journal* reader's eyes to glaze over. Yet all these subjects were covered in a story that was both readable and entertaining.

I didn't see Peter's story at the time. Weeks later it arrived with a letter from the *Times* deputy foreign editor who asked: "Why can't we have stories like this in the *Times*?"

I was livid. Surely this editor knew exactly why the *Times* didn't have such stories. The *Times* foreign desk wouldn't let a correspondent waste so much time on a story that might not pan out. The *Times* would never have allowed a story of this importance—the possible breakup of a nation—to be written in a way that was entertaining or fooled the reader into thinking it was about camel races.

Later, I sent my editor Peter's camel-race story rewritten the way it most likely would have turned out in the *Times*—straightforward and full of self-importance:

Islamabad, Pakistan—Having lost East Pakistan in a disastrous war with India that created the nation of Bangladesh, Pakistan is threatened by regional forces that could pull it apart, according to a variety of sources.
Interviews of dozens of government officials, foreign diplomats and ordinary Pakistanis paint a picture of a nation faced with possible disintegration. . . .

The forces of Balkanization can be illustrated by looking at an annual camel-racing competition in Sibi, a small town in Baluchistan.

As I sat in the third-floor bedroom in the giant cottage in town rereading the file I'd brought from New York about people who sell fog, I couldn't help but think again about the differences between my *Times* and *Journal* editors in their approach to this story.

At the *Journal,* all I had to say to my editor was that I had found a bunch of guys who make and sell fog.

"Do it!" he said.

The process would have been much different at the Times when I worked there. To write about fog-making for Science Times, the Tuesday science section, I'd have to stress new research discoveries in the science of fog. If I told the editor of that section that my story was mainly about people who sell fog-making systems, he might say:

"Oh, that sounds like a business story. But I can't spare you to write a piece for the Business Section right now. So why don't you write a memo we can pass on to them and you can get back to science."

The Journal let me follow stories wherever they led and poke into obscure crannies to find them. In this case, I found an advertisement for fog-making equipment in *World's Fair,* a quarterly magazine for people in the business of putting on international exhibitions and for world's fair buffs. The ad was placed by an outfit called "Mee, the fog people," a California company that had figured out all sorts of uses for man-made fog.

I called up the founder of the company, Thomas R. Mee, a former navy pilot and cloud physicist who got into the fog business in 1969 by creating a permanent cloud over the Pavilion of the Clouds at Expo '70 in Osaka, Japan. To do that he had to build the world's first fog-making system.

Mee went on to build thousands of fog systems. The Bronx Zoo bought some. Dolly Parton's theme park, Dollywood, in

Pigeon Forge, Tennessee, bought some. Mee told me that man-made fog can cool off backyards, tennis courts, and even golf courses in the western desert. Fog, he said, cools hot, dry air by drawing out heat energy as it evaporates. Wind, however, was a problem. Wind could blow your cooling fog away.

I found another company that made fog-machines. Called Atomizing Systems Inc., it was in Ho-Ho-Kus, New Jersey. I called up its founder, Mike Elkas, and he told me that he got into fog in the late 1970s, when big meat companies switched from real smoke to "liquid smoke" to cure their bacon and other meats. He said he also sold fog to greenhouses for humidity and furniture factories for dust abatement.

I went out to see Mr. Elkas, and he showed me how fog-making machines worked by pumping water under pressure through a tiny hole in a nozzle. The stream is smaller than a human hair. It is aimed at a tiny metal pin point that splits the stream into molecules light enough to float. Fog!

The nemesis of fog-makers is dirty water that clogs nozzles. Cheap water-filtering technology made fog making possible. What made Elkas a success was his "patented ruby orifice." He showed one to me. It looked like a microscopic, one-hole shower head. It was a hole drilled by a laser through a wafer of industrial sapphire. Sapphire doesn't wear out quickly, and, with properly filtered water, doesn't clog.

Back in my New York office, I did some more fog reporting on the phone. But I didn't immediately write the story. Another, more timely, story came up. I set fog aside, figuring I could get around to it again sometime over the summer.

Now I sat in the natural fog of Maine and wrote.

Ho-Ho-Kus, N.J.—Forget little cat feet.

That's the first thing you learn in the fog business: Nature is no competition. Its delivery systems are lousy. It has a few niche markets: San Francisco Bay romance, London mystery, Maine coast pea soup. Otherwise, nature gives fog a bad name. It confounds commerce, befuddles shipping, closes airports, causes lethal highway pileups.

On the other hand, the kind of fog people pay money for comes in on new high-tech delivery systems. Fog users want it here and now—pea soup on demand. And demand has never been higher. Demand for fog?

Sure, fog is cool.

I wrote about light-show fog used by rock bands, smelly land-fill fog, outdoor air-conditioning fog, smoke-free nightclub fog, funeral fog, theatrical fog, hospital sanitation fog, apple storage fog, and textile factory dust-reduction fog.

Nature's fog is a cloud on the ground. It consists of water drop-lets, each about one-tenth the diameter of a human hair, or 10 to 35 microns (a micron being a millionth of a meter). It doesn't feel wet. It evaporates before falling to the ground. Anything bigger than 50 microns is mist. Mist is wet. It falls. Fog makers dump on mist. Misters give foggers a bad name.

Man-made fog comes in two varieties: real and fake . . .

Fake fog, also known as theatrical smoke, has been around since olive leaves were burned for effect in the Greek theater. Real smoke, dry ice and mineral oil mist gave way in recent years to glycol-based fluids that are heated until they vaporize and can be whooshed out on cue. Easier to control than water fog, these systems boomed as rock bands drew bigger audiences and moved outdoors. Fans wanted to see something besides ant-sized performers. Fog created curtains on which light shows could dance.

Elkas and Mee had told me that the Walt Disney Co. bought more fog-making equipment than any other single customer. The artificial environments of theme parks seemed more real bathed in fog, they said. Fog was also good for keeping theme park cus-tomers cool while they did what most theme park customers did the most: wait in lines.

I finished a draft of the story that afternoon.

★ ★ ★

Frankie's brother, Des, his wife, Lucinda Ziesing, his children, Caitlin, Ryan, their children, Alexander and Cooper, the family's yellow lab, Ray, and a nanny had moved into the house on Somes Sound in the afternoon of the morning we had moved into town.

Frankie's sister, Joan, her husband, George, their children, Frances, George Jr., and Amos, their yellow lab, Gloria, and a nanny were arriving at the camp near Pretty Marsh toward the end of the week.

FitzGerald family summer reunions had gotten a lot more complicated since the days when Desmond FitzGerald, Sr., brought his children to Somes Sound for picnics. In those days, there were one or two adults and four children. Now there were eight adults and nine children, and coordinating the schedules and logistics for those who wanted to get together for walks, boat trips, picnics, and dinners was always difficult and often impossible.

We found Des's family in Northeast Harbor one afternoon, eight-year-old Ryan explaining to his father why life wasn't all that much worth living without a set of Topps baseball cards containing the complete roster of each team in the Major Leagues. Such a set happened to be for sale in a village store. Father asked son why he needed the set. Son explained with notable logic and detail. Negotiations ensued. Father's wallet emerged from pocket. Son became a very happy eight-year-old.

That night, all the FitzGerald adults went to dinner at the Burning Tree, a restaurant in Otter Creek. Des, Lucinda, Frankie, and I ordered a bottle of wine and waited for Joan and George. Joan called to report that George's flight had been fogged out of the Bar Harbor airport and diverted to Bangor. They would be late. We ordered another bottle of wine.

Joan and George arrived at nine-thirty. We ordered. The food was wonderful. As for the conversation, I had difficulty concentrating. After a couple of glasses of wine and a meal, I got sleepy. After four glasses of wine and a very late dinner, I got very sleepy. I was tuning in and out of the table talk. At one point, I tuned in enough to hear Des, Joan, and Frankie talking about "what to do with the house." At first I thought they were talking about some house somewhere else. Then it dawned on me that they were talking about the house on Somes Sound, the FitzGerald house.

I almost choked on my wine. They were talking about Frankie's place! I couldn't believe what I was hearing. I woke up in a hurry. Joan was saying that she had been thinking about selling her share in the house for some time. She said selling made more sense now that she and George had gotten their Pretty Marsh camp. Des said he had been thinking about selling, too. He said his family enjoyed coming over from Camden in the summer. But the limited time he spent on Somes Sound didn't justify his share of the annual upkeep. On the other hand, he said, he wasn't sure he wanted to sell the house because it held fond family memories. It was a repository of family photographs and books that had belonged to his father and mother.

Joan said she felt much the same way about the family aspects of the house. Frankie said she had even had thoughts about selling, especially when the bangers and pounders got loud at Jurassic Park. Des said he had thought from time to time about getting another, larger place in some less popular and less expensive part of the Maine coast. With such a place, all the brothers and sisters and their children and dogs and nannies could live at once, re-creating the community they once had shared.

When their father had died, the children built the house in the woods that was a kind of shrine to the memory of their parents. In that house, as young adults, they were together as a family. Gradually, however, they had grown up, gotten married, and become involved in their own families, and the togetherness that was the FitzGerald house became a warm memory. Was it possible to restore it now? Should the now scattered family get another place somewhere else and try to re-create it? What should be done about the memory? That's what the conversation was about.

The spouses, George, Lucinda, and me, kept our mouths shut. I didn't know what George and Lucinda were thinking, but I knew what I was thinking: "You people must be nuts! I know family togetherness is important. I came from a family with very little of it. But, hey, children grow up, families come apart, new families begin, and life goes on. Memories or no memories, abandoning Frankie's place is the dumbest idea I've heard in years!"

The conversation drifted into the possibility of selling shares of the house. If Des and Joan sold, could Frankie and I buy? The short answer was no. We couldn't afford it. If Joan and Des wanted to sell any time soon, they'd have to sell to outsiders. I was getting depressed fast. As the dinner check arrived, I imagined some nouveau tycoon handing over a fat check to the FitzGeralds, waving them good-bye, ushering in a bulldozer, demolishing the house, and putting up a mansion. Frankie's place gone without a trace.

"Boy, what a summer," I said in the car on the way home. "First, Jurassic Park. It's starting to look like a hideaway palace for the sultan of Brunei. Then, a heinous crime against Ahuan and the alleged perp denies it. Now, this!"

We talked about Joan's and Des's seven children.

"They should decide what to do with their grandfather's place and Buddha's house," I said. "They're going to own it sooner than you'd like to think. They're going to need space. We're just temporary occupiers. Like the ants and mice."

What I was feeling went back to my own childhood. Frankie's place had become a home to me. Now they were talking about making me homeless again.

Eleven

Adjusting to life in town took a little doing. Things felt mixed up the next morning. Frankie said she felt like she'd gotten up on the wrong side of the bed. I struggled to take a bath in a tub, on hands and knees, head under the faucet, then with my back to the bottom of the tub, knees high. I had forgotten how to do it.

Nobody else in the house was home. Frankie walked off to the store to buy some breakfast muffins and came back marveling at all the morning people she'd seen but didn't know. She had grown up in Northeast Harbor over many summers. But the people in the village this morning were strangers because we never went to town in the mornings.

I was the real outsider, and I figured that as long as I had a week to spend in town I'd read some more books about the place and its inhabitants.

Historically, Northeast Harbor had been one of the summer epicenters of the American aristocracy, a place where college presidents, Episcopal bishops, prep school headmasters, and scholars gathered with writers, artists, and the wealthy inheritors and brainy new magnates who eschewed the social life of Bar Harbor. It had changed a great deal but it remained a nest of WASPs. Indeed, this very acronym for white Anglo-Saxon Protestant was coined by a man who had lived for many summers in a pink cottage on Lower Hadlock Pond, just north of the village. His name was E. Digby Baltzell. He was a sociology professor at the University of Pennsylvania who wrote about America's upper classes, mainly in Philadelphia and Boston, and he didn't mind living among his subjects.

When I first came to Northeast Harbor with Frankie, I paid little attention to its summer inhabitants. I heard Frankie's friends describe them variously as "high WASPs" and "proper Bostonians" and "snooty Philadelphians," but in those early summers I met very few people who seemed to qualify. Foraging for groceries and newspapers, or attending the odd porch-bender or dinner in Northeast Harbor, I kept an eye peeled for a "high WASP" and listened for the sound of a "proper Bostonian." Just as Frankie consulted her birding books for distinguishing features, I turned to WASP guidebooks. They told me to look for men wearing pink or green trousers and having "aquiline noses." In his book *Old Money: The Mythology of America's Upper Class,* Nelson W. Aldrich, Jr., wrote that if I came upon chummy people who occupied frayed and somewhat seedy cottages and clubs, I was on the right track. And I should always be on the alert for tedium:

> "Boring" is the commonest word in Old Money's social vocabulary. But the insult is mild compared to those that are hurled at the Old Money class from outside—that it's "stuffy," "old-fashioned," "pompous," and "stupid." They're all richly deserved, the inevitable reward of a social group that often prefers to inherit the company it keeps rather than choose it."

I had met my share of run-of-the-mill WASPs in Northeast Harbor over the years. Their names are usually a giveaway: Schofield, Minturn, Hamilton, Bradley, Whitney, Warrington, Denholm, Burnham, Crawford, Crompton, Stockton, and Granville. Those were their first names, their given names. Their given names, middle names, and family names all looked like last names. Hardly a Bob, Bill, or Dick was among them. Looking at the Northeast Harbor

Directory reminded me of Calvin Trillin's story about growing up as the son of a Jewish grocer in Kansas City and arriving at Yale to discover students with names like Thatcher Baxter Hatcher.

Genuine High WASPs and snooty Philadelphians, in contrast to plain WASPs, seemed to be an elusive species. In my summers at Frankie's place, I'd never encountered any. Or if I had, they'd fooled me. Now, with a whole week in the village, I figured I could see and hear some up close, like camping out on a pond to study pied-billed grebes.

Northeast Harbor's reputation as a hotbed of simple Christian living had frayed a bit since 1880, when founding fathers Eliot, Curtis, and Doane built their summer houses. As described by Samuel Eliot Morison, the early summer residents were educators and clergymen who lived in modest cottages intermingled with the fishermen and farmers along the shore. Their houses had neither electricity nor telephones. Like the locals, they pumped their own water and chopped their own wood for heating and cooking. Morison noted that the early settlers had tried to aggregate relatives, friends, and fellow educators and clergy into their village, people who shared their idea of a virtuous simplicity that stood in sharp contrast to the crass hedonism and conspicuous wealth increasingly on display in Bar Harbor. Every effort was made to keep Northeast Harbor's character distinct from Bar Harbor's, he wrote: "It used to be said that to be a summer resident at Bar Harbor you needed money but no brains; at Northeast Harbor you wanted brains but no money."

When land in or around Northeast Harbor came up for sale, efforts were made to sell it to what Morison called the "right people." He wrote of hearing a story about a real estate agent who in the 1880s had an offer to sell an entire farm to a less than reputable financier. When one of the village's pioneer settlers, Captain Samuel Gilpatrick, heard who the proposed buyer was, he quashed the sale by saying, "We have some very fine people here now in Northeast Harbor, including a bishop and three college presidents. We don't want any Wall Street riffraff!"

Among the "very fine people" who joined the summer rusticators of Northeast Harbor, I soon discovered, were Parkmans and Peabodys, Frankie's relatives. I'd picked up bits and pieces of their history over the summers, but now I mined the books in the library for more. I knew that Mr. and Mrs. Henry Parkman were the earliest of Frankie's ancestors—they were her grandmother's parents—to have a summer cottage. They came in the 1880s. Endicott Peabody, Frankie's great-grandfather, rented cottages in the village. I knew he was the founder of Groton School, but I didn't know he was, as described by Baltzell, "the most-famous headmaster in the English-speaking world," or why. When in residence, he preached at St. Mary's-by-the-Sea and was very much at home in the community, having educated many of its members.

Peabody was a descendant of one of the founding clans of puritan Massachusetts. The Peabody ancestors, John Endicott and Joseph Peabody, came to Massachusetts from England early in the seventeenth century. John Endicott, a Puritan, landed at Naumkeag in 1628 and became governor of the Massachusetts Bay Colony. Francis Peabody came to Ipswich in 1636 and settled in Boxford, and during the colonial period his fourteen children and their children made names for themselves as soldiers, teachers, lawyers, and clergymen. It was Joseph Peabody, born in 1757, who built the first fortune in the Peabody family. As a privateer, preying on British ships during the Revolutionary War, he was taken prisoner and later severely wounded in battle. He went on to amass a merchant shipping empire, his small, fast schooners circling the globe with cargoes of silk, sugar, hemp, indigo, tea, and spices. He made enormous amounts of money ferrying opium between India and China. His shipbuilding and trading workforce was said to number seven thousand. He lived in grand style, ate good food on fine china, drank fine wines in crystal goblets, and sat on furniture made of rare woods. Peabody's fleets suffered from Jefferson's trade embargo from 1807 to 1809 and during the War of 1812, and when he died in 1844 his empire was much diminished.

It was George Peabody, of Danvers, Massachusetts, a member of one of the poorer branches of the Peabody family tree, a school dropout and lifelong bachelor, who became the richest and most famous member of the family. He started out as a New England merchant and in 1837, after floating a large loan in London for the city of Baltimore, became a London banker. In 1854 he made Junius S. Morgan his partner. Before Peabody died in 1869, he became a prominent philanthropist on both sides of the Atlantic, giving away more than $8 million. After his death, his firm's name was changed to the J. S. Morgan Company, later Morgan and Company. The firm invited Samuel Endicott Peabody over to London as a partner. His son, Endicott Peabody, was thirteen years old at the time and in the spring of 1871 he entered Cheltenham School and stayed for five years. He went on to Trinity College, Cambridge, tried investment banking at his grandfather's firm, Lee, Higginson and Co., hated it, and went on to Harvard Divinity School. After seven months of missionary work in Tombstone, Arizona Territory, Endicott Peabody set about founding a school on the model of an English boarding school. In 1884, he founded Groton School. Its board of directors included his father, Samuel, and his father's business associate, J. Pierpont Morgan, a man who sailed his legendary yacht, *Corsair,* to Mount Desert regularly.

Endicott Peabody, the Rector, presided over Groton for fifty-six years, educating boys who would become some of the most influential men in America, including the two Roosevelt presidents (he married Eleanor and Franklin). He and his wife, Fanny, hobnobbed with some of America's richest and most powerful people, but they lived simple lives. They had five daughters and one son. The son, Malcolm Endicott, followed his father into Episcopal Church ministry, becoming Bishop for Central New York, based in Syracuse. He married Mary Parkman and they had five children: Mary (Marietta) Endicott Peabody, Endicott (Chub) Peabody, George Lee Peabody, Samuel (Sam) Parkman Peabody, and Malcolm (Mike) Endicott Peabody. The Bishop and his wife built their house in Northeast Harbor in 1924 and afterwards spent their summers there. They lived without extravagance, and they taught their children that to live the same way was virtuous.

On our second day in Northeast Harbor, we went to the swimming club for lunch. It was my first visit. In the dozen years I'd been coming to Frankie's place, I never set foot in the place. The swimming club was an affiliate of the tennis club, a private club to which members paid dues. Opened in 1896, the swimming club was the first institution in which Northeast Harbor summer people segregated themselves from the local population.

The closest I ever got to the swimming club was driving by. The longer I went without visiting it, the less I was inclined to visit it at all. Years passed. Not going became a matter of principle. The swimming club was the social center for summer people. It was a hangout where they went not only to swim but to see other people, to swap gossip and to while away a morning, or an afternoon. While I had nothing against this as a form of recreation, it didn't much suit either Frankie or me. The argument Frankie always made for going to the swimming club was that you could actually swim there. I argued that the idea of driving all the way to town to go for a swim seemed kind of silly when Somes Sound was right out front, ready for a quick kerplop day or night, high tide or low.

"No," she'd say, "I mean swimming swimming."

She explained that you could actually swim at the swimming club because it had a freshwater lap pool filled with warm water. The club also had a saltwater swimming area that had been walled off from Somes Sound around the turn of the century. Seawater was pumped into this area where the sun warmed it up to several degrees above the temperature of the water in the sound.

You could jump into the warm seawater and swim around to your heart's content. If swimming had been a favorite form of exercise for me, I suppose I would have headed to the club regularly. But I wasn't much of a lap swimmer and the idea of swimming for exercise struck me as a misuse of time better spent walking trails or playing tennis.

I caved in and went to the swimming club as an act of journalism. I would investigate, I told myself. I would observe. If I were lucky, I would spy a snooty Philadelphian in full snoot.

We arrived just after one o'clock and found the place full of people. The club was surprisingly austere, even decrepit, just as Aldrich had written it would be. I looked over weathered decks and unkempt sand and warmed to the place immediately. Above the seawater swimming area was a lap pool and a large deck. The deck was crowded with adults and noisy children. I warmed a bit more toward the club after being told that children were booted out of the lap pool during the noon hour and again between five and six o'clock so adults could swim in peace.

I made my way to the men's changing room, slipped on my suit, and emerged. Frankie was already swimming in the saltwater pond. As I walked down a set of wooden steps and got wet I had to admit that the water was comfortable. I had no impulse to scramble out. We swam for half an hour. My only discomfort was wearing a swimsuit. It felt clingy.

For lunch, we joined Jamie and Susanna at a table under an umbrella on the open deck. We ordered club sandwiches and iced tea by writing them down on a piece of paper and exchanging it at the order window for a number written on another piece of paper. When our order was ready, our number lit up on a board beside the order window.

A couple of men who looked vaguely familiar to me sat at separate tables nearby. One of them, Jamie point out, was Douglas Dillon, secretary of the treasury in the Kennedy and Johnson administrations. The other, he said, was Paul Nitze, a senior Pentagon official during the same period and the dean of strategic arms negotiators.

"This place is amazing," Jamie said. "Where else could you be sitting with Paul Nitze at a table on one side, Douglas Dillon on the other, neither one paying the least bit of attention to the other."

A couple of former Washington heavies ignoring each other was routine at the swimming club, I learned. Jamie pointed out a couple of banking tycoons seated at other deck tables. He identified for us a couple of nouveau tycoons, too. Frankie said the people she recognized were mainly members of old WASP families who had been summering in Northeast Harbor for generations.

"See any snooty Philadelphians?" I asked.

Most of the summer people I came to know in Northeast Harbor over the summers were Frankie's friends. Some of them were writers and artists, others were publishers, architects, and professors. A few were lawyers and investment bankers, and a few more were active or retired government servants, mainly diplomats. These people were well off, but I didn't think of them as being rich. Many of them rented summer houses. In some cases, two or three couples would share a house.

Not that there wasn't serious money around Northeast Harbor. All you had to do was look at the yachts and the shorefront houses to realize that plenty of people had plenty of dough. But the people who had it didn't flaunt it. The price of houses and summer rentals rose gradually, but houses were much more affordable in Northeast Harbor and Mount Desert than they were on Martha's Vineyard and the Hamptons on Long Island. In the mid-eighties, however, things had begun to change. Mount Desert began to be discovered, as it had been in the century before, by New Money. The Hamptons, Martha's Vineyard, and Nantucket were full up, and newly wealthy outsiders could either barge in with unseemly wads of money or look for new places. In the case of Mount Desert, they found a new place that was an old place. A New York financier named William Stewart, Jr., bought a house and four acres of shorefront land across Sargeant Drive from the Northeast Harbor Golf Club. The house was fairly large and grand by Northeast Harbor standards, but not by Stewart's. He tore it down and built a ten-thousand-square-foot replacement valued at $2.3 million. A few years later, that seemed like a pittance.

By the mid-1990s the town of Mount Desert, which includes the villages of Northeast Harbor, Seal Harbor, Otter Creek, Pretty Marsh, and Somesville, had become one of the richest municipalities in Maine. Even though Mount Desert had little industry and few businesses, the value of its property, consisting mainly of homes and land owned by summer people, made it rich.

As property values continued to rise, year-round residents and long-term summer residents faced a dilemma. They could keep their property or sell it, make a bundle, and move off the island. It happened more and more. As local people moved away, they commuted to their jobs on the island. They drove onto Mount Desert each morning and drove off each evening, creating rush hour congestion. Local housing became less and less affordable. The year-round population on Mount Desert became smaller and smaller. The island, like other places with large summer colonies, was losing its community.

Being temporary villagers gave us a respite from the Jurassic Park bangers and it made me feel decadent. There was no FitzGerald Survival School, no exercises on the front porch, no running, no kerplops into Somes Sound, nothing arduous at all. We didn't even have to cook. Roxana had hired a student cook from the Culinary Institute of America. Meals were awash in exciting cream sauces. Jamie cooked too. He was famous for his grilled leg of lamb. When he agreed to grill one while we were in residence, I followed him from start to finish, taking notes.

Life in town was leisurely. We slept late. We ate breakfast late. We walked to Main Street and wandered through the galleries and the boutiques. We drove off to Southwest Harbor to check out an antiques store and take a mountain walk. It was amazing to me how much time there was in a day when you didn't write. One afternoon we played three sets of tennis with Jamie and Susanna and showered at the club. On other days after mountain walks we would stop by the swimming club for nice long soaks. I began to think that the swimming club was a pretty nice place.

One evening we went to a concert at St. Mary's-by-the-Sea Episcopal Church. The church choir sang Bach chorales. At intermission we slipped back to the cottage for a glass of wine. This town living wasn't bad. It was also, in a way I never would have imagined, a revelation. My Indiana Jones–like sleuthing into the WASP culture of Northeast Harbor had led to a discovery that scared the daylights out of my inner farm kid. After quizzing WASP-watching veterans, venturing into the recesses of the library, thumbing through brittle tomes on colonial history, I asked a third-generation Northeast Harbor veteran exactly who on the island qualified as the quintessential High WASP.

"Oh, that's easy," she said. "You're living with her."

On Sunday morning, we slept so late in the guest bedroom on the third floor of the big cottage in town that by the time we got up, took baths, and went downstairs, everyone else had gone out to play. We warmed up a couple of blueberry muffins, made some coffee, read the *Times,* packed, cleaned up our room, wrote a thank-you note, and drove back to Frankie's place.

We found Des and his family packing, haphazardly. Ryan and Caitlin were yelling at each other. Lucinda was on the phone. Alexander, age three, and Cooper, age two, were running around the living room and the front porch, chasing each other, jumping onto the couch, jumping off, and squealing. Ray, the yellow lab, was making a feeble effort to keep up with the boys.

Watching this family in action was exhausting. I couldn't imagine how the parents kept their sanity. I couldn't imagine what it was like to raise two small boys and two older children, run a family, manage a business, and have a life at the same time. I couldn't imagine how this family, the picture of anarchy, would ever get packed and move out of the house.

Slowly but surely, later than sooner, Des and Lucinda got everybody going. This family was like a supertanker, I thought. The captain has to issue an order for a turn half an hour before the turn actually begins. Eventually, the nanny changed the little boys' clothes and packed up their toys. Ryan and Caitlin gathered their things. The adults policed up the house. Before long, two vans were stuffed with stuff. Then they were further stuffed with people and Ray the dog. Finally the FitzGerald convoy pulled away.

In its wake, we discovered a disaster area of scattered toys, half-eaten candy, Cheerios sprinkled hither and yon, sticky floors, bundles of unused diapers. The house was in disarray. A hurricane of two- and three-year-old kids had blitzed the place. It needed a lot more work. We went at it.

In a back bedroom, I peered into the wastebasket and saw a gooey soup. I leaned closer and sniffed. It smelled like melted sugar. In the bottom were sticky lumps of what looked like melted ice cream, half-eaten candy, and little mounds of congealed sticky syrup. I picked up the wastebasket, turned it toward the window light, and looked closer. In the syrupy goo were three mice. Dead mice. It looked like the mice had jumped into the basket after the sweets, gotten stuck, and couldn't get out. I felt sorry for them before realizing that the residential mice had just enjoyed, no doubt, the best week of their summer. The two little boys, cavorting around the house with all sorts of food and candy, had dropped a banquet of delectable morsels all over the place.

Twelve

Halfway up Eliot Mountain the trail gets steep and narrow as it winds through stands of young spruce and fir so thick that they blot out much of the sunlight. It was there on our afternoon walk where Frankie let out an uncharacteristic yip and scurried into the underbrush. She had spotted a curious mushroom.

Eliot Mountain lies just south of Acadia Park and on the edge of Northeast Harbor. It was named after Charles Eliot, the former Harvard president, who once owned it. It is actually more hill than mountain, and it lacks the grand vistas offered up by many of the other mountain trails on the island. But Eliot is a heavily forested and intimate place to walk, cool on hot days, and usually a good place to find wild mushrooms.

Frankie eventually emerged from the thicket with a big smile and a scraggy-looking, softball-sized coral mushroom that was faded orange in color—a hue we didn't associate with this family of fungus, which made it suspect. The coral specimens we usually found, and made into soup, were grayish brown. Frankie held this one up to my nose. I sniffed. It had a deep, earthy smell—a good sign.

When we got back to the house, Frankie rushed to the bookshelf and began leafing through wild mushroom field guides. She leafed and leafed before settling on a candidate of the genus *Ramaria* that looked very much like her prize. It was labeled "edibility not known."

I cut a tablespoon-sized chunk out of the specimen, carried it to the kitchen, turned on the stove, melted some butter in a skillet, and tossed it in. The mushroom began to sizzle and give off a wonderful smell. When it turned golden brown, I speared it with a fork, cut off a tiny piece, and tasted it. I gave Frankie a bite.

"Delicious!" she said. We waited for an aftertaste. Sometimes a metallic taste comes on, something akin to licking a piece of zinc.

"Nothing," I said. Frankie wasn't sure if she tasted faint metal or not. We looked at each other with what-to-do-now expressions.

"I say we serve it up on some toast to our next dinner guests and see what happens," I said. She laughed. I put Frankie's mushroom into a paper bag in the refrigerator, where it would stay while we mulled.

I got my first taste of wild mushrooms as a boy back on the farm in Michigan. One weekend in May, my uncle from the city came for a visit, took a walk in our woods, and came back to the house with a double handful of morels. I'd never seen them before. They looked strange to me, more like dark brown sponges than the toadstools I kicked in the cow pasture. They smelled like the inside of a sneaker after practice. My uncle sliced them, fried them in butter, and gave us all a taste. They had a strong, earthy taste—nothing a ten-year-old got excited about. But I remembered it.

We arrive on Mount Desert Island too late for the morel season. Morels fruit in the early spring. But dozens of other species pop up from underground threads called mycelium throughout the summer and fall on the island. Some are edible and delicious. Others are poisonous and deadly. The trick is figuring out which is which. Actually, it is more of an adventure than a trick, an exploration into the realm of unknowns and uncertainties in which self-confidence and doubt wage war in one's mind. To find, examine, identify, and declare a wild mushroom edible is the first step. The second step is the one that counts. For those who then plunge a batch into a skillet of melted butter, stir them through sweat and sizzle to golden perfection, and then devour them with a self-confident gusto that masks grave second thoughts, wild mushrooms have a flavor the gastronomically timid will never know. The timid, of course, will also never know the consequences of eating a mistake.

To bridge the chasm between self-confidence and doubt, shroomers, as wild mushroom hunters refer to themselves, band together to learn and share knowledge of mycology—the study of fungi. The shroomers invite neophytes to join their local associations, attend lectures, and come along on mushroom walks or forays. Many of these clubs are affiliates of the North American Mycological Association, which publishes *Mycophile,* a mushrooming newsletter, and *McIlvainea,* an annual journal for "serious" amateurs. Most of the local clubs publish newsletters too. *Spores Illustrated,* for example, is the newsletter of the Connecticut–Westchester Mycological Association, which calls itself COMA for short. This is a little inside joke, of course, and indicative of shroomers' sense of humor.

Experienced shroomers show beginners how to tell the difference between edible species such as morels, chanterelles, black trumpets, chicken-of-the-woods, and hedgehogs from poisonous species such as death caps, fly agarics, and false morels. In some areas, hunting and fishing guides supplement their incomes by taking people on mushroom hunts. In Michigan during one spring morel season, I paid a guide one hundred dollars to take me on a half-day foray. This seemed expensive at the time, but my guide thoughtfully found and showed me a false morel. This lookalike species contains a toxin called monoethylhydrazine, an ingredient in early rocket fuel that, when consumed, can cause acute poisoning and even death. My guide's unspoken point was that his services were much cheaper in the long run than, say, a liver transplant.

Mistakes are easy to avoid if you stick to a few hard-to-confuse species and adhere to a hard-and-fast rule of shrooming: if in doubt throw it out. Doubt is a warning bell, going off in a good shroomer's mind when something isn't quite right. Our friend Calvin Trillin, the writer and eater, says his warning bell rings when he hears or reads the phrase "central nervous system."

Shroomers teach beginners to use common sense. For example, as a general rule it is best to avoid eating species of wild mushrooms with common names that contain the word "death." Yet there is an exception: the horn of plenty, a delicious cousin of the chanterelle that the French call *trumpet de mort* (trumpet of death).

On Mount Desert Island, several edible species of mushrooms can be found that are difficult to mistake for inedible species. Chanterelles are plentiful and easy to identify with their chalky-orange funnel-shaped caps. They smell vaguely of apricot, taste mildly of pepper, and make terrific appetizers when fried in butter and served atop squares of toast, as well as fabulous soup. But I have also found a scaly chanterelle on the island. It is usually large and, while some people eat it without ill effect, it is mildly toxic to others.

Boletes are ubiquitous on the island and are easy to spot because they don't have gills on the undersides of their caps. Their undersides look like fine sponges. Many members of the genus *Boletus* are edible, and a few species, such as *Boletus edulis,* are delicious. *Boletus edulis,* known as porcini in Italy, cep in France, and steinpilz in Germany, is the most sought after mushroom in Europe. On Mount Desert we find other species of *Boletus* that are almost as tasty, but some cook up into slimy goo. Eating them produces what they call in the food trade "unpleasant mouth-feel." A few species of boletes are poisonous but easy to identify. Forst's bolete, for example, has a red cap that quickly bruises blue when cut or pinched.

Coral mushrooms abound on Mount Desert. They usually look like miniature versions of the branching coral found on coral reefs.

A large bunch might be the size of a fist, although I've found inedible species as big as a head of cauliflower. With a little trial and error, we found two species, one grayish brown and the other light tan, that were edible and delicious. They made the best soup of any mushroom on the island, including chanterelles.

Every now and then we came across a bright reddish-orange lobster mushroom or a batch of hedgehogs. These were both delectable and relatively easy to identify. But for every species that is easy to identify we found dozens that were devilishly difficult to pin down.

The bookshelves at Frankie's place held a sizable body of literature on fungi. There were half a dozen field guides, the oldest a 1974 copy of *The Mushroom Hunter's Field Guide, Revised and Enlarged,* by Alexander H. Smith. It was one of the first guides for nonexperts, initially published in 1958. A professor of botany at the University of Michigan, Dr. Smith was the editor of *Mycologia,* an academic magazine of fungi researchers, from 1945 to 1950, and president of the Mycological Society of America in 1950.

"For years," he says in its introduction, "I refused to write a field guide to the common edible and poisonous mushrooms, because field characteristics alone are not sufficient for accurate recognition of our native species."

Dr. Smith believed that people should not eat wild mushrooms without identifying them scientifically, by using a microscope and consulting technical literature. But people in growing numbers were collecting and eating them anyway, with no help from science. So Dr. Smith changed his mind.

"Would a well-devised field guide give mushroom hunters better protection against serious mistakes than they now have?" he asked himself. His answer was yes.

The guide that Dr. Smith produced was so unusual when it came out in 1958 that it was noticed outside the fraternity of fungi scientists. Donald Malcolm reviewed it for *The New Yorker:*

> It is hard to understand why mushroom hunting has been neglected by lovers of dangerous sport. Surely the equip-

ment required is not prohibitively expensive, for it consists merely of a knife to trim and peel the quarry, and a paper bag to put it in. Some cautious hunters also carry a coin, which they toss to determine whether a doubtful specimen is poisonous or not, but my experience suggests that it is not worth the added expense. Since equipment presents no obstacle, we must conclude that our sportsmen have been put off by the fact that the mushroom, when tracked to earth, does not indulge in obvious dramatics, such as roaring and leaping about. Yet the peril to the sportsman is perfectly real, and not like the dangers of the safari or the roller coaster, which are largely imaginary. For the hunter's only protection from the mushroom is a quick eye and an infallible judgment, in the exercise of which he soon acquires a quiet fatalism that might arouse envy in one of Ernest Hemingway's heroes.

Malcolm recommended Smith's book somewhat backhandedly: "This guide may not represent a great advance in accuracy over the tossed coin, but it will, I think, provide ideal reading for the winter months, when time hangs heavy on the mushroom hunter's hands and he has little to do but polish his stomach pumps and set them out in gleaming rows against the coming season."

Dr. Smith himself must have harbored some doubts about whether his guide would suffice to allow the nonscientific shroomer to identify wild mushrooms accurately because he included in its introduction this disclaimer: "It follows that neither I nor the publisher accepts responsibility for mistakes that have unfortunate results. People interested in the scientific identification of fleshy fungi must learn to use the technical literature and this involves having access to a microscope and being able to use it."

Such disclaimers can be found in all subsequent field guides to wild mushrooms. Ardent mushroom hunters aren't put off. To them, these warnings neatly sum up the adventure and uncertainty of shrooming.

"If any doubt remains about the edibility of a species, do not eat it," writes Gary Lincoff in the National Audubon Society's *Field Guide to North American Mushrooms.*

The Mushroom Book: How to Identify, Gather, and Cook Wild Mushrooms and Other Fungi, by Thomas Laessoe, Ann Del Conte, and Mr. Lincoff, contains detailed photographs of wild mushrooms from many angles to make identifying easier. The volume is prefaced with a publisher's note: "If in any doubt about the edibility of species do not cook and eat it."

Mushrooms of North America, by Roger Phillips, a comprehensive guide with more than a thousand color photographs, tells readers directly after the title page that "Neither the publisher nor the author accept responsibility for any effect that may arise from eating any wild mushrooms." Then, as if to underscore the point in his introduction, Phillips lists symptoms of mushroom poisoning: "They may show up as one or a combination of the following: stomach pains, diarrhea, vomiting, sweating, chronic thirst, hallucinations, slowing of the heartbeat, liver failure, coma."

All field guides clearly label some mushrooms "deadly poisonous" and others "edible and choice." Of the former, the most notorious is *Amanita phalloides,* which has a pale-greenish to yellowish cap often streaked with gray, a white veiled stem, broad gills, and a white volva. Write Laessoe et al.: "It is particularly important to be familiar with this fungus, since just one mistake could be fatal." Of the latter, mushroom eaters disagree, but *Boletus edulis,* with its pale-to-brown bunlike cap and bulging stem, is delicious and, as Phillips writes, is "one of the best-known edible fungi."

Between "deadly poisonous" and "edible and choice," however, is a vast center of the fungal spectrum where a kind of middle muddle occurs in which the guidebooks resort to weasel words and phrases such as "edible, but not recommended," or "edibility not known." I always wonder how edibility gets known unless the authors of guidebooks simply fry up a batch of edibility-not-knowns, eat them, and document the results—if possible—in the morning.

The fungal spectrum is also littered with look-alikes that aren't alike, and telling one from another can be difficult if not impossible. To do this, Frankie mined the guides, reading their descriptions carefully. She pawed over them, specimen in hand, comparing every nook and cranny and stem striation with the photos and descriptions in fine print. If she had had a microscope, she would have used it. If she had taken a class taught by Dr. Alexander H. Smith, she would have been an "A" student.

I found it much easier to identify a mushroom by looking at its photograph than by reading its description. It's hard to mistake a chanterelle from its photograph. The chanterelle's written description, on the other hand, seems almost impenetrable: "Cap 4–15 cm broad, broadly convex when young, becoming plane to depressed or vase-shaped in age; surface smooth or occasionally cracked, not viscid . . ."

When trying to identify a new specimen, I leafed through the photographs looking for a resemblance. If I found a likely match, I looked it up in the Peterson Field Guide, written by Kent H. McKnight and Vera B. McKnight, which has handy edibility symbols beside each species. A little black cooking pot next to a species means this mushroom is "edible for most people." A little black pot inside a circle with a line through it means "not recommended." A little skull and crossbones means "poisonous." If my specimen didn't have a skull and crossbones beside it in the Peterson guide, I skimmed the other guides, including Dr. Smith's. If these guides said "edible but not recommended," or "edibility not known," I usually tossed out my specimen. When I felt confident, if not brave, I'd cut off a chunk, fry it up in butter, and take a bite—a small bite.

My favorite field guide was *Mushrooms Demystified: A Comprehensive Guide to the Fleshy Fungi,* by David Arora, an engaging expert with an attitude I liked. Arora is a confidence builder. He advises readers to think positively, pointing out that of the thousands of species out there, "only five or six are deadly poison-ous!" He says that once you get the hang of it, telling a Death Cap from a chanterelle is as easy as telling "a lima bean from an artichoke."

"Like driving, swimming, walking, or breathing, mushroom-eating is only made dangerous by those who approach it frivo-lously," Arora wrote. He blames lurid media headlines and a "fungophobic" medical profession for perpetuating the wild mush-room's loathsome image.

> Bring home what looks like a wild onion for dinner, and no one gives it a second thought—despite the fact that it might be a death camas [a poisonous member of the lily family] you have, especially if you didn't bother to smell it. But bring home a wild mushroom for dinner, and watch the faces of your friends crawl with various combinations of fear, anxiety, loathing, and distrust! . . .
>
> For there are few things that strike as much fear in your average American as the mere mention of wild mushrooms or "toadstools." Like snakes, slugs, worms and spiders, they're regarded as unearthly and unworthy, despicable and inex-plicable—the vermin of the vegetable world . . .
>
> This irrational fear of fungi is by no means a universal trait. The media and the medical profession have done their part to perpetuate it, but they are certainly not responsible for its origin. To a large extent, we inherited our fungo-phobia from the British.

The British live on a damp island where mold, mildew, and mushrooms hasten decay of everything from dead trees to crops to shoes to building walls. In England, mushrooms were so de-spised that few were given common names. All were labeled as toadstools. Eating them was, until recently, contemptible. In contrast to continental Europe, where edible mushrooms were and are beloved, in England they were maligned as foul and loath-some instruments of disease, decay, and death. As an example,

Arora quotes this passage from the creator of Sherlock Holmes, Sir Arthur Conan Doyle: "A sickly autumn shone upon the land. Wet and rotten leaves reeked and festered under the foul haze. The fields were spotted with monstrous fungi of a size and colour never matched before—scarlet and mauve and liver and black— it was as though the sick earth had burst into foul pustules. Mildew and lichen mottled the walls and with that filthy crop, death sprang also from the water-soaked earth."

Some years ago I found an article in *Mushroom, The Journal of Wild Mushrooming* entitled, "There ARE Toadstools in Murder Mysteries." The article dealt with mushrooms used as murder weapons in novels, and it was written by Dr. R. E. Reinert, an avid mycophile and retired psychiatrist. Dr. Reinert had collected and read all the murder mysteries he could find in which mushrooms played a part in the crime. He discovered that as often as not they were written by British authors, and set in the English countryside.

Dr. Reinert delighted in pointing out cases in which the author had selected the wrong mushroom for the job. In *Documents of the Case,* written by Dorothy Sayers and published in 1930, for example, an accountant is found dead in an isolated cottage and a partially eaten plate of cooked mushrooms is found near the body. The authorities presume the man died after "consuming a dish of venomous toadstools." They identified the mushrooms as *Amanita muscaria,* or fly agaric, which contain the poison muscarine. Much muscarine is found in the victim's stomach.

Wrong shroom, wrote Dr. Reinert. *Amanita muscaria* is a bad choice for two reasons. First, cooking destroys its muscarine. Second, even if these mushrooms were undercooked experts don't think they contain enough muscarine to be lethal to humans. The mushroom is commonly called fly agaric because farmers in the old days cut it up into pieces and put them in a bowl of milk in their milking barn. The milk infused with muscarine. Flies drank it and died.

Dr. Reinert praised two murder mysteries in which the authors chose *Amanita phalloides,* or death cap, as the murder weapon.

It was an excellent choice by knowledgeable authors who "seemed to know their mushroom fairly well," he noted. They were aware that death caps grow in woods, not meadows, fruit in August and September, and make their victims ill in two stages, first causing gastrointestinal pain, nausea, and vomiting and then liver destruction. He quotes Gordon Wasson, a renowned mushroom scholar: "When it comes to real murder, there is only one kind of mushroom worth considering: *Amanita phalloides.*'"

When it comes to escape, on the other hand, Dr. Reinert points out, *Amanita phalloides* is not so good because its deadly symptoms can begin to occur only a few hours after this mushroom is consumed. The perpetrator might not have enough time to abscond cleanly. For a leisurely getaway, Dr. Reinert recommended another family of shrooms. "As for giving the poisoner plenty of time to get to the hinterlands," he wrote, "it would be hard to beat those *Cortinaarii* which contain orellanine which may take days or weeks to destroy kidneys."

One weekend, an old friend of Frankie's came to the island to visit and we went for walk on Pemetic Mountain in the park. An interior decorator, he had a keen eye for color and texture and as we were walking and talking he spotted a cinnamon-tan mound of something in the woods about forty yards off the trail. We headed for it. It was a dense clump of mushrooms growing from a decaying birch trunk on the forest floor. The mushrooms had gills, their caps were dotted with flakes, and their stems were scaly—all signals for turning on the caution light. But these specimens were young and beautifully formed. I said that I had recalled spotting this species in the guidebooks.

"So let's take one home and check it out," Frankie said.

"Just one?" I said. "What if it's a keeper? We're not going to come all the way back here to get the rest, that's for sure."

I picked a dozen mushrooms off the log and popped them into a paper bag.

Back at Frankie's place, I got out the Phillips guidebook, looked through its photographs, and found our prize: a brown-spored

agaric named *Pholiota squarrosoides*. It was a perfect match. I read
the text and found the word I was looking for: "Edible."

I looked up *Pholiota squarrosoides* in two other guidebooks and
found similar matches. I got out the frying pan. I chopped one
up and fried it in butter. I took a bite. Delicious! I fed a piece to
Frankie.

"Oh, that's good!" she said. We waited for a metallic taste to
invade our mouths. None. I took another bite. Frankie took
another bite.

"Definitely a keeper," I said. I fried the rest in butter and turned
them into a very good soup.

After dinner, as I was returning the mushroom guidebooks to
the shelf, I pulled out David Arora's guide and looked up *Pholiota
squarrosoides*. I couldn't find it at first. Instead, I found the scaly
Pholiota, or *Pholiota squarrosa*. I looked at its color photograph. It
looked the same. I read its description. It seem to be the same—
until I came to the section on edibility:

"Not recommended. Some people eat it regularly but others
have suffered severe stomach upsets and old specimens are often
rancid-tasting."

I rushed into Frankie's room.

"How do you feel?"

"Fine."

"Well, don't panic," I said, reading her the Arora passage.
She grabbed the book to read for herself.

"Wait a minute," she said, reading down the page into the fine
print.

"Listen to this: 'Other species: *P. squarrosoides* is a very similar and edible scaly species with a somewhat paler cap and mild
odor . . .'"

We didn't know which one we had eaten, and we had no
leftovers to reexamine. We stayed up late that night, listening
carefully to abdominal rumblings, awaiting the first feelings of
nausea or a stab of pain down near the belly button. Nothing
happened.

A few days later I phoned David Arora in California. I had interviewed him previously for mushroom stories I had written for the *Wall Street Journal*. I described our specimens.

"You ate *that?*" he exclaimed.

Uncertainty and doubt continued to pop my brain with each questionable mushroom that found its way back to Frankie's place. Still, I remembered some useful advice I had found in an article in *Mushroom, The Journal*. The author of the article observed that while the timid eat only foolproof species (*always cooked, never raw*), he noted that the more daring "have a wider range, feeling that a little diarrhea is worth the new experience." Which reminds me: *Neither the publisher nor the author of this book accept responsibility for any effects that may arise from eating any wild mushrooms.*

The day after I'd put Frankie's faded-orange coral mushroom in the refrigerator, I went through the guides once more, then pulled out the specimen and announced bravely, "I'm making soup." Frankie didn't laugh.

CORAL MUSHROOM SOUP

Clean 1½ cups of coral mushrooms, carefully removing moss and spruce and fir needles. As with all wild mushrooms, it's best to conduct a visual inspection by slicing off a part—or slicing a stem lengthwise. Some people don't feel comfortable eating a mushroom if its stem or cap is laced with little tunnels created by larval friends who had discovered it first. To determine how much live protein may be occupying a shroom, try this test: Put the mushroom slices in a lightly oiled pan, flat sides up, and turn up the heat. If little white worms assemble in an irregular dance formation and begin gyrating on the tops of your specimens, toss them out.

Chop the shrooms you decide to eat into thumbnail-sized pieces. Sauté in a frying pan in a combination of olive oil and butter until the moisture is steamed away and they begin to crackle slightly. Crank in some freshly ground black pepper.

Meanwhile, in a saucepan heat up a can of chicken broth until hot but not boiling. Dump shrooms from the frying pan into the broth, oil and all, and turn the heat down to low. (You can add 2–3 tablespoons of dry sherry, but I don't.) Add ½ cup of milk. The milk adds body and turns the broth light brown, which is crucial for spotting the spruce or fir needles floating on top. Skim off as best you can. Serve hot, but not so hot that the milk curdles.

The soup was delicious, and we went to bed with just enough lingering uncertainty to make us feel like cutting-edge shroomers.

Thirteen

We set out for Frenchboro the next morning in *Scoop,* skimming across a calm sea at twenty-five knots. We stopped along the way near a tiny granite islet to watch a colony of harbor seals, then sped on. Frenchboro is a lobstering village on Long Island, situated eight miles off the southern tip of Mount Desert. It was one of our favorite places to visit in the summer. Frankie's old friend Gilbert owned land and a beautiful house on the island, and his wife, Ildiko, had invited us there for a picnic. When invitations like that turned up, even Frankie's work ethic failed.

Frenchboro was one of the last working villages left on the islands of Maine. Forty-five year-round residents lived in the village, most of them lobster fishermen and their families. At the beginning of the twentieth century, some three hundred islands off the Maine coast had working villages. By the end of the century only fourteen were left, and Frenchboro was among the smallest.

When we arrived at the entrance to Frenchboro's narrow harbor, I cut back *Scoop*'s motor and we idled in. The harbor extends nearly half a mile into the north side of the island. Hills rise steeply on each side of it, providing shelter from winds blowing off the sea. On the hilltops a dense spruce forest rings the harbor like a collar. The village was built around the harbor. Along the water's edge, fishing docks perched in varying states of repair, some freshly planked and piled high with lobster traps, others barely standing or badly listing, their planks rotting. Decaying hulls of old lobster boats rested on or alongside some of the docks. Small houses, most of them covered with peeling white paint, dotted the hills on both sides of the harbor. A Congregational Church, a white clapboard school, and a small museum sat at the top of the harbor. A car-ferry dock perched on pilings on one side of the harbor entrance. Ferries made the forty-five-minute run from Bass Harbor on Mount Desert to Frenchboro twice a week. Frenchboro had no stores. Islanders took the ferry, or their own boats, to shop on Mount Desert and the mainland.

I eased *Scoop* up to a wooden float at the Lunt & Lunt wharf on the harbor side opposite the ferry dock and Frankie hopped off with a line to tie up. Several floats were roped together at the base of the wharf's ramp. This was where lobstermen sold their catches. On top of the floats, doors opened to porous tanks in the water below where live lobsters were stored. The floats were stacked with wooden boxes used to transport live lobsters to wholesale and retail outlets on the mainland.

We climbed the ramp to the deck of the wharf. Gasoline and diesel pumps stood on the harbor side of the wharf. The Lunt family sold fuel to lobster boats, mainly, but other boaters in need were free to buy some. They also sold bait for lobster traps.

In the center of the wharf stood Lunt's Dockside Deli, a carry-out restaurant open in July and August. The Lunts sold steamed lobsters, lobster rolls, chowder, crab salad, chips, other snacks and soft drinks to islanders and visitors. Customers could eat at two picnic tables on the deck outside.

David Lunt came out from behind the counter to greet us. A seventh-generation islander in his fifties, he managed the wharf and knew Frankie well from her many visits over the years. Dave was Frenchboro's mover and shaker. His family dominated commerce on the island. He headed the Frenchboro Future Development Corporation, an economic development group organized to help the village survive.

* * *

Frenchboro was settled early in the nineteenth century as a convenient base for fishing in the Gulf of Maine and the Georges Bank to its south. Settlers caught Atlantic cod, halibut, haddock, and sole on day trips to nearby waters in rowboats and small sailboats. Some of them sailed far offshore in large fishing schooners and were gone for weeks at a time. They made extra money by cutting island trees and selling lumber. They collected round rocks along the shoreline and sold them as paving stones. They started dairy farms and sold butter and cheese, raised sheep and sold their wool, and grew potatoes. But it was fishing that kept the village populated and prosperous for a century.

By 1835 the village had a population of more than one hundred and fifty people, and in 1842 it had its first one-room school. The mid-nineteenth century was Frenchboro's golden age. Dean Lawrence Lunt, David's son, tells us in his history of Frenchboro, *Hauling by Hand,* that in the second half of the nineteenth century two big fishing companies operated in the harbor. The island's population hit its peak in 1870 at one hundred and seventy-six, enough people to keep two, and sometimes three, general stores in operation. After that came an era of slow decline. Fishing boats from Canada and Massachusetts plied the Gulf of Maine and the Georges Bank in ever-increasing numbers. As their catches grew, competition became fierce and Maine's fishing industry went downhill. Frenchboro's population decreased slowly. The village still had one hundred and nineteen people in 1940. But by 1960 there were only fifty-seven.

Keeping Frenchboro alive became a struggle, and keeping the Frenchboro Elementary School open became a crucial element in that struggle. Losing the school would be fatal to the village because families with school-age children would be forced to move off the island or send their young children to attend boarding schools on the mainland, as high school students did. Without a school, mainlanders with children would be unlikely to move to the island.

In 1964, the island's leaders hatched a scheme to populate the school with pupils by importing fifteen foster children from the mainland and boarding them with local residents. State education officials called it a bad idea, in part because they worried about the long-term effects on the foster children of having to use the school's outhouse in winter. The scheme was implemented, and it worked. But it proved to be a temporary fix. The student body at Frenchboro Elementary continued to decline, hitting a low ebb in the winter of 1979 when the only pupil was Dean Lunt. Instead of spending money to heat the one-room school building for a single student and teacher, Lunt sat through his classes at his teacher's kitchen table.

Attracting a teacher to Frenchboro was a lot easier than keeping one. Dozens, if not hundreds, of teachers responded to advertisements in education magazines for a qualified teacher to come to an island off the Maine coast and teach in a one-room schoolhouse. Keeping a teacher over the winter was the hard part. Through the heart of the school year, Frenchboro is a bleak, isolated, and forlorn place. Thick, dark, low clouds blanket the sky from horizon to horizon. The sun, if you saw it at all, disappeared in the west in the middle of the afternoon. Whatever propelled a teacher to take the job—idealism, adventure, dreams of an idyllic life—could quickly drain away.

Lots of Maine teachers applied for the job. The problem with them was that if they moved out to the island, settled in, started the school year, and then began to have doubts about their decision as winter set in, they could quit. They could get on the ferry and go home, no big deal. After a while, the wise men of Frenchboro, led by David Lunt, figured that they had to hire their teachers from as far away from the Maine coast as they could find them. The town advertised nationally and caught the interest of teachers in the Midwest and other places where teaching on a Maine island seemed like a dream come true. To someone in Kansas or Ohio, Frenchboro sounded blissful.

Teachers recruited from the Midwest or beyond made major commitments in coming to Frenchboro. They had to pack up and move themselves and their families a long way to the island. Quitting in a fit of despair during an ice storm in February was easier for a teacher from Bucksport, Maine, than it was for one from Omaha, Nebraska. But teachers from far away got worn down, too. It just took a little longer, or so villagers hoped. Eventually the teacher realized that Frenchboro, like the rest of Maine, was ten months of winter punctuated by July and August, and that living on an island off the coast of Maine in the winter was not for the faint of heart. After a year or two or more—and more was always Dave's goal in recruiting them—the teacher would begin to wonder what life was like in, say, Florida. Then Dave and his committee would have to start all over again.

In the mid-1980s, Frenchboro tried a homesteading plan to attract new families to the island. Islanders formed the Frenchboro Future Development Corporation, got a federal community development grant, and built six houses on one-and-a-half-acre wooded lots on the hill above the west side of the village on donated land. The corporation would rent the houses for $375 a month and occupants who stayed three years could buy them for less than they had cost to build and make mortgage payments of $312 a month.

Word got out. Frenchboro's scheme was written up in the supermarket tabloids. Thousands of people fed up with crime, traffic, and the mainland rat race thought they wanted to live on a remote and beautiful island off the Maine coast. Hundreds filled out a ten-page questionnaire and paid a $25 application fee. Twelve finalists came to Frenchboro in the spring of 1987 for interviews and to see the island firsthand. Six families were chosen. Three of them moved onto the island in December of 1988. Two more came later. Most of the homesteaders didn't last long. They couldn't adjust. More families who wanted to try island life were chosen to replace them. By the mid-1990s, of eleven families who had come to Frenchboro, three remained, and they were headed by lobstermen from the mainland.

The lobster was the mainstay of Frenchboro's modern economy and Maine's fishing industry. Lobsters had been part of the American diet long before European settlers arrived. Colonists ate lobster. But the crustaceans were so ubiquitous along the New England shoreline that they were considered to be trash fish, edible but with no commercial value. In 1607 English settlers at the Popham colony at the mouth of the Kennebec River reported gaffing fifty lobsters in less than an hour, anthropologist James M. Acheson notes in his book *The Lobster Gangs of Maine*. Lobsters were everywhere, and they were huge: five-footers were reported.

Lobsters have to be marketed live or processed. Their carcasses develop sickening toxins soon after they die. Live lobsters caught locally were sold in colonial markets in Boston and New York. But to get lobsters to market in quantity over any distance required the development of a boat with seawater tanks that could keep them alive in transit. These boats, called smacks, first appeared in Long Island Sound in the late 1700s and moved up the coast. It wasn't until the smackmen arrived in Maine in the 1820s that the state's commercial lobster industry began.

Until the notion of fishing for lobster came to Penobscot Bay, lobsters were ground up and used for garden fertilizer or chopped up and used as bait for much more valuable fish such as mackerel, cod, and halibut. When fishermen began catching lobsters, they sold them for two cents a pound. Frenchboro's fishermen didn't start catching and selling lobsters until 1880. As Dean Lunt tells it, eight local fishermen switched to lobstering between April and August of that year. Each man set out fifty traps and earned about seventy-five dollars.

Canning made lobster fishing boom in Maine, and it almost ruined the fishery. The first of twenty-three canneries opened in Harpswell in 1844. The canneries were rapacious, taking all sizes of lobster, and harvests began a steep decline. In 1872, the state government responded by imposing size limits on catches, outlawing the harvest of egg-bearing females, and closing the fishery for two-and-a-half months each year. The regulations and declining harvests made canning less productive and profitable. Canneries began to shut down. By 1895 all of them had closed. Demand for lobsters went down and so did annual harvests. As a result, lobster stocks began to recover, but the recovery took decades. The two world wars and the Depression helped by keeping demand down. In 1930, according to Acheson, lobstermen could get only three cents a pound for their catches. Many of them quit setting traps.

For many years the recovery was gradual. But in the 1980s, a remarkable resurgence began, with harvests climbing to forty million pounds annually. By the end of the 1990s, yearly hauls had almost doubled again. No one was sure why. Some marine scientists believed that overfishing in the Gulf of Maine explained it in part. With fewer fish eating lobster larvae and small lobsters, more of the crustaceans survived to adulthood. Other experts noted that lobstering isn't really fishing; it is farming, aquaculture. Lobstermen put food into millions of traps and lower them to the bottom. Small lobsters walk into a trap, eat, and walk out. Larger lobsters are hauled up and removed from the traps. If they are under the legal size or females carrying eggs, they are tossed back to grow larger and hatch more lobsters. Still, by the end of the century, many marine scientists warned that lobsters were being overfished. If they were right and the catch collapsed again, Frenchboro would be in peril.

Over Diet Cokes at the Dockside Deli, we asked Dave about the latest news on the island. He nodded to the other side of the wharf. Beyond stacks of lobster traps, past the deli, on the other side of the dock from the gas pump, over near a pile of lumber and several piles of what some people would refer to as junk, was a partially restored shed. Hanging on the shed walls, inside and out, were oil paintings of the Bass Harbor lighthouse, Frenchboro harbor, the headland of the village, lobster boats, and island landscapes and seascapes. These paintings, Dave told us, were the work of the husband of the new schoolteacher. He was an artist and a potter. He and the teacher had arrived from Missouri last fall. The only reason there wasn't a lot of pottery around for sale, Dave explained, was that some kiln parts the husband needed to fire his clay work hadn't showed up. Dave said he hoped the kiln parts would turn up soon so that the teacher's husband would be happy. Dave smiled.

Dave didn't have to explain. With the current teacher, everything was going well except for her husband's missing kiln parts. Dave Lunt had gone out of his way to create an art gallery on his wharf to keep the teacher's husband's spirits high. Now you could buy gas, a lobster roll, or an oil portrait of the wharf. Dave had even gotten the art bug himself. He was offering sand dollars from the beach on the other side of the island for a dollar apiece.

Soon, Gilbert was guiding his launch, full of other picnickers, up to the Lunt wharf. We held his lines while his guests disembarked. He parked his boat on a mooring and rowed his dinghy back to the wharf.

Gilbert was one of three summer people who had built houses on the island. He was a successful businessman, an ardent conservationist, and something of a human aggregation device. He organized all sorts of outdoor activities. He planned daylong walks over Mount Desert's mountains, stopping for a picnic lunch and a swim in a freshwater pond. He went hiking, biking, running, and kayaking. Sometimes he did them all in a single day with whoever had the stamina to keep up. He ran up and down mountain trails most mortals walked. He bicycled around the carriage roads for miles, then launched his kayak and paddled for hours at sea.

The picnics Gilbert and his wife, Ildiko, had on Frenchboro became a ritual. Guests assembled at a dock in Northeast Harbor. There precisely at eleven A.M., a chartered lobster boat and Gilbert's launch would load up and depart on a journey of an hour and a half out the Western Way and through small islands, some with colonies of seabirds and harbor seals.

When Gilbert and the others arrived, we joined them and set off on a walk—a traditional prelunch constitutional that came to be known over the summers as Gilbert's forced march.

Long Island's shoreline is eleven miles around and Gilbert was always eager to show it off. He led his charges, offering commentary on shore life, pointing out scenes, reminding them to keep up the pace or watch their step.

We set off along a path on the north shore of the island heading east. The crisp sea air cut into our nostrils. Seabirds were everywhere. Gilbert said we were walking on the longest path of undeveloped shoreline anywhere in the state of Maine, longer than any seaside path in Acadia National Park. The mountains of Mount Desert loomed in the distance.

After two hours of walking we were less than a third of the way around the island and starved. We started grumbling. Gilbert reluctantly led us on to a path that cut across the center of the island, back to the village, and over a hill to his house. Under an umbrella around a table flanked by deep beds of moss and rock-lined pools, we wolfed down a buffet of salads made of fresh lobster and crabmeat catered by Lunt's Dockside Deli. On the way home, Frankie and I bought two pounds of steamer clams from Dave Lunt and pushed off.

With the wind at our backs, the passage to Somes Sound took only forty-five minutes. We did a little fishing at the mouth of the sound. Frankie baited the hook on a hand line with bacon, tossed it in, and within seconds pulled up a crab.

Fourteen

Suddenly mushrooms were everywhere, and berries were no-where. Local strawberries, so sweet, succulent, and abundant at $3.50 a quart when we arrived, vanished in mid-July. Raspber-ries were scarce and finding them was hit-and-miss. The king of Maine berries, the blueberry, was late.

Frankie was perfectly willing to suffer this berry-less interreg-num with bananas. Not me. I was having berry withdrawal pangs. I was ready to take drastic measures to find berries. I was ready to go up Route 3, over the causeway, and onto the mainland, the world! Up in that direction were vegetable stands, farmers' mar-kets, and lots of guys who sold fruits and vegetables out of the backs of their pickup trucks. If there were any berries to be had, that's where I'd find them. We might have to go as far as Ells-worth. Ellsworth is the region's mercantile center. It is where Down East Maine does its big shopping. Highways funnel into it from all over Maine.

Just thinking about going to Ellsworth was evidence of some desperation on my part. Days of isolation in the woods made Ellsworth loom as a mighty metropolis. And the longer I stayed in the woods, the bigger and more complex it became. I called it the Greater Ellsworth Metroplex. I thought of its bustle, traffic jams, acres of hot asphalt parking lots, shopping malls, McDonald's,

Burger King, Kentucky Fried Chicken, and the L. L. Bean outlet store. I thought of Doug's Shop'N'Save, where the shopping carts were so big they reminded me of supertankers. Ellsworth even had a new Wal-Mart, a store so huge you could get lost in it. Ellsworth made my head spin. Here was a knot of urban frenzy only half an hour up the road. My goodness, the population of the place was more than five thousand!

Frankie didn't think we'd find any berries, but she enlisted in my expedition so she could buy some new tennis shoes.

We set off just before noon, crossing the Thompson Island Bridge into bumper-to-bumper traffic. We inched past roadside lobster pounds, with their belching outdoor steamers. The traffic was so heavy by the time we passed the Bar Harbor airport in Trenton that we figured Ellsworth would be gridlocked. Compared to our neck of the woods, of course, a stop sign was a form of gridlock. But I had a plan. We would stop at places on the right side of the road going into Ellsworth, turn around, and do the same thing heading out. No left turns into traffic.

Before we got to Ellsworth we passed through a zone I called the People's Republic of Fudge Moccasins. The highway between Mount Desert and Ellsworth was lined with shops selling lawn ornaments, maple syrup, blueberry soap, bayberry candles, and, of course, genuine Indian moccasins made in the People's Republic of China. You could eat lobster rolls, play miniature golf, buy name-brand towels cheap, and get Christmas decorations year-round. A restaurant featured "Maine Luau." Kart Land offered rides in go-karts that were souped down to make them go slow. Acadia Zoological Park (adults: $5; kids and senior citizens: $4) had real live Buffalo Bill–type bison, caribou, and a genuine Maine moose. Seacoast Club Adventureland combined water slides, miniature golf, and other wholesome recreational activities for the entire family. Not exactly Disneyland. More like Disneylot. But if you had kids in your car, you could kiss several hours good-bye.

At one point, a man set up shop along this route making sculptures out of trees with a chain saw. He worked in the parking lot of a towel outlet. We'd passed him many times over the years and mulled whether his creations would fit the bill as Christmas presents for our friends. His name was Ray Murphy, and one summer the *Ellsworth American* did a feature story on him. Murphy claimed to be the "World's Original Saw Sculptor." Self-taught, he had been wielding a chain saw since he was eleven years old. He went on the road with it in 1963, turning tree trunks into all sorts of animals and birds. He created eagles out of white pine or cedar, bears too. Out front one summer sat a huge pine log that he had fashioned into two bears. Murphy claimed it was his forty thousandth sculpture. Who could argue? Some lucky buyer, he liked to say, could walk off with it for almost nothing, like buying an early Picasso. Murphy said one of his pieces was already in the Smithsonian.

"I'm a rarity and I know it," he told the *American,* adding that his plans called for sculpting the world's largest totem pole, at least two hundred feet tall, thus ensuring an entry into the Guinness Book of World Records. After that, he said, he wanted to open a theme park.

Then one summer he disappeared. He eventually turned up over on Route 1, in a lot next to the Irving gas station and John's Used Tires between Ellsworth and Hancock. He said he had moved there because too many people who drove to or from Mount Desert Island along Route 3 stopped to gawk but didn't buy. These were fancy people who didn't appreciate his art. The folks who traveled Route 1 deeper into Maine, he said, were more serious shoppers who saw the investment potential in collecting his pieces.

Along Route 3 we passed store after store advertising fudge. These places sold fudge as though fudge were an extremely rare and missing portion of the American diet. Some of the biggest signs along Route 3 advertised fudge. I could imagine a dizzy traveler, eyes glazed over from too many hours at the wheel of his motor home, slamming on the brakes, screeching to a stop, looking up toward heaven, and saying, "Fudge, thank you Jesus!"

Between the fudge signs, I spotted a handwritten sign on the right-hand side of the road that said "Raspberries" out in front of a Bart's Greenhouse.

"Raspberries," I shouted, "thank you Jesus!"

"Raspberries, boy are we glad to find them," I said to a big man behind the counter, presumably Bart himself.

"We hurried 'em this year," he said. "We're about done with 'em."

"What about blueberries?"

"Blueberries is late," he said. We bought two quarts of raspberries, along with two blueberry muffins and a loaf of seven-grain bread.

"Thank you berry much," I said. Bart winked.

We went up a hill and down the other side past Chinese and Thai restaurants, a muffler shop, a speedy lube place, and a couple of motels with CANADIANS WELCOME signs out front. We entered Ellsworth's suburban mall district of fast-food joints, gas stations, discount drugstores, auto parts outlets, supermarkets, and acres and acres of asphalt parking lots.

Our first stop was at J&P's farm stand near the junction of Route 1 and Route 3. We bought peas and new potatoes. We bought peaches that cost an arm and a leg. When I complained to the proprietor, Pete Mayo, he said, "Those peaches are worth every penny. Those peaches are guaranteed."

"Is that a money-back guarantee?" I asked.

"That's taking it a bit far."

We stopped at Life Sports, a store for serious outdoor persons. Life Sports sold Patagonia clothing and gear for backpackers, kayakers, campers, and rock climbers. It had lots of hiking boots and tennis shoes. Frankie looked over the tennis shoes while I ogled the Polartec long underwear. We looked at jackets and shorts, shirts and socks, rain gear and canoe paddles. Overwhelmed by the choices, we were seized by indecision and left without buying anything.

The traffic outside Life Sports was bumper to bumper in both directions as far as the eye could see. We waited several minutes for a gap between cars, then darted into it. We waited through five changes of the traffic light at Main Street before we could turn left into the historical center of Ellsworth and over to Rooster Brother, a kitchenware store. Frankie looked at plates and silverware. I headed for the toasters. Our year-old Black & Decker had been acting up, doing whatever it wanted to our morning toast regardless of how we set its dial. Sometimes the toast came out burned, sometimes not even brown, sometimes a bit of both. I looked over a $50 Braun bagel-sized "Multitoast HT 70 Type 4107 toasting system" made in Germany, and bought it.

Rooster Brother was the farthest we needed to go into the Ellsworth maw. From there, we began our retreat, reversing direction and heading up Main Street and turning south on High Street toward Mount Desert. We had several stops to make on the right side, the first at Willey's, a store that sold clothing, fishing gear, guns, and shoes. Frankie found some Reeboks for tennis. I found a pair of Nike "all-conditions" leather and fabric beauties that were much too complicated and expensive to be called walking shoes. They were, it said on the box, a "footwear system."

By now we were both getting hungry, so as I drove south along High Street I pulled into the Burger King. We got out of the car and walked inside and looked at the overhead menu. I order a Whopper with cheese, fries, and a Diet Coke.

"I'll have the same," Frankie said. When the orders arrived, we carried them on trays outside to a picnic bench in the sun. There, Frankie told me something astonishing. She said she had never eaten at Burger King before. She revealed that she had never eaten a Big Mac before either, or, for that matter, anything else at McDonald's or any other fast-food outlet sold. Never!

But why? I asked. Surely, living in Manhattan and on Mount Desert hadn't isolated her totally from the Whopper-eating masses out there in the Interstate World.

"No, but it helps," she said. Besides, this was junk food, she said, and if it was to be eaten at all it should be eaten sparingly. This seemed to be a corollary to her Maine lobster axiom.

"So, how was it?" I asked as she chomped into her cheese-burger.

"Delicious."

My thoughts exactly.

"Up to a point," she added quickly, as if to keep her enthusiasm in perspective.

At Doug's Shop 'N' Save, our next stop, we loaded a giant cart with $110 worth of groceries. Next: Wal-Mart, where Frankie searched and searched for typing paper.

"It's obsolete," I told her. A sales woman pointed her in the right direction.

We bought a wok, a vegetable grilling tray, plastic hangers, two packs of chewing gum, and two quarts of Quaker State 10-W-30 motor oil.

Back at Frankie's place, we congratulated ourselves for having survived the Greater Ellsworth Metroplex. We had quite a haul. I unpacked our new Braun Multitoast HT 70 Type 4107 toasting system and stationed it on the kitchen counter. Frankie looked it over, seeing the words "Electronic-Sensor" written on its side.

"I'm going to name this thing Star Wars," she said.

Northeast Harbor in late afternoon seemed positively serene in comparison to Ellsworth. Our first stop was the library. The Northeast Harbor Library was one of the best little libraries around, and Frankie was one of its best customers. She found it easier to use than the big libraries in New York City. To do the research for her book she had to read a lot of transcripts of congressional hearings, and she found that the Northeast Harbor Library could track them down and borrow them through the inter-library loan program. The library contained a good assortment of novels, histories, biographies, and books on current affairs. What I liked most about it were its books about Maine and Mount Desert Island. In its local collection were diaries of former residents and summer people, some privately published, some original handwritten volumes. It had many old maps, drawings, and photographs of the island and the village. It had collections of the minutes of town meetings and village improvement societies back to the turn of the century. It was a marvelous font of local knowledge, with an entire wing packed with local poop. If you needed local information in a hurry and didn't have time to look it up yourself, you could ask the chief librarian, Robert Pyle. Chances were he'd know it or where to put his finger on it.

We popped upstairs and spotted Pyle in his office. He threw up his hands in greeting.

"How are you? How's your work coming? How's the Volvo?"

"We're fine," I said.

"The work is coming," Frankie said.

"The Volvo is purring along nicely," I said, "although I did back into a post in the bank parking lot the other day and put another dent in the bumper."

"I know that post," said Pyle. "Around here we call it the Saturday Evening Post."

Pyle was a town character. He knew everyone, and if you met him on the street he always had a pun, joke, or story to tell. He was big and tall, with a full face, a furrowed brow, a full white beard, and a pipe clenched between his teeth. Pyle looked like a sea captain played in the movies by Burl Ives. Born near Philadelphia, he grew up in Searsport, at the top of Penobscot Bay, and spent summers on Little Cranberry Island, where his family had a cottage. His family moved to Northeast Harbor when he was a teenager. He attended Mount Desert High School and worked summers as a soda jerk at the drugstore in Northeast Harbor. Graduating in 1964, he went on to get a degree in English from Ricker College in Houlton, Maine.

Pyle had the distinction of being one of the world's few pistol-packing librarians. He began a part-time career in law enforcement as a summer patrol officer for the town of Mount Desert in 1969 and worked for many years as a volunteer constable. In the early days he wore a uniform, with a side arm and radio strapped to his belt and a broad-brimmed campaign hat on his head, and he looked less like a jolly sea captain and more like a man you didn't want to mess with. As a daytime librarian and moonlighting cop, he was, no doubt, the only law enforcer in the area with a working knowledge of both the Dewey decimal system and the Police Response Code. He said he never knew when his knowledge of both numbering systems might come in handy, but he had figured out one scenario. He explained that 822.33 was the Dewey decimal system number reserved for William Shakespeare, the only author with an exclusive number. The number 10-53 in the Police Response Code means that someone is under suspicion of operating a motor vehicle while under the influence of alcohol.

"So," said Pyle, "if I heard 822.33 and 10-53, it could only mean that Will Shakespeare had come back to life, gotten drunk, and been pulled over trying to drive home."

It was Pyle's local knowledge that helped clear up one of the mysteries of Mount Desert. It had to do with spelling. At one end of our main road was a road sign that read "Sargeant Drive." At the other end was a sign calling it "Sargent Drive." At first, the latter spelling seemed right because next to it was a Sargent Cove and a Sargent Point. Not far away was Sargent Mountain, down which flowed Sargent Brook. Most of the maps called the drive, the cove, the point, the brook, and the mountain Sargent, too.

I'd heard polite arguments between summer residents over the spelling of the drive. Most of them preferred "Sargent," a name that was evocative of the American painter John Singer Sargent, instead of "Sargeant," which brought to mind Sergeant Bilko, the bumbling noncommissioned officer of stage, screen, and television. "Sargent" was the logical name and the preferred one. It was just the wrong one.

Pyle first referred me to a book, *Mt. Desert: An Informal History,* published in 1989. He had written a chapter in it about the history of an area between Somesville and Northeast Harbor that was once called Somes Sound Village. In that village, Pyle wrote, was the family of a Mr. J. S. Sargeant, a farmer who owned most of the land north of Sargent Mountain and for whom the mountain, brook, cove, and point were named.

Then there was Samuel Duncan Sargeant, the chief fund-raiser for the Somes Sound Road, built between 1897 and 1901 along the water's edge at a cost of $10,929.73. Mr. Sargeant died suddenly in 1903 and Somes Sound Road was renamed "Sargeant Drive" in his honor.

Pyle told me a number of stories about his career in law enforcement. He claimed that when he became a reserve patrol officer twenty-five years earlier, his first major act was to ticket his boss, the chief, for going the wrong way on Main Street. Early in his dual role as librarian and policeman he encountered two tourists, an elderly couple, in the library. He told me that they had stopped in after lunch on a Friday in autumn to look at photographs of Mount Desert scenery—views they couldn't see that day because they were blanketed in fog. Pyle, a cordial host, showed them photos, manuscripts, and other things in the archive, and told them story after story about the village and its history. The couple stayed on and on. The library's five o'clock closing hour came and went. Pyle finally told them he had to go, so they left, too.

After locking up the library, Pyle, as was his habit, stopped at Don Hagberg's drugstore on Main Street for coffee. No one was in the front of the store. Pyle heard Hagberg in the back filling prescriptions and rather than bother the druggist, he went behind the soda fountain and got his own coffee. Just then the couple from the library walked into the drugstore and saw him.

"Do you have a twin who is a librarian?" the man asked. Pyle laughed. They ordered coffee and English muffins. Pyle served them, took their money, and rang up the sale on the drugstore cash register. "We chuckled all the while about the fact that in a small Maine town people are liable to have multiple talents," Pyle told me.

On Friday nights in those days, Mr. Pyle became Officer Pyle at six o'clock and went on patrol in the police cruiser. He said good-bye to the couple, shouted to Don in the back of the drugstore, went home, took a shower, and put on his police uniform. Traffic was light that night, so after cruising around in the police car for a few minutes, Officer Pyle pulled up to Peddar's corner on the edge of town and turned on his radar gun. A few minutes later, a car came whizzing down Ice House Hill on its way out of town. The radar clocked it doing fifty-eight miles per hour in a thirty-five-mile zone. Officer Pyle flipped on his blue flashers and siren and roared after the vehicle. It pulled over and stopped. He got out of his cruiser, adjusted his belt, donned his flat-brimmed campaign hat, grabbed his flashlight and clipboard, and strode purposely forward to confront the speeder and his passenger.

"Good evening," he said. "I'm sorry to detain you. Do you know why I stopped you?"

The driver looked up. It was the same couple!

The man stared at Pyle.

"Jesus Christ!" he shouted. "Isn't there anyone else in this goddamn town?"

Before I left the library, I asked Pyle what was new in the local law enforcement world. Not much action, he said, just a couple of fender benders.

"That's a 10-55," he said.

"Which reminds me," he went on, "what ever became of your case?"

"I didn't know you knew," I said. He rolled his eyes.

"Of course, I knew," he said. "I was there."

As a law-enforcing librarian, he explained, he had his police radio turned on that afternoon when the report came in. Since the library is just up the hill from Brown's, he radioed in and volunteered to check it out. He jumped into Lazarus, his forty-five-year-old pickup truck, drove down the hill to the scene of the crime, and discovered neither a perpetrator nor a perpetratee. He asked the people at Brown's what had happened, got a description of the vehicles involved, and asked which way they'd headed out of town. With that information, he immediately knew to whom they belonged. He reported in on his police radio.

I told Bob that the matter was in the hands of my insurance company.

"It's an open and shut case, right? We've got her dead to rights, don't you think?" I didn't know what an open and shut case was or what "dead to rights" meant, but I had watched enough TV cop shows to mouth law enforcement lingo.

Bob raised an eyebrow. It was his "don't-be-so-sure" eyebrow.

After visiting the library, Frankie went to the bank and I picked up the papers at McGrath's. On my way to the Pine Tree Market, I ran into Gunnar Hansen, another one of Northeast Harbor's characters. Hansen stood six-feet-four and weighed two hundred and seventy pounds. He was a big man with a gentle demeanor. In summer, he padded around town in untucked, short-sleeved shirts. He wore a beard sometimes and when his salt-and-pepper hair was long he pulled it back into a ponytail.

Hansen was a writer, a dedicated student of Herman Melville, and Pyle's best friend. He lived in a house next door to the library and served on various library committees and on its board of trustees. He performed other civic duties, too, and had once been a volunteer fireman. To supplement his income from writing, he worked off and on as a carpenter and at other part-time jobs. Hansen was born in Iceland, grew up in Texas and Maine, and studied English at the University of Texas. In the mid-1970s, after attending graduate school in Austin, he came to Northeast Harbor to write. He started writing magazine articles, selling them to *Yankee, Down East,* and other periodicals. He worked as an editor for *Maine Magazine.* He wrote several books, including *Islands at the Edge of Time,* about barrier islands on the Atlantic and Gulf coasts. Published in 1993, it got good reviews and was well received by nature historians.

What most of Northeast Harbor's residents, summer people, and visitors didn't know was that Gunnar Hansen had another life, a secret past. He was once known as the scariest man in the world.

"Kids knew," he told me. "It was secret knowledge they passed around. You'd see ten-year-olds talking, and every so often one would get up enough courage to come up and ask."

The French novelist Marguerite Yourcenar lived in the village and she knew Hansen but didn't know about his secret life. But Grace Frick, one of Yourcenar's translators, found out and confronted him.

"In New York City, fifteen people were murdered yesterday," she told him sternly, "and it's your fault!"

Hansen's other life grew out of a part-time job he'd taken one summer as a grad student in Texas. One afternoon, he dropped in on a casting call for a movie that was going to be filmed in and around Austin. He auditioned and walked out with the part of a character called Leatherface, a retarded, psychotic killer, in what was to become one of the most famous horror movies of all time, *The Texas Chainsaw Massacre.*

The 1974 film was based loosely on the 1957 exploits of Ed Gein, a deranged Wisconsin farmer. It revolves around a rural Texas family of unemployed slaughterhouse workers, including Leatherface. Handy with a chain saw, he dispatches four victims in the course of the eighty-four-minute film. Shot on grainy sixteen-millimeter film, the movie was produced and directed by Tobe Hooper for $250,000. It opened to mixed reviews. Critic Rex Reed called it "the scariest motion picture I have ever seen." *Harper's* magazine said it was "a vile little piece of sick crap." Writers of articles in specialized "splatter-genre" magazines loved it. One of them called it "The Gone with the Wind of Meat Movies."

The Texas Chainsaw Massacre became a cult classic. It made the character of Leatherface into a horror film supercharacter. It turned the chain saw into an American metaphor, as in "chainsaw politics" and "chainsaw management." The movie earned, by one estimate, $50 million. It made some people rich, but Hansen was not among them. He made less than $3,000 from it including the $200 a week he was paid during four weeks of filming.

Fans of the movie knew Hansen's name from the credits but they did not know his face. Throughout the film, his character, Leatherface, wears a mask supposedly made out of dried human flesh. Most people in Northeast Harbor and Mount Desert Island hadn't seen the movie by the time Hansen arrived to take up his career as a writer. Most of those who had seen the movie didn't connect Hansen to Leatherface. But ardent fans did. He got enough strange phone calls to persuade him to unlist his phone number for a while. Sometimes fans of the movie would turn up in Northeast Harbor asking where he lived. Aging bikers, members of a faraway gang, made the pilgrimage one summer more than a decade after *The Texas Chainsaw Massacre* came out. They rode into town on their Harley-Davidsons asking for Hansen's whereabouts.

At first, when other horror filmmakers offered him parts in sequels, Hansen turned them down. Later, a monthly horror-film magazine called *Fangoria* published an interview with him. Offers poured in. He took a part in a 1987 spoof called *Hollywood Chainsaw Hookers*. Other low-budget roles followed. In the late 1980s Hansen discovered that horror festivals, commercial haunted houses, and haunted mini-theme parks were booming. He learned that horror-movie stars were in demand at such venues. There was money to be made in celebrity appearance fees. In 1992, he was hired for a month of appearances at Spookyworld, a Berlin, Massachusetts, haunted hayride theme park. After that, celebrity appearance offers began to roll in.

By the time I got to know him, Hansen was in his fifties and was using his old movie fame to help sustain himself as a writer. Every year as Halloween approached, he took up what he called his "shadow life," going on the road to make paid appearances at horror-film conventions and spookfests. He found that he could earn $20,000 and more in appearance fees and by selling and signing photographs of himself. It wasn't exactly a killing (so to speak), but it was more profitable (and less work) than grinding out freelance magazine articles.

"I can go back to my novel and filmscript and live on this money for months," he told me.

One October, I followed Hansen to Sacramento to write a story for the *Wall Street Journal* about his other life. There, in the California state capital, he was paid $2,500, plus expenses, to appear for two days at the Carnival of Horrors Festival in a city park. He sat behind a long row table with other horror-movie stars, including Reggie (*Phantasm*) Bannister, Kane (*Friday the 13th*) Hodder, Richard (*Halloween II*) Warlock, and Carel (*The Addams Family*) Struycken. He signed autographs (free) and sold photographs ($5) of himself as Leatherface and himself as Gunnar Hansen (he didn't dress up as Leatherface because he didn't own rights to the character).

Nearby, vendors sold horror comics, videos, T-shirts, and jewelry. Horror films played nonstop. The U.S. Post Office sold "Classic Movie Monster" commemorative stamps. There was a haunted house and horror rides. The Nightmarez Torture Salon did horror-makeup jobs. A madeup slit throat cost $13, bullet wounds, $3.25. The most popular makeup was vampire bites, at $7.50 each. Kids tossed Ping-Pong balls painted to resemble bloody eyeballs at targets for prizes. A psycho-rock band, Death B4 Decaff, played horror-movie music. It took a sense of humor, and a need for a supplemental income, to go on the road each year. Hansen set up a website called "Gunnar Hansen's Cave" for interested fans.

Hansen, the writer, avoided chain saws, although he once agreed to fire one up and pretend to saw a woman in two for the opening of a bar in Key West.

"I had no idea how dangerous chain saws were when we did *The Texas Chainsaw Massacre*," he said.

Indeed, when a tree blew down on Hansen's garage one September, he summoned Herb Watson, the barber of the forest, to cut it up with his chain saw and haul it away.

"We've never compared notes," Watson told me. "And I haven't seen the movie."

Fifteen

A few nights later, it rained. This wasn't pitter-patter rain. This was a serious drenching. It began with pounding drops on the roof that jolted us awake in the middle of the night. The pounding increased in intensity until it sounded like a steady, all-encompassing woosh that became sleep-inducing background noise. It eased a bit at dawn, but continued its steady drumbeat on the roof and porch into the morning.

We spent more time at breakfast and on the reading pile when it rained. I refilled my coffee cup and opened a copy of *Preview,* a throwaway that billed itself as the "arts & entertainment guide for the Maine coast."

"Listen to this," I said. "On September 10 the Ellsworth Library is devoting an entire day to cooking with zucchini. How can we possibly miss that!"

"Easy," she said.

"If they were devoting the whole day to cooking with eggplant," I said, "you'd be there in a flash."

The *Bar Harbor Times* reported the visit of a nuclear submarine, the USS *Groton,* to the Winter Harbor Lobster Festival on the previous Saturday. But the sub had departed almost as soon as it had arrived. Earl Brechlin, the *Times* editor, nosed around and discovered that the submarine had lost its anchor while trying to moor in the harbor, then departed in haste, leaving the anchor behind.

Brechlin wondered how much a nuclear submarine anchor costs, noting that "a custom nuke sub anchor is not the kind of thing you can just run down to Hamilton Marine in Searsport and buy off the shelf." He decided to find out.

"Little did I realize that I was about to embark on a telephone journey into the deepest, darkest equatorial heart of the bureaucracy that is our representative form of government," he wrote. He called the Electric Boat Company in Groton, Connecticut, got transferred three times, and then was told that no one there was authorized to reveal this "proprietary information." He called the navy base in Groton. No help. He called the Pentagon, was referred to "Public Affairs," which referred him to Navy Public Affairs. He called Navy Public Affairs. They said somebody would call back. He called the General Accounting Office. The operator switched him back to Public Affairs, which put him on hold for ten minutes then told him to call the Coast Guard. They told him to call NSIAD, which stands for National Security and International Affairs Division. Finally, a navy officer called from Norfolk, Virginia, and said he'd found a parts catalog that put the price of an anchor at around $25,000.

"New or used?" Brechlin asked. The officer didn't know.

Rain fell, off and on, for two days and nights.

"Tomorrow," I told Frankie, "the weather is supposed to clear up. If it does, we're going to sea. We're going to go find the USS *Groton*'s anchor."

We had plotted lots of expeditionary adventures in *Scoop* over the summers, many more than we ever managed to begin. We had never gone to Blue Hill by boat, or across Penobscot Bay to visit friends who lived on other islands, or to Camden, where Frankie's brother lived.

But as the weather brightened the next morning, I made plans.

"I have to work," Frankie said. I put my foot down. "Look, it's a Saturday, as in weekend, as in recreation, as in fun," I said.

"Okay, great," she said, getting up from the breakfast table. "Let's go around three."

Three?

"We're going on a major journey, an historic, pathfinding expedition into the unknown, crossing a lot of open ocean in a small boat, and you want to go at three o'clock?"

"That's right, I have to type," she said, heading for her Remington.

"So, you're actually willing to cut your workday down by one hour?" I asked with mock incredulity. "I'm certainly glad Lewis and Clark didn't have your work habits."

By three-thirty, we were buzzing down Somes Sound in *Scoop,* headed for Winter Harbor and Schoodic Point. They are on the east side of Frenchman Bay from Mount Desert. I thought we might be able to see, at first hand, what was happening to the seagulls Russ Wiggins had waxed poetically about when the Schoodic Point dump was closed. Frankie got out the chart and plotted our course while I checked *Scoop*'s fuel supply.

We cruised out between Bear Island and Sutton Island, sped past Seal Harbor, and up the east side of Mount Desert island. A thin haze hung in the air and we couldn't see all the way across the bay to Winter Harbor. We could, however, make out Egg Rock, with its lighthouse, and we made for it. This was virgin territory for us. We were seeing Mount Desert Island and its rounded mountains from a new angle, and in the haze they looked much bigger than usual.

From the east side of Egg Rock, we headed for Winter Harbor, cutting through some small islands and following a lobster boat past some rocky shoals, then turning north into the harbor itself. As the lobster boat surged straight ahead, we veered left toward an aggregation of moored yachts and the Winter Harbor Yacht Club. A giant stinkpot from Philadelphia was pulling away as we idled up to the club's float dock. As we moved in, we saw a woman on the dock and a man tying up a dinghy. He turned and looked up. I knew that face.

"Is your name Dick?" I asked.

"Sure is," said Richard Dudman. "And this is my wife, Helen." He paused. "You look familiar. Who are you?"

We introduced ourselves.

"I've read all your books," he said to Frankie. Then, looking at me, he said, "I remember. You came to see me before you went to Asia, and I've been reading you ever since."

"Thanks," I said. "You were a great role model."

Richard Dudman was famous among journalists. He worked for the *St. Louis Post-Dispatch* and was one of the best reporters in Washington during his era. He'd traveled out of Washington to many of the world's trouble spots, too, and came to Southeast Asia to cover the Vietnam War when I was there with the *New York Times*. During the 1970 invasion of Cambodia, Dudman, along with Elizabeth Pond of the *Christian Science Monitor* and Michael Morrow of the Dispatch News Service, were captured by Viet Cong soldiers and held for forty-seven days as suspected spies.

Eight years later he interviewed Pol Pot, the notorious Cambodian communist leader. "For a mass murderer, Pol Pot seemed strangely refined. When he shook hands with me, in the Western manner, his fingers felt slim and delicate," Dudman wrote. "With most other Cambodians I had met, shaking hands was like grasping a handful of thick hot dogs."

Dudman retired in 1981 at the age of sixty-two, then moved from Washington to Ellsworth, where Helen had bought a radio station. In the winter they lived in Ellsworth. In the summer they lived in Islesford, on Little Cranberry Island, off the southern tip of Mount Desert.

"We're on our annual cruise," he said, pointing to their little sailboard moored a short distance away. Unlike annual cruises that began in New York or Boston and ended in Winter Harbor, this one began at Islesford, ten nautical miles away.

"We're going to have dinner here and spend the night, then sail back to Little Cranberry in the morning."

"That sounds like my kind of annual cruise," I said. "None of this two weeks at sea in the rain and fog."

We shoved off, promising to visit them on Little Cranberry. Dudman had become a pillar of the Maine business community. He had mysteriously parlayed his interview with Pol Pot into a seat on the Maine Lobster Promotion Council. My idea was to debrief him about his work on behalf of Maine lobsters. He'd be able to supply facts and figures to bolster my ongoing argument with Frankie that by eschewing lobsters we were hurting the local economy.

Dick told me later that one of the major accomplishments of the Maine Lobster Promotion Council was to get people to not think of them as "bugs." Historically, they were called "bugs," which they are technically, being arthropods and, thus, closely related to insects. It was the council that also came up with the idea of calling lobster "the ultimate white meat." If chicken was promoted as "white meat" and pork was promoted as "the other white meat," then the lobster was surely "the ultimate white meat." The council launched a big advertising campaign starting with ads in seafood trade magazines. The National Pork Producers Council, which had come up with the phrase "the other white meat" for pork, took offense. It claimed that the lobster people were guilty of trademark infringement and filed a lawsuit. Dudman said he and other council members got letters from New York lawyers containing the word "forthwith." Since the pork people and the lobster people were in two different states, the lawsuit was filed in federal court. The "ultimate white meat" became a federal case.

At the Maine Lobster Festival in Rockland that summer, lobster supporters put on anti-pork street theater. They borrowed a pig, named it Spam, and put a saddle on it. They strapped a lobster called Leroy to the saddle. The lobster rode the pig around for a while to demonstrate who was boss, at least in Maine. The pork people eventually settled out of court after the lobster people agreed to make cosmetic changes in its "ultimate white meat" ads.

That's when the Maine Lobster Promotion Council went overboard. It began sponsoring a contest for new lobster recipes. The contest, called the Great Taste of Maine Lobster cook-off, was held each summer in the kitchen of Blaine House, the governor's mansion. Instead of classic steamed or boiled lobster with drawn butter, the winning recipes were more complicated. First prize one summer was lobster risotto with fresh tomato and basil. Second prize was a creamy lobster and mango bisque, with sugar cane–skewered, tamarind-lacquered lobster satay garnished with wontons and toasted coconut, served with Korean kimchee!

We never made it to Schoodic Point. Heading out of Winter Harbor, we found ourselves facing a strong head wind and an incoming tide. The sea got bumpy and the temperature was dropping. As we passed Egg Rock and turned toward the southwest, I noticed an enormous bank of fog moving in from the open ocean. From afar it looked slow-moving, but as we sped past the buoy at the southeast tip of Mount Desert Island I could see that it was coming in rapidly behind us. We were in a race by the time we passed Seal Harbor. The fog was chasing us. *Scoop* was barreling along at twenty-five knots but the fog kept moving faster. We were losing the race.

Suddenly, *Scoop's* engine sputtered and died. The boat drifted with the incoming tide as the fog began to engulf us. I took some quick compass readings: the heading for the buoy between Sutton Island and the Cranberrys; the heading beyond that for Somes Sound. We had charts of these waters, but we knew that once the fog bank surrounded us it would be blindman's bluff all the way home, if we got home at all. This kind of thing happened all the time: boats trapped in the fog, lost, adrift or tied to a buoy through the night. If fogged-in boaters had a marine radio aboard, they could call the Coast Guard and the Coast Guard would respond, mounting a search-and-rescue operation if necessary. If the lost boat were adrift in the fog, its radio could save it. The Coast Guard could hone in on its broadcast signal. If the occupants of the drifting vessel could fire their emergency flares at the right time and pinpoint its location, rescue vessels could find it. Sometimes the Coast Guard made its rescue efforts seem easy while making the occupants of the boats they rescued feel embarrassed for having gotten into a situation where they needed to be rescued. Sometimes the Coast Guard rescue efforts failed and lost boats were never found.

My hands were stiff with cold as I grappled with the gas tanks. I pulled the empty tank out from under the seat and snapped off the line connector. I pulled the spare gas tank out from under the seat and snapped the fuel line to it. Then I pumped the rubber bulb in the gas line to make sure it was full and turned the ignition switch. The engine erupted to life and settled into its faithful purr. I pushed the throttle forward into gear, slowly turned the boat toward the compass heading I had noted for the buoy between Sutton and Little Cranberry, and eased ahead. The fog had come in fast and it was way ahead of us now. We pushed on slowly and cautiously, looking and listening for boats, watching for rocks and the shoreline. If the fog was moving in faster than we were, we would be in it for a long time. Getting through it could take hours. This was ominous. We eased ahead. After several minutes, we popped out of the fog, which had stalled near the entrance to Northeast Harbor. As Frankie rubbed her stiff, numb fingers, I pushed the throttle forward, the engine roared, and we sped for Somes Sound. We were home before dark. It was getting colder.

Life in the woods at Frankie's place in late August was about as nice as it could be with a population of monstrous metal dinosaurs roaring and grunting and hissing and banging next door. The weather had cleared, bringing mornings that were warm and sunny and afternoon breezes strong enough to keel the sailboats on the sound so far over that they looked like they were about to capsize. The air was so dry and crisp that the saltshaker actually poured again. The days were noticeably shorter, the evenings chilly enough to put the fireplace to work.

Most nights, sitting in front of my computer after dinner, I listened to my marine radio. I began to listen to conversations between boaters a few days after we bought our Whaler. Our friend Jamie had shown me his new handheld two-way VHF radio called a SI-TEX Marine Radiotelephone Model HH200 and demonstrated how to transmit and receive "traffic" on it. Traffic is boater-speak for talk. I went straight to Village Electronics in Southwest Harbor and bought my own and began "monitoring" traffic. I tuned in to Channel 16, the international calling and distress frequency, which boaters "monitored" and used to contact one another.

"Northeast Harbor harbormaster, Northeast Harbor harbormaster," I heard somebody say.

"This is the Northeast Harbor harbormaster, Whiskey X-ray Zulu Five Three Six, to the vessel calling. Switch to Zero Nine." Then the first voice said, "Roger that. Going Zero Nine." I quickly tuned my radio to Channel 9 and listened to the caller ask the harbormaster if any moorings where available for that evening.

My HH200 had preset channels beginning at one and going through 28, then running again at 60 and going through 88. It had nine WX (for weather) channels. I gradually got to know my way around the channels. The Coast Guard station in Southwest Harbor monitored Channels 16, 21, 22, and 23. Boaters called the Coast Guard operator about problems ranging from emergencies at sea to lost dinghies or missing buoys. When callers on 16 forgot to switch to another channel and began making small talk, the Coast Guard operator usually came on to remind them politely but firmly that Channel 16 was to be used only as a contact and distress channel, not for chat.

I carried my radio on and off our boat. I listened to it while I was shaving. I listened to it at my desk. I listened to it while jumping off the rocks into Somes Sound in the mornings. I listened to it while gathering mussels.

I listened to weather reports on Channel WX2 broadcast by NOAA weather radio announcers who spoke in gravelly voices and in local accents. When they gave the forecast for the fishermen out on the Georges Bank, they sounded as though they had spent a lot of time out on the Georges Bank themselves.

"Good morning, this is the voice of the National Weather Service broadcasting to you from the international jet port in

Portland, Maine, over NOAA weather radio," the announcer would say. He would proceed to give a general forecast for the state, and then he would zero in on the midcoast of Maine, our region. After that, he gave the temperatures in various cities as far away as New York, then he would go on to reports from automated stations along the Maine coast such as the one on Matinicus (pronounced Ma-TIN-a-cus) Rock, where the wind was often from the southwest. For the offshore forecasts "from the Gulf of Maine out to the Hague Line," which is where Canadian waters begin, he'd give wind speeds in knots instead of miles per hour.

Then another man would come on to broadcast the ozone report, which I found particularly puzzling. Apparently lots of ozone in the higher atmosphere was good but in the lower atmosphere it was bad. I never could get the hang of it. On the other hand, I had no trouble understanding the "haying advisory": "Mostly sunny conditions will result in good to excellent drying conditions for southern areas. High pressure will build across the entire region resulting in good to excellent drying conditions for Friday and Saturday." I wondered whether there were people on boats listening in who would rush home to make hay while the sun shined.

One day when I was listening to the weather on channel WX2, I heard an announcer say, "The coast of Maine is closed to the taking of mussels, European oysters, surf clams, soft-shelled clams, and carnivorous snails and whelks from Cape Elizabeth to the New Hampshire border. The coast is also closed to all species of shellfish from Moose Cove in Truscott to the Canadian border with the exception of Cobb's Cook Bay. For more detailed information, please call the Maine Department of Marine Resources at 289-6550." I called and a man told me some of these places were closed because they were polluted and were undergoing a poisonous plankton bloom called a red tide. I looked at a map of the coast and discovered that Somes Sound wasn't in one of the closed areas.

Frequently, a voice would come on Channel 16 and make an announcement like this: "This is Camden Marine holding traffic for the vessel *Key Largo, Key Largo, Key Largo.* Please shift and answer Two Six or Eight Four for traffic. Camden Clear."

Channels 26 and 84 were used by Camden Marine Radio, a shore-based service that allowed boaters to place or receive ordinary telephone calls by calling in on their marine radios and getting patched in to the land phone network. The only drawback to callers was that anyone with a marine radio could tune in to channels 26 and 84 and listen. In fact many people found listening to such calls was a major side benefit of having a marine radio.

I tuned in the Camden Marine Radio channels a lot. The operators were very courteous and friendly. They sounded cheerful when placing calls, looking up phone numbers, and offering advice. They sounded like friendly aunts. Callers ranged from confident sailors who used marine radio lingo perfectly to obvious novices. Some of them sounded like William F. Buckley, others like truckers. Some fishermen and lobstermen talked in such heavily accented voices that I imagined them encrusted in barnacles.

Amazingly, many of the callers didn't seem to realize that they were talking on an open channel. One morning during that first summer I beeped up to Channel 26 and heard a woman say, "Darling, I have great news. You got the appointment. The president sent a personal letter."

The yachtsman she was talking to quickly interrupted. "Thanks for telling the entire Maine coast the news," he said. "Don't say another word. I'll call you from a land phone as soon as I can and get the details."

Boaters, I learned quickly, like to "check in" with their wives, children, homes, offices, and investments, not necessarily in that order. When the New York Yacht Club was in Southwest Harbor, I beeped in to the middle of a conversation between a boater and a colleague at his office:

"We've been in fog for two or three days. What did the market do today?"

"It's up twenty-three points. Anything else I can do for you?"

"Just bring the market up some more. That's all. Over."

Sometimes boaters called their office and didn't mess around with pleasantries.

"Hi. Where's the long bond and what happened to the market today?"

Boaters talked all the time about how they loved being out to sea away from their offices and work. But they also seemed to want to be needed. Often, they'd "check in" in hopes of hearing from people who were having difficulty getting along without them. Nothing seemed to cheer up some boaters more than to hear someone say, "Oh, thank goodness you called!"

Parents on boats called their children back home a lot. They said they were just "checking in," but it sounded as though they were checking up, and some of their children gave them short shrift.

One evening, I beeped on to the Camden Marine channel just in time to hear a child ask, "Why did you call?"

"Just called to hear your voice and make sure everything is okay darling. . . . Here's Dad. He just wants to say hello. Bye.

"Hi sweetie, we're having a good time. You have any news for us?"

"No, not really."

"All right darling, we love you."

"Okay, bye."

Parents on land liked to check up on their children at sea, too.

One late afternoon, I tuned in to a conversation between a mother on land and a son on a boat:

"Are you all right? How's the weather up there? It's terrible down here. It's torrential rain here. Where are you?"

"We're off Northeast Harbor at Great Cranberry Island. It was pretty fun."

"Oh I'm glad sweetie. Where do you go to next?"

"We're going up to Roque tomorrow and then we'll be back a day after that or so . . ."

"How's your breathing?"

"My breathing is fine mom. We went climbing up a mountain . . . and swam in Sargent Mountain Pond."

"Oh, that's wonderful sweetie. . . . Are you putting on lots of sun lotion?

"Well Ma, there's not much sun to worry about the last few days."

Moms on some occasions seemed to forget about the welfare of their child and revert straight to self-interest. Once I heard an enthusiastic young man tell his mother, "We caught another bluefish today. We made so many filets we couldn't eat them."

"Fine, just don't bring any bluefish home to us. I don't want it. I don't like it. I won't eat it."

Listening to conversations on Camden Marine Radio made me realize that it wasn't just our friends who wanted us to come on their boats. Boat people were always trying to get others to join them on their boats. They called their friends up and down the coast inviting them to come aboard for drinks or a meal or a sail or cruise, speaking as though being invited onto a boat was a rare treat.

Shore people, on the other hand, were shore people for a reason. The reason was they didn't want to be on boats. Shore people didn't wait around for boat people passing through to invite them on board, although boat people seemed to believe that was the case. Sometimes a great deal of diplomacy was needed to get friends on to boats.

Once, I heard a woman on a boat say, "We are having a lovely fish dinner here and we'd love to have you out here with us. An hour or so makes no difference. Over."

The woman on shore replied, "I just don't think we can because I've got my three children and I just don't see how we can, you know, kind of leave them. Over."

The boat lady pressed.

"Couldn't we come to you and have a drink, then we could all come back to the boat for supper? We don't want to impose, so why don't you come aboard for dinner? Don't you want to leave your children, get away from them for about an hour and a half or so? Over."

"The problem is Bill has been away for four days, and I just don't think I can grab him at the ferry and tell him we're going to go on a boat for dinner. I just think he'll probably think he has to be with the children."

"We understand. We hoped to persuade you. Anyway, we'll come in and say hello."

The shore woman then pressed a counteroffer.

"We're having a chicken dinner and I'm just going to go out and buy another roast chicken and we'd love to have you here on shore with us, we really would. Why don't you guys do that?"

"All right, you've persuaded us."

Listening to Camden Marine Radio could be exciting. If a boater called in a medical emergency or was lost at sea or without power and adrift, the operator would set to work contacting the Coast Guard. Then listeners like me would flip to Coast Guard frequencies to listen to the rescue operation get under way. Sometimes the dramas played out over several hours.

One day, on impulse, I called Camden Marine Radio from a land phone to find out more about its operation. I talked to Charley Foote, actually Charles M. Foote III, who was thirty-two years old and general manager. He told me that Camden Marine was a private company started in 1970 by three full-time boat pilots who guided large ships around Penobscot Bay and needed to make telephone calls from the ships from time to time. To patch in the ship-to-shore radio calls to land telephone lines, they had hired Marge Knight to run the service out of the basement of her house in Camden. She became Camden Marine's chief operator. For a while, Helen Andrews, the bookkeeper, ran the service out of her house on Ragged Mountain. In 1986 the Foote family, including Charley, his parents, and his wife, bought the company and moved it into a nondescript house on Route 1 in Rockport.

Camden Marine transmitted from a tower situated thirteen hundred feet above sea level and had the range to handle ship-to-shore radio traffic across the central Maine coast from Portland in the west to the Canadian border to the east. Fishing boats off Nova Scotia and out on the Georges Bank and beyond could get through to the station when the weather was right.

During the busy season, from around the first of July through Labor Day, eight operators—six women and two men—ran the station two at a time from six in the morning until midnight. Many boaters were getting cellular phones. Calls on cell phones could be dialed directly. But at the time I talked to Foote, cellular service went no farther Down East than Portland. As cellular service spread, he told me, Camden Marine would still have its place because boaters liked having an operator who knew the local area and could track down local contacts and services, and help in an emergency. Camden Marine was a security blanket. Its operators regularly got calls for help from people on boats that had gone aground, or on which someone had had a heart attack. Once, Foote told me, a sinking fishing boat had been unable to contact the Coast Guard but did get through to Camden Marine operators who connected the stricken vessel through to the Coast Guard over land lines. The boat was saved.

The only talk on marine radio I found more interesting than the conversations on Camden Marine was fisherman talk. Sometimes they talked to one another late at night in the Gulf of Maine or out on the Georges Bank. One night I tuned in Channel 80 and heard a monologue:

"I only got one-and-a-half tows [of his net] in tonight, so maybe I'll do a little better tomorrow . . . Seems like she's [his boat] got a lot of pressure in the engine. I remember last year when I fed my dipstick in she was blowing it back out, pumping it back out. She's got too much pressure, she's blowin' a lot smoke out . . . have to drain the hull. Sometimes she'll get water and shit in there, and oil . . .

"The day runs weren't as good as the ones tonight, still got some real nice size hakes, real good, maybe just because its nighttime or something, I don't know . . .

"I don't know I may go shrimping if I don't go back to Alaska . . . Last year I guess we done okay. I's just thinkin' of moneywise. I guess we caught our share, but Jesus Christ when it [the price] got down to sixty cents or fifty or whatever we was getting, we was just givin' them away. So we got out of that like the third week in February and went for spring fish. Had a few good trips but didn't do a hell of a lot until end of March, I guess, first of April, something like that. Had some good trips. Ben made a couple of trips with me Down East and then he quit. I've had the boat since March. June was kind of dry. Best I done all spring was a run of four. One week I done pretty good . . . after that, I mean nothing, man. So hopefully maybe this trip will turn things around. I got a clear head now. Before I didn't know what the hell was going on. I didn't know whether it was me or the gear or there just weren't any fish. So I just had to get the hell away from it for a couple weeks. So I don't know if I'm any better off. I can think a little better anyway. I really didn't plan on it. I was pretty sick for a week and a half so I really didn't have much choice . . .

"I don't even know what the hell prices have been the last couple weeks . . ."

I had no idea who he was talking to. Still he was telling who-ever wanted to listen that fishing was no pleasure cruise.

Sixteen

Frankie's place, the FitzGerald camp, Buddha's house, whatever you called this nest in the woods, worked its magic on me over the summers in ways that were difficult to explain. It was more than a summer house. It was the place where we created a life together, a loving home that had been missing from much of our lives.

Frankie and I came from separated families. Our parents divorced when we were young children. We didn't talk about this much, but it drew us together in unconscious ways. Our fathers were gone when we were young. We lived with our mothers, but they were usually somewhere else. Their love was rationed. They weren't around when we needed them. We were alone in strange places, with relatives in my case, with servants in Frankie's, crying ourselves to sleep.

My mother left my father when I was two years old and took me to live with my grandparents while she worked. In those days, day care didn't exist. It was difficult to raise a child and work at the same time. So for the next six years I lived with a combination of relatives, first my grandparents, then with an aunt and uncle. My mother came to see me on weekends.

Frankie's father was in Asia fighting the Japanese until she was five years old. Her parents divorced when she was six. Before her seventh birthday her mother had remarried and moved from New York to Ditchley, an enormous estate near Oxford, England. Before the move her mother, who had a career and a hectic social life in New York, didn't have much time for Frankie. After it, Frankie was relegated to one of Ditchley's twenty-nine bedrooms. Finding her mother wasn't easy. Her father, meanwhile, was an ocean away in Washington.

The happiness I felt being with Frankie in Maine was not easy to admit or express. I had told Frankie about feeling threatened by happiness.

"Sounds like when you were little," she had said. "When your mother came to see you, she made you happy. Then, when you were happy, she went away again."

Frankie's place became a spiritual home for me as well. I felt the hold it had on Frankie and her brother and sister. I didn't think of myself as a very spiritual person, but sometimes things happened that seemed more than merely coincidental.

Marietta Tree, Frankie's mother, died at 3:30 A.M. on Thursday, August 15, 1991, at New York Hospital after a glamorous life that ended in a painful battle with breast cancer. She was seventy-four. Her last words to Frankie were loud.

"Get me out of here!"

Six days later we carried a small tin box containing her ashes to Northeast Harbor. We flew in rough weather from New York to Bangor, the plane dodging a hurricane named Bob that was racing up the East Coast. Marietta's brother George conducted the funeral service the next afternoon at St. Mary's-by-the-Sea, where their father and grandfathers had preached over many summers and where Marietta was married to Desmond FitzGerald. On the following morning Marietta's four brothers, Chub, George, Sam, and Mike, and their wives and children, other relatives, and close friends gathered at the Peabody plot at Forest Hill Cemetery, just north of the village, for an interment service. Frankie and her half sister, Penelope, taped Marietta's red leather appointment calendar for 1991 to the tin box of ashes and placed it in a small grave. Prayers were read. Good-byes were said. The tin box was buried.

That evening, back at Frankie's place, the phone rang at seven-thirty. I picked it up. My uncle was calling from Midland, Michigan.

"Sorry to bother you, but I thought you'd want to hear this," he said. "Your father is trying to find you."

"Well, why doesn't he just call?" I said. "Did he lose my number or something?"

"No, not that father," my uncle said, referring to my stepfather, Fred Sterba. "Your *real* father."

My real father? I had no memory of a real father except for my mother's rare comments about how awful he had been as a husband. On my sixteenth birthday, he'd telephoned from Detroit, where he lived. I didn't know it at the time but the call had been arranged as part of their divorce arrangement. He talked to me for less than five minutes. It was a stilted conversation. I listened and said little. He said he thought that I probably didn't care about him and that I probably didn't want to see him. I didn't say anything in response, but he was right. He was, in my mind, a stranger, a man my mother had kept me away from and didn't want me to know.

That phone call was the last I had heard from him. After that, I had no idea where he was or how he was. And, thanks to my mother, I didn't much care. As I got older, my curiosity grew. I wondered about his family, where his grandparents and parents were from, what they did, whether he had brothers and sisters. I wondered if he'd remarried. I wondered whether he had more children.

On the phone my uncle told me he had received a letter from my father asking for his help in finding me. My first thought was to see the letter. I asked my uncle to fax it to me in the morning. We didn't have a fax then, so I gave him a fax number in town that would receive it for one dollar, and hung up the phone, shaken. I hurried into Frankie's typing room.

"You're not going to believe this," I said, recounting the call. "This is spooky."

"How can you wait till morning?" she said.

She was right.

I called my uncle back and asked him to read me the letter. My father's name was James Walter Watts. His letter was short. He said he had found my uncle's name and address in a Michigan phone book and decided to write in hopes of finding "my son, James Sturba." My mother had so removed him from my life that he didn't know how to spell my name.

I asked my uncle to tell me what he knew about my father, and about his relationship with my mother and me. My uncle told me that my mother left my father because he drank heavily and became abusive. He hit my mother. He spanked me when I cried. My grandmother had been against the marriage from the start, he told me. My mother was only eighteen when she had a fling with Watts, who was ten years older. They eloped, and Granny never forgave her. My uncle said Granny was merciless about it, calling my mother all sorts of names that he wouldn't repeat to me.

My uncle told me that he had already called directory assistance for Ocala, Florida, where the letter had come from, and gotten a telephone listing for James Walter Watts. I copied it down, said good-bye, hung up the phone, and sat at my desk wondering what to do.

I took a deep breath. I didn't know what I was feeling, but I was feeling something. I pretended to be calm in front of Frankie, putting on my foreign correspondent's demeanor—stay cool in dicey situations and appear not to be apprehensive or frightened, try not to sweat. My conscious mind was trying to operate in this way, but my unconscious mind had taken over. This was not some war, a coup d'état, or a riot. This reached back to feelings about being alone in a dark room in a strange house. This was about my broken home, living with relatives, a mother who visited on weekends. This was about getting a stepfather with a temper and little tolerance for talk about needs and feelings. As I stared at the Florida telephone number, what I felt was a child's fear of being hurt.

I squeezed Frankie. The summer had been exhausting enough already. Coping with a Marietta's final weeks and days had taken its toll on Frankie. She was stoical on the outside. But we both felt drained. After the service at Forest Hill Cemetery I wanted to exhale.

Now this. Just hours after having said good-bye to Frankie's mother, I was about to say hello to my father. But I wasn't ready to pick up the phone. I felt as though I had climbed to the top of a very high diving platform, looked over the edge, and didn't want to jump. Frankie didn't say anything. She didn't have to. Her eyes told me what had to be done.

I picked up the phone and dialed the number in Florida. It rang three times.

"*Hell*-oh."

It was an old man's voice. It was gravelly. It sounded sleepy.

"Hello," I said. "Is this Walter Watts?"

"Yes it is," he replied.

"Hello Walter," I said. "This is Jim Sterba, your son."

I was so nervous I was shaking. I realized later that by calling myself Sterba I was distancing myself from him. But by calling myself "your son," I was doing the opposite. He could have taken those words either way.

"Hey, Jim," he said. "I'm awful glad you called."

This was an inviting thing to say, I thought. I relaxed a little.

He had something of a Southern accent. He said he was seventy-nine years old. I asked if he was in good health. He said he played golf three times a week. He told me he and his wife had moved to Florida from Michigan when he'd retired fourteen years ago. Frankie, hovering over my shoulder, sensed the conversation was turning mundane fast. She grabbed a pencil and paper and began scribbling questions.

"Why did he want to find you now?" she wrote.

"Why didn't he try to contact you earlier?"

"What was he feeling now?"

These were hard questions for me to ask. What I asked him instead was how he came to write that letter to my uncle asking for help in finding me.

Walter told me that he and his wife drove from Florida to Michigan nearly every summer to visit his wife's relatives. This summer, they went in July, taking their time, stopping for meals and staying overnight in motels. On the last day of their journey north they stopped in Midland, Michigan, for lunch and, as was his habit, he looked through the phone book for the name Sturba. He found no such name. But he continued thumbing and came across the name of my uncle. He copied down my uncle's address and phone number. Later, he said, his wife urged him to write the letter.

"Jim, I felt very badly about not having made contact with you earlier," he said. "But, you know, for a long time I figured you didn't want anything to do with me."

I didn't know what to say. I looked up at Frankie.

"I love you," I told him. "I want to come down and see you soon."

"You do that," he said.

Two weeks later I was on an airplane to Florida for a reunion with a stranger. I flew from Bangor, via Providence and Atlanta, to Gainesville. From there I rented a car and drove south on Interstate 75 to Ocala. Along the way I passed stately thoroughbred horse farms, their pastures and paddocks lined with immaculate post-and-rail fences. I passed billboard after billboard advertising retirement communities. Ten miles beyond Ocala, I came to Exit 67, which Walter had said I couldn't miss because there was a billboard advertising the Don "Big Daddy" Garlits Museum of Drag Racing, which was nearby. I turned off the highway and drove two miles down the road to the entrance to a real estate development. I wound through a subdivision of bungalows.

At three-thirty in the afternoon I found the right address. A short, bald man with white hair around his ears stood in the front yard of a white one-story house made of concrete blocks. I pulled into the driveway and hopped out.

"Is that you, Walter?" I asked. He came over. I shook his hand.

"You can do better than that," he said. We hugged, but only briefly.

He had a round, full, ruddy face with drooping jowls. He looked something like George Shultz, President Reagan's secretary of state. I didn't think he looked much like me, but I wondered whether he looked as I would at his age.

Then a short, thin, white-haired woman came out of the front door.

"This is my wife, Agnes," Walter said. I hugged her. We went inside, and Walter pulled two cans of Budweiser out of the refrigerator, handed one to me, and motioned for us to sit down around a table in a sunny, glassed-in porch.

We sat across the table as strangers. Seeing Walter in the flesh triggered no old memories of him. I felt tense and stiff. Whatever he was feeling didn't register on his face.

"How was your trip?" he asked. "Did you find us all right?"

"Yeah, no trouble," I said. "It's pretty hot, isn't it?"

"Not as hot as it was last month," he said.

The awkward small talk went on for several minutes as we sipped our beers. I began asking him questions. How long had they lived in the house? Did they like it? Who were the neighbors? I gradually found myself acting like a reporter questioning a source, playing journalist again to overcome shyness. I felt much more at ease across the table from my father as a nosy reporter than as a shy son.

I had wondered about the health of his family for a long time because it was a question I was often asked and couldn't entirely answer. Every time I moved to a new place, a new doctor would give me a physical examination, draw some blood for testing, and then sit me down across his desk and ask, "Is there any history of heart trouble in your family?"

I asked Walter about family heart trouble.

"Nope," he told me. "Nobody in the family has had a heart attack yet."

Walter and Agnes Watts lived in a retirement community of several thousand people called Marion Oaks. It consisted of tens of thousands of acres of sandy scrub pine forest with clumps of houses here and there and many empty lots waiting to be sold. Marion Oaks had two churches, two shopping centers, and a Winn Dixie supermarket. Its prime attraction was the Marion Oaks Country Club and its eighteen-hole golf course. Most residents lived in single-story houses made of concrete blocks and bricks. Many of the houses had patios that were screened to keep a vigorous local insect population at bay.

Walter told me that many of the residents were retirees from the north like himself. He said he and Agnes were living in Detroit in 1978 when they saw an advertisement for Marion Oaks in the newspaper and stopped by a motel to watch a movie about it and hear a sales pitch. The salesman offered them a free trip to Florida to see the place for themselves. They accepted, bought a lot two miles from the golf course and picked out a model of a small house to build on it. Two years later, Walter and Agnes moved in. Plenty of empty lots around theirs stayed empty for years. Lots around the golf course filled up with houses first. But the vast expanses of scrub pine went unmolested by other retirees who were supposed to flood in and keep real estate values high. A decade after Walter and Agnes arrived, Marion Oaks remained an unfinished community. In the early 1990s, houses were on the market for $50,000 or less. Gradually, those houses were sold not only to retirees but also to younger couples with children seeking affordable homes. Marion Oaks became a diverse, if isolated, community.

I stayed for three days. I tried to get Walter to tell me his likes and dislikes, what he thought of various politicians and issues in the news. For a man of seventy-nine he had a quick and alert mind. He read the local newspaper each morning. He watched news, sports, quiz shows, and Lawrence Welk reruns on TV. He had lots of videotapes of movies he'd recorded. He subscribed to *Smart Money* magazine and he read a lot of books, mostly mystery novels from the local library. But he didn't want to talk about his opinions, except on sports, and I couldn't understand why until I thought about myself. As a reporter, I didn't discuss my opinions with people I was interviewing because I had to try to be objective and because I didn't want to turn off a source by blurting out what I thought. Walter seemed to be doing much the same thing: he didn't want to risk saying something that might make me dislike him.

He stubbornly refused to talk about his life. I kept prodding, but I didn't get anywhere until Agnes helped me.

"Come on, Walter," she said at one point. "Your son wants to know. He's interested. He's here. He deserves to be told."

Walter didn't know much about his ancestors. He said he'd heard stories about a Watts who came to Virginia, from England or Ireland, then moved to West Virginia sometime before the Civil War. This Watts was said to be a "horse trader," a euphemism, at the time, for swindler or worse.

Over lunch on the second day of my stay, Walter began to talk about his childhood. He was one of seven children. His family was Methodist and lived in the hills of West Virginia near the town of Huntington, on the Ohio River.

"We didn't have nothin'," he said. He described his family crowded into a tiny house with no plumbing, adults and children taking whatever work they could find to get by. Walter's father would go off for weeks or months at a time to work on construction gangs, building iron bridges, rail lines, anything that paid a wage. The girls took in sewing. The boys tended crops of potatoes and beans and took odd jobs. In this way, the family got by, until the Depression.

The Depression cut off much of the work Walter's father did and the money it brought in. As economic conditions went from bad to worse, the family became desperate for enough cash to hold itself together. But jobs were scarce locally and people began to migrate wherever the latest rumors had it that they might find work. Walter's younger brother, Ernie, then eighteen, heard there were jobs in the automobile industry in Detroit. With bus fare from the family, he took a Greyhound north. Weeks went by. Finally, a letter from him arrived back home. He had gotten a job that paid eighteen cents an hour! Better still, he knew someone who might have a job for Walter. Walter, then twenty, was on the next Greyhound.

Ernie and Walter lived together in a small flat and worked as laborers in one of the gritty factories that supplied parts for Detroit's automobile assembly lines. They sent part of their paychecks home to their family each week. Walter eventually learned how to use lathes and other machines used to turn out parts for cars. He became a tool-and-die maker, a skilled trade that gave him lots of steady work. Cars were redesigned to some extent for every model every year. New tools and dies had to be made to stamp out new parts. Walter's skill gave him job security and good pay. He worked at various automobile-parts feeder plants around Detroit until he retired.

It was Agnes who turned the conversation to the subject of Walter and my mother. As she cleaned the lunch leftovers and plates from the table, she told me that Walter talked often about contacting me but the last time he actually made an effort to see me was when I was eleven years old. He had filed a petition in a court in Detroit asking a judge to allow me to visit him so that he could take me to see his dying mother. My mother, in response, told the court that she disapproved, and the judge sided with her.

"He seemed to give up after that," Agnes said. "I kept pushing him to keep trying to see you, but your mom didn't want him to interfere with your lives." She looked at Walter across the table.

"It was my fault," said Walter.

"He wasn't good to your mom," Agnes said. "He drank too much."

When Walter proposed to Agnes, she put her foot down about alcohol.

"I told him he'd have to straighten up before I married him, and he did," she said. "He straightened right up and that was that. He hasn't had anything stronger than beer to drink since."

I asked if they had children.

"Oh no," Agnes said. "I was thirty-five when we got married, too old to have kids."

Walter told me he thought about me a lot over the years. But he asked me nothing about what had happened to my mother and me after we left him. I wanted to tell him all about it but I wanted him to ask first. I wanted to tell him how much hardship the separation had caused us. I wanted him to know that we survived without him. I wanted to lay all this out for him, but I didn't get the chance until our last dinner together on the eve of my departure.

Agnes brought it up. She asked what my childhood had been like. I answered her and looked at her, ignoring Walter. Then I noticed that Walter was paying close attention so I looked at them both. I told them I didn't remember the early years when my mother and I moved from Detroit a hundred miles north to Sanford. I told them what my mother and grandmother, and various aunts and uncles, had told me. Granny was a divorcee herself and she wanted my mother to admit she had made a mistake and beg for forgiveness. My mother had no choice but to obey. She needed work to support herself and help taking care of me while she got back on her feet.

At first my mother took part-time house-cleaning jobs. Then she got a job working fulltime as a waitress in a restaurant and did housework on the side. But these jobs took her far away from the cottage where I lived with Granny on the lake. Eventually, my mother took a job in an Autolite battery factory in the town of Owosso. My uncle Ken and aunt Bessie lived there with two infant sons. My mother moved me in with them. Uncle Ken had come back from World War II with one leg, and he was in and out of the Veterans Hospital a lot. He became a watch repairman. I lived with them for three years, attending school at Washington Elementary, only a block down the street. My mother visited on weekends. One day, Uncle Ken fixed my Mickey Mouse watch, and then an ambulance came and took him away. My mother said he had cancer. I never saw him again.

When I was eight years old, my mother married Frederic J. Sterba, a man she had met at her factory. They both worked the night shift, she on the assembly line, he in machine repair. I was the ring boy at their wedding. They borrowed $2,200 from his older sister and bought a sixty-acre farm north of Owosso near the village of Ashley.

The farm was rundown, its fields overgrown with bushes and small trees, its buildings dilapidated. The farmhouse was a four-room woodframe rectangle with tarpaper and asbestos siding. The man who sold the farm was something of a hermit. He's raised chickens, and though a large concrete chicken coop sat not far from the house he didn't use it. He kept his chickens in the farmhouse. The smell of chicken shit inside was ovewhelming. For several weeks after Fred and Gert bought the place, they commuted to it on weekends to clean the inside of the house. They scraped chicken manure off the floor and from between the floorboards, scrubbed down the walls, washed everything with ammonia, set out deodorants, and burned incense to rid the house of the smell.

For a while living on the farm was like camping out. The house was wired for electricity but it had no running water or plumbing. Fred set up a portable bottled-gas stove for cooking. He installed a potbellied stove in the living room that burned wood and coal. Our toilet was a two-hole outhouse out back under a big oak tree. We pumped water by hand from a well on a neighbor's property across the gravel road and carried it in pails, two at a time, to the house. We heated water on the stove, and took baths in a galvanized tub once a week.

The farm had only fifteen acres of cropland. The other forty-five acres were scrub forest and meadows for pasture. Fred bought a small tractor, an old plow, a disc and drag to work the ground. We planted a large vegetable garden behind the house. We partitioned off part of the chicken coop, installed stanchions, and acquired the first of half a dozen dairy cows. We built a pigsty behind the chicken coop and bought four piglets to raise. In this way we settled in to a life together, a life of subsistence farming supplemented by the paycheck from Fred's night-shift factory job.

I loved the farm. I loved being together with my mother and her new husband. We were a family. We had two dogs, sometimes three or four. We had lots of cats and I had a pet goat. I roamed the woods, playing cowboys and Indians, and war. I learned to be a farmer, to care for animals and grow vegetables. I learned how to milk cows and got so good at it that I could squeeze a teat and propel a stream of milk horizontally across the barn into the open mouth of a waiting cat. I learned how to bale hay, how to load a hay wagon, how to stack bales in the chicken coop so that air could circulate through them to keep them dry. Fred taught me how to drive the tractor and his old Buick, a heady experience for an eight-year-old. He taught me how to use tools, how to fix tractors and farm machinery, how to take apart small Briggs & Stratton engines and put them back together without having any parts left over. He taught me how to shoot a .22, and how to hunt partridge and rabbits and deer. Eventually, my half brother, Ken, was born.

Fred made me work hard. Because he left the farm each day at two-thirty in the afternoon to drive twenty-five miles to his factory job, he wasn't around to do the evening chores, and milking the cows quickly became drudgery. Because he didn't return from his job until after midnight, he slept through the morning chores. The daily farm work, thus, fell to my mother and me. Because Fred tried to work high-paying overtime shifts in the factory as well, he was often unavailable for farm work on the weekends. Though my mother and I did the twice-daily chores, other farm work would pile up. Fred would squeeze in a few hours here and there. I would help him. Sometimes he was irritable. Sometimes he would get mad, swear, and throw a tool. His irritability spilled over into family conversations. He didn't like to hear about personal problems or feelings. He didn't like to talk things out or argue. He got angry for reasons I didn't understand. When he got angry, he would threaten to leave the farm and my mother and me, forever. It was scary. Much later, I came to realize that he was very insecure and that he thought bringing up problems was the same as making accusations against him. To foreclose the possibility of Fred exploding in anger, my mother and I kept quiet. We kept our problems and feelings inside.

A yellow school bus picked me up in front of the farm after morning chores and delivered me back before evening chores. In the mailbox out front I found an envelope each month with a check in it from J. Walter Watts for thirty-two dollars. The check was a child-support payment from someone my mother rarely mentioned. She now had a new life, and while it wasn't an easy life it was better than her old one.

One day early in my new life on the farm, Fred and Gert sat me down and solemnly told me that I had to choose whether I wanted to be a Watts or a Sterba. My mother made it clear that, in her mind, it would be better for family togetherness if my name was Sterba, just like hers. I agreed to the change, and she told me that I could now call Fred "Dad." What I didn't find out until much later was that my mother and Fred had ruled out a formal adoption. They thought that if he tried to adopt me as his son, my real father might raise an objection in court or, worse, stop paying the thirty-two dollars a month in child support. So instead of adoption, I simply used the name Sterba. For the first eight years of my life I was James Paul Watts. At my old school, kids called me Wattsy. Now, I was James Paul Sterba. At my new school, kids called me Sterbs. Only many years later did they hire a lawyer to file a simple change-of-name petition at the county courthouse.

I told Walter and Agnes that after years of trying to make a go of the farm without very much success but with a lot of very hard work, Fred and my mother decided to quit farming. They sold the farm and bought a big, old house in Owosso not far from the factory where he continued to work. We moved in. Ken and I shared a bedroom. I felt liberated. No more cows to milk. I was now a city kid, a boy of leisure, and I turned my attention to schoolwork, books, and sports. I grew up and went off to college, leaving behind the tensions of living in our dysfunctional family. Ken eventually followed me.

When I finished telling this story, I turned back to Agnes and asked her to tell me about the moment Walter decided to write the letter to my uncle inquiring about me. She said that as Walter got older, he wanted more and more to find me. She urged him on. But he didn't know what to do, or where to look, after all the years. He told himself that I probably wanted nothing to do with him. He doubted that he would ever find me, and his doubts discouraged him from trying. On their drives to Michigan, they talked about making an effort.

"He wanted to find you and see you before he died," she said.

"Now you never mind!" Walter said loudly. He rose from the table, turned, and walked away toward his bedroom. He seemed to be weeping, but I couldn't see his face.

Seventeen

One morning in the last week in August, we woke up to the howls of a stiff north wind. It was blowing whitecaps down the sound and buffeting my porch crops. We ate indoors. As I turned the pages of the *Ellsworth American* over coffee, I came to a story about prices at the Portland Fish Exchange. Cod was going for $1.07 a pound, on average, it said, and fishermen had brought in 138,700 pounds of dabs.

"What's a dab?" I asked.

"A what?" Frankie peered up from deep inside the *Times*.

"A dab. It's some kind of local fish."

"Never heard of it. Ask Mr. Stanley. Maybe it's good in bouillabaisse."

"Bouillabaisse!" I said. "That reminds me, when are we having that big dinner?" I had completely forgotten our invitation, weeks before, to Gilbert, Ildiko and six other friends to come over for fish stew.

"Oh my god," Frankie said, dashing for her datebook.

"Oh my god," she shouted from the bedroom, rushing back. "It's tonight."

We looked at each other.

"Don't panic," I said, glancing at my watch. "We've been training all summer for this. Ten people. Last minute. Piece of cake. Call Linn and ask her to bring two more chairs. Get the extra knives and forks out of the back closet."

I studied the tidal chart tacked to the kitchen wall beside the stove. High tide was 6:54 A.M., which meant low tide would be around one P.M. I could gather some mussels then. We could get lobsters, scallops, and fish at Mr. Stanley's. I relaxed.

This dinner was going to fit my philosophy about cooking for guests perfectly. Pulling together a meal at the last minute was the way to have fun cooking, not spending days or hours in a cold sweat. Cooking dinner for six or eight people need not be an ordeal. Pulling a meal together late takes wrist and confidence, that's all. We'd pick up ingredients while in town, and I'd start cooking no earlier than six o'clock for guests arriving at seven-thirty. No muss, no fuss, and no panic.

At one o'clock, I grabbed a pail and climbed down to the low-tide rocks in front of the house and filled it half full of mussels. Back on the porch I cleaned them, setting aside thirty small black "show" mussels. The others I steamed and cleaned, removing the meats.

We went to the village at four-thirty. Mr. Stanley sold us lobsters, scallops, halibut, and hake. A dab, he told me, was like a flounder, but smaller. Not much call for them, he said. We drove back to Frankie's place, popped the seafood into the fridge, and went for a walk. Back home shortly after six o'clock, I went to work on Somes Sound bouillabaisse.

I started by making a rouille. I had not made a rouille in three summers and I had never come close to pronouncing "rouille" correctly. Frankie, a French speaker, reminded me of this often. To my ear, the first part of the pronunciation approximates the sound of a smoker clearing his throat in the morning. I consulted Julia. I turned to her rouille page, read it, and closed the book. This recipe produces about a cup.

ROUILLE

Seed a red bell pepper, cut it in fourths, and put it into boiling water along with two unpeeled new potatoes slightly larger than golf balls. Boil 5–8 minutes until potatoes are tender.

Into a food processor put 4–6 cloves of garlic, four shakes of dried chili flakes (or 2 tablespoons of hot oil), ½ cup of a combo of fresh thyme leaves stripped from their tough stems, chopped fresh oregano leaves, and tarragon. When the potatoes are done, put them in the food processor along with the pepper and a quarter cup of olive oil. This mooshes up nicely into a spicy paste. Set aside. (You can make this ahead and refrigerate, but serve it at room temperature.) Just before serving, stir in another tablespoon or so of olive oil and 3–5 big tablespoons of hot broth from the stew. Pass the rouille immediately after serving the stew.

My recipe for bouillabaisse was adapted from one for *cioppino di pesce,* adding a few wrinkles of my own, including a cup of periwinkles for sound effects.

BOUILLABAISSE

Ingredients: 30 show mussels, 2 cups of mussel meat, 2 small lobsters, steamed, 1 pound of scallops, 1½ pounds of halibut, hake, or haddock. Plus onions, tomatoes, garlic, potatoes, cilantro, and parsley. From the porch, I gathered thyme, basil, oregano, and tarragon.

Pour half a cup of olive oil into a wide—at least 12 inches wide— and deep pot. Add two medium, roughly chopped onions. After they sizzle for a few minutes, add 6 cloves of chopped garlic (always remember Calvin Trillin's line: with enough garlic, you can eat the New York Times). *Then add ½ cup of chopped parsley, and 2/3 cup of a chopped combo of fresh thyme, tarragon, oregano, and basil and a couple of shakes of chili pepper flakes. Once the onion wilts, add a large can of Italian peeled whole tomatoes (or 2–3 fresh ones cut into eighths, skins, seeds, and all) and a bottle of clam juice.*

(I quickly realized as my mixture heated that I didn't have near enough stew sauce for eight people, so I added another bottle of clam juice, a can of chicken broth, and an 8-ounce can of tomato sauce.)

Cook sauce for 10 minutes, add half a dozen quartered new potatoes, simmer for 10 minutes, then turn it off. (Don't fill the pot with liquid because it's amazing how fast it fills up once you start adding the seafood. You can always top it up later with more chicken broth, clam juice, or tomato juice, which I recommend in that order.)

Meanwhile, steam 2 small (one-pounders) lobsters and let them cool. Cut their tails into three parts, pull off the front claws and arms, cracking their hard shells with a hammer but otherwise leaving them intact.

About half an hour before serving, bring stew to a slow boil, then add the shelled mussels. Then in succession every 3–4 minutes, I add the show mussels in shells, the periwinkles (which fall like sinkers to the bottom), the whole lobster claws and arms, and a pound of scallops (big ones cut in half). Then, in the last 5 minutes, add a pound and a half of halibut (or whatever) cut into ice cube–sized pieces (add this last so that it won't flake into tiny bits with stirring). And, finally, add ½ stick of butter. (As far as butter is concerned, see garlic rule.)

Also 5 minutes out, add the juice of one lemon, lots of fresh ground pepper (you can use lemon pepper, too) and almost a cup of the chopped fresh herb combo: tarragon, cilantro, basil, oregano, and thyme. And a few more sprigs of chopped parsley. (Last-minute herbs do wonders. Indeed, lots of last-minute tasting and adjusting with more lemon juice, lemon pepper, or various fresh herbs is the secret to making this dish taste, in the bowl, alive.)

We also boiled some ziti al dente to serve as a base, and Frankie toasted some fresh croutons as a topping. But you can use toasted French bread as a base as well.

We put the big pot on the table and Frankie ladled the stew into bowls. The periwinkles sounded like marbles. We served hot crunchy bread and red wine, salad and cheese, and blueberry pie.

The wind shifted in the night and calmed down. In the morning, there was a light breeze from the southwest. We went about our morning routine. After stretching and bending on the porch we set off up the lane. Around the third bend, as usual, Fifi of the North charged at us in a growling, barking fit. We grabbed sticks. The big poodle backed off. My dog-biscuit peace initiative wasn't working.

I had been bribing Fifi with a beef-flavored Milk Bone dog biscuit from the Pine Tree Market for two weeks. Each morning, I'd put a Milk Bone in my jogging shorts and at the right time toss it to Fifi—stick firmly clutched in the other hand. Fifi ignored the Milk Bones while we passed, but they were gone by the time we jogged up to the main road and back. Yet my offerings had no effect on Fifi's antagonistic behavior toward us.

On this morning I tossed out a Milk Bone again.

"I say give it up," said Frankie. "All you are doing is rewarding aggression."

Back home Frankie reminded me about the story of the red setter that used to chew the rug in Richard Nixon's Oval Office. To divert the dog, the president would give him a dog biscuit. One day, after watching this happen several times, Henry Kissinger, Nixon's national security adviser, interrupted.

"Mr. President, you are teaching the dog to chew the rug."

Frankie was right. Besides, my heart wasn't in befriending Fifi. I gave the rest of my Milk Bones to the squirrels. We ate breakfast on the porch. A chipmunk joined us.

Every summer toward the end of August the biggest stinkpot in the realm arrived in Northeast Harbor. It was named *Highlander* and was owned by Malcolm Forbes, the patriarch of the *Forbes* magazine clan. Northeast Harbor was a stop on the *Highlander*'s annual cruise along the Maine coast to promote *Forbes* magazine and, perhaps, scratch up a little advertising. It was a faint echo of J. P. Morgan's visits on the *Corsair*. The *Forbes* minions always phoned ahead and got local pillars of the summer community to invite Mount Desert's finest for a dinner cruise. This summer, whoever pulled together the invitation list put our names on it.

The summer people turned out in coats and ties and party dresses, prepared for gaiety. Some of them came prepared to sublimate, temporarily, their utter disdain for monstrous motorized seagoing vessels.

Northeast Harbor was carved out of granite by God and glaciers for sailboats. Each summer, though, big motorboats escaped their domains in Florida, New Jersey, and elsewhere and ventured north like illegal aliens, fouling Maine's vistas and harbors in an annual blight more predictable than a red tide. This was what people who knew a spinnaker from a jib said under their breath.

These gargantuan tubs crowded into Northeast Harbor in August, occupying slips and moorings, and giving the place all the charm of a floating trailer park. The *Highlander*'s stay each summer was brief, usually a weekend, and I thought it served two useful purposes. First, when its green and gold hull, 151 feet long, eased up to the main dock with a green and gold helicopter, two cigarette boats, and two big BMW motorcycles lashed to the deck, the *Highlander* turned the other stinkpots in the harbor into toys. This, I presumed, gave their owners a mild dose of humility. The second useful purpose was personal. Surely among all these grand invitees I'd find a Philadelphia snob or two. They'd eluded me all summer.

At precisely seven o'clock that evening, a bagpiper wearing a kilt stood on the upper deck and piped guests aboard. A young man in a white officer's uniform stood at the foot of the gangplank checking off names on a guest list as they moved patiently in line. One behind another, they mounted the gangplank, climbed to the main deck, and walked into the salon, where a receiving line of Forbeses greeted them with handshakes. Malcolm Forbes himself was a no-show. The line snaked past a guest book, where another white-uniformed young man dutifully monitored the guests to make sure they signed in before they made their way to the bar.

Once on board, Frankie signed the guest book and moved on. I signed slowly, looking at the names of the guests. I found Bass, Ford, Pierpont, Peabody, Mellon, Astor, and Rockefeller. Oh boy, I thought, if names like these were aboard, snooty Philadelphians had to be hanging off the gunnels.

We came upon a bar and spotted Paul Nitze sitting to one side. I sidled up to him and was about to introduce myself when he, thinking that I was a waiter, asked for a vodka and tonic.

"Yes sir, right away sir," I obliged, heading for the bar.

When I returned with his drink and a glass of wine for Frankie, Nitze, who was eighty-seven years old, was telling Frankie about his afternoon tennis lesson.

The *Highlander* crew operated with military precision. They boarded their guests, moved them around decks and through lines, served them drinks, fed them a buffet dinner—all the while casting off, cruising out to sea, and returning to the dock—and got them off-loaded within a schedule that must have been planned down to the last ten seconds. Just watching them was tiring. As I sat with plate in lap, Mrs. Astor came over and sat down next to me. She was in her nineties but incredibly spry. She began asking me all sorts of questions. When talk turned to China she told me about living in old Beijing before the revolution. She lived there with her father, a Marine major attached to the American legation. I was so flattered to be talking to her that I forgot to keep an eye peeled for Philadelphians with their noses in the air.

Labor Day weekend was closing in fast. On Friday morning, early, Frankie's old friend Boyden called to ask us to play tennis at eleven o'clock on Monday morning. I told him we worked during the day and suggested we play in the afternoon. He said that would be too late. He had to catch a plane back to Washington that evening. Then he said, "It is, after all, Labor Day, the workers' day of rest. Even back in 1982, when I was named one of the ten most boring bachelors in Washington—a glum workaholic, they called me—I didn't work on Labor Day!"

"Well, I'll appeal to Frankie's sense of solidarity with the working classes—we'll be there," I told him.

Over breakfast, I picked up the *Bar Harbor Times* and discovered Earl Brechlin's front-page follow-up story about the $25,000 anchor that the nuclear submarine, the SSN *Groton,* had lost on August 13 while trying to get to the Winter Harbor Lobster Festival. A salvage operation was under way, Brechlin reported. The navy had dispatched a 280-foot, tug like vessel, with divers, to scour the bottom, locate, and grab the anchor. This effort seemed a bit much, since some local fishermen had already found the anchor and tied a buoy to it.

I listened to NOAA Weather Radio on my marine radio to get the latest installment of the soap opera that played out all summer in our skies—the weather war between the Canadians and the Bermudans. The Canadians bombarded us with high-pressure fronts of cold, dry air, which made for sunny days and chilly nights. The Bermudans bombarded us with high-pressure fronts of warm, moist air, which produced damp days and warm nights. When these two weather systems joined in battle near us, the results could be rain, thunderstorms, heavy winds, and rough seas. When one front or the other was occupying the skies over us, the weather was stable. But the stability lasted only until the other side attacked.

These battles were chronicled in detail and repeated around the clock on NOAA Weather Radio. All I had to do to get the latest was tune in. Sunday morning's weather news was good and bad. Good because Bermuda was counterattacking and the temperature would probably rise. Bad because Bermuda's counterattack was ginning up a big storm. NOAA Weather Radio was forecasting big-league foulness, with heavy rains and winds in the night, and issued a "weather advisory" warning boaters and fishermen offshore. Strong winds were expected to kick up seas, creating waves with crests sixteen feet high! That was big. In all the years of shaving and listening to NOAA Weather Radio, I had never heard of waves cresting at sixteen feet. That was almost as high as *Scoop* was long!

The storm moved in. By afternoon we heard the first rumbles of thunder in the distance. They sounded like Frankie's rumbling Remington behind a closed door. Just before midnight, the wind began to howl and big drops of rain began to pound the cedar roof shingles. The rain grew more intense into the night. We snuggled deep under blankets and a goose-down comforter.

The rain lasted all night, easing to sprinkles as the day broke.

"There's only one thing to do on a morning like this," Frankie said at around eight o'clock, rolling over and burying her head under the comforter. An hour later, I announced that I was getting up in preparation for our eleven o'clock tennis date.

"Yeah, wetsuit tennis," said Frankie. She added, "I was wide awake at eight, like Pavlov's dog."

"Yes," I said, "but you didn't leap out of bed. That's the secret, instant up, immediate alert."

"Such a Boy Scout," she said, burying her head under the comforter.

I decided to set a Scout-like example by throwing back the covers and leaping up and dashing into the back bedroom, where I slipped into my FitzGerald Survival School uniform and set about stretching in the living room. The phone rang. Tennis match canceled. I completed my sit-ups and plunged out into the rain. From inside the house it always sounded and looked as though it were raining harder than it was because the roof shingles tended to amplify the sound and the rain runoff from the roof poured off onto the porch right in front of the windows. Once outside, I realized the rain was light, if chilly, and I started up the lane dodging huge puddles of water everywhere. The rainwater had washed pine needles into berms, which held the water in place like little dams.

On my return trip, I stopped at Jurassic Park. Stacks of plywood sheeting had arrived, along with the modern equivalent of two-by-fours made out of pressed, glued-together wood clips. This was the first direct evidence that the builders were going to put up a wood-frame house. Some big steel I beams had been laid in place on top of a huge foundation, and some two-by-eight wooden planks had been bolted on top of the concrete. Over to the side, I noticed that a portable toilet had arrived and I wondered how the workmen had managed without it earlier. Looking around, I could see no sign of the alleged swimming pool.

Out in front, the dock was already beginning to weather, a process helped by our neighborhood population of seagulls. The dock had become a gull social center.

NOAA Weather Radio said two more days of even stronger winds and more rain were on the way. The wind picked up all morning. By noon the whitecaps on the sound were as big as I'd ever seen. The wind howled in from the north and northeast.

"It's a nor'easter," Frankie said that afternoon as we drove to Northeast Harbor. Nor'easters could be big, powerful storms. A lone Coast Guard patrol boat churned up Somes Sound, battering through five-foot crests. The road near the golf course was littered with snapped branches and pinecones.

We drove into the village and around by the Fleet Dock to get a look at the open ocean. The sea churned. Huge waves crashed on to the rocks. All over town downed tree branches littered the streets.

Back home we found a message from Frankie's uncle Mike inviting us to a family meeting the following evening. He said he knew that most members of the Peabody clan would be leaving Mount Desert for home very soon and he wanted to tell us about a "unique opportunity" at the cemetery before he left. Most of the Peabodys who vacationed on the island had gone home. Besides Mike and his wife, Pam, the only other members of the family still on Mount desert were Uncle George and Frankie.

The Peabody plot was a parcel of real estate thirty-five feet long and thirty-two feet wide situated among the newer headstones at the south end of Forest Hill Cemetery. The cemetery, which was next to Acadia Park just up Highway 198 from Northeast Harbor, contained many old headstones etched with the names of some of Mount Desert's earliest settlers—Savage, Fernald, Gilpatrick, Tracy, Smallidge, among them. The remains of a number of summer residents were buried in Forest Hill too, including the historian Samuel Eliot Morison.

The cemetery real estate market is something a clergyman gets familiar with after a while, and Uncle George shrewdly bought into Forest Hill before plot prices skyrocketed. George bought the first of four sections of the Peabody plot in October of 1986 for $600, a steal. Five years later he bought two more parcels, adjacent to the first for $900 each, still a bargain. The three parcels formed an L-shaped plot. George offered members of the Peabody family a chance to buy into it at cost.

Frankie's mother was the first in the family to occupy the Peabody plot. In the years since her ashes were buried there, Frankie had arranged for a small, granite gravestone to be engraved and put into place. She planted some wild roses and a clump of birch saplings. Nothing was done, otherwise, to landscape the property. The Peabody plot was, in fact, a rather scruffy patch of grass, weeds, and wild strawberries not totally out of character with the family's traditions of parsimony. Family members talked over the years about making the gravesite look more respectable with more shrubbery and landscaping. But nothing much happened until Uncle Sam said he and his wife, Judy, wanted in. Unlike the other members of the family, including George, Frankie, and Mike, his wife, Pam, and their family, who preferred to have their cremated ashes interned, Sam and Judy wanted their remains buried intact in coffins. Although there was plenty of room in the plot George had assembled for ashes, coffins could make the fit a bit snug. As it happened, a square of land adjacent to the Peabody plot was for sale. George acquired it in 1994 for Sam for $5,000, an inflationary price for a little more legroom. (Uncle Chub had made burial arrangements for himself and his wife, Toni, in Groton. With Sam's purchase, the Peabody plot went from the shape of an L to a rectangle. With the participation of Sam and Judy came more pressure for improvements because Judy, who envisioned an afterlife in a more manicured glade, declined to commit herself to spending eternity in the Peabody plot not up to her standards.

The most important task was to find a suitable family stone to anchor the gravesite, and Uncle George and Uncle Mike had been thinking about such a stone for years. They didn't want to buy one, however, and they didn't want one that was cut, squared off, and polished. They wanted to find a stone of Mount Desert granite and they knew where to look.

Along the shore in front of the Peabody cottage in Aunt Hannah's pasture on Gilpatrick Cove sat dozens of pink granite stones, and among them George and Mike had picked out several candidates for the Peabody plot. They varied in size, and the final choice depended in part upon what sort of engraving the family members wanted on the stone. They eventually decided to keep it simple, the name "Peabody" etched in.

In the years that followed Marietta's death, however, Uncle Mike and Uncle George discovered that moving a suitable stone from Gilpatrick Cove would involve a major and expensive amphibious operation. They began to look at an alternative source for stones. Eventually Uncle Mike found a man who moved around heavy things, including large rocks. His name was Doug Gott, and he was known in the construction business as a "heavy contractor."

At six o'clock the next evening, we arrived at the family meeting at Uncle Mike's. The youngest of the Peabody uncles, Mike was an energetic, take-charge guy. He developed real estate around Washington and had been a senior official in the Department of Housing and Urban Development. Mike was anxious to make some progress on the Peabody plot and he introduced us to a man named David Graves.

Graves lived on Manchester Road and was famous for his woodpile, the neatest pile of split hardwood logs in Northeast Harbor and, perhaps, in the entire state of Maine. Not a single log stood out from the tightly stacked pile. So perfectly aligned were the split logs within it that the woodpile had the look of a sculpture. When passersby spotted it, they often slowed down. Sometimes they stopped their cars, and stared at it in disbelief.

Graves was also the caretaker of the Graves family plot at the cemetery, right across a narrow asphalt road from the Peabody plot, and he kept it so green and manicured that it put all the plots around it to shame.

Before turning to Graves, Mike said he had some very good news about the headstone. He had gone over to Doug Gott's place, surveyed his extensive collection of pink granite rocks, and made a couple of preliminary choices. Gott had tagged the choices so Frankie and Uncle George could go look them over. Once the right stone was selected, Mike said, Gott would take it to Ellsworth, get it engraved, bring it back to Mount Desert to the cemetery, and place it on the plot. He would do all this, Mike said, for about two hundred dollars, not including the cost of the stone itself, which was about thirty. Smiles filled the room. This was the kind of bargain that could light up an entire room of Peabodys.

Mike called on Graves, who said he worked on the Graves cemetery plot at least twice a week except in winter. Mike said his idea was to hire Mr. Graves to do the same thing for the Peabody plot. But first the Peabody plot needed a face-lift: about a foot of its tired topsoil would have to be dug up and carted away, replaced with fertile topsoil, and either seeded with grass or covered with sod. After that, a landscape architect could draw up a plan for trees and shrubs. All of this, Mike went on, wouldn't be cheap. This thought cast a pall over the room. George suggested further study. Frankie suggested that the meeting be adjourned.

Back home, I built a fire. The wind howled. Rain splattered on the roof. Somes Sound rocked and rolled. Fog moved in, thickening as evening approached. It was going to be a dark and stormy night. And a romantic one. I made dinner.

MUSSELS WITH CHORIZO SAUSAGE

I amended this recipe from one we came across in the New York Times, *steaming the mussels separately first, draining them, and then adding them to the sauce and blending them in. The idea, again, is to avoid having the seawater inside the mussels dilute the sauce too much when they open. The chorizo, or, for that matter,* almost any hot sausage from Spain, Portugal or Italy, adds zest and body.

Cut one 8-inch link of chorizo sausage in half lengthwise, then cut the halves into pieces ½ inch wide, yielding 32 bite-sized pieces. Cut the white part of a whole leek into ¼ inch sections. Thinly slice 2 large cloves of garlic.

Heat a tablespoon of olive oil in a wok and add sausage and leeks. Sauté 5 minutes and add garlic. Sauté another minute and add 1 large fresh chopped tomato (seeds too, please, I believe in fiber), 3 chopped sprigs of fresh porch oregano, stems removed, and a handful of fresh thyme leaves. Simmer for 2 minutes before adding one 8-ounce bottle of clam juice, ½ cup of white wine, and 2 tablespoons of butter.

Steam about 3 dozen mussels in a covered large pot in about half an inch of boiling water for 6 to 8 minutes—essentially until they foam up and over the covered lip. Drain and add immediately to wok sauce, stirring the mussels and shells to coat them with the sauce. You can sprinkle on some fresh chopped parsley at this point if you want. Add freshly ground black pepper.

Serve in soup bowls over pasta (penne in this case, but squiggles or bowties or rigatoni would do nicely). With chianti.

As a small side dish, we also had fresh steamed string beans. Then salad and oven-heated sourdough bread.

It rained all night. The wind howled. The fireplace worked overtime.

Eighteen

On the morning after Labor Day, the last drop of an all-night rain hit the roof shortly after eight and as I tossed awake I had the sensation of being left behind. Mount Desert Island had emptied. In the last days of August, the caravans of early summer reversed direction, and a grand exodus climaxed over the holiday weekend. Vacationers departed in great streams of campers and motor homes. Summer people gathered their children and dogs, stuffed their cars, vans, and sport utility vehicles with the toys of summer, strapped kayaks and mountain bikes to roofs and hatchback racks, and decamped. They rolled north, across Thompson Island over the Trenton Bridge to the mainland, then forked west and southwest down interstate highways toward Boston, Philadelphia, New York, Washington, and beyond. They packed suitcases, drove to the Bar Harbor airport, and boarded shuttle flights, chartered planes, or private jets. They headed home to jobs, schools, weekend football games, and the beginning of a new season.

"Why is it that I always used to think of fall as a beginning—and now I think of it as an end?" Frankie said as we assembled on the porch. (The FitzGerald Survival School didn't stop with Labor Day.) "I suppose it's because I used to think summers were boring, but I don't anymore." Good thing. We had five weeks more at Frankie's place.

It rained off and on for the next several days. The woods were soggy, the air heavy with moisture, the ground spongy from rain. Great pools of water had collected in low spots just outside the house. Pine-needle berms terraced the lane. Rivulets had washed out gravel on the steeper slopes of the lane. One morning after an all-day, all-night downpour, NOAA Weather Radio said six inches of rain had fallen. Driving along Sargeant Drive, I passed water cascading over granite cliffs, waterfalls that hadn't existed all summer.

One of the nice things about a hard rain was that it brought the commotion next door to a halt. No pounding, roaring, and banging. But during light sprinkles, the crew of carpenters hammered on. One weekday morning, not a single truck was parked at Jurassic Park as I trotted by soaked. On the way back, I turned in for a look.

Despite the foul weather, much had changed. A plywood floor had been laid over the massive foundation, and on this wet morning an inch of rainwater covered it. Between an inner and outer foundation fine gravel had been poured as fill. The yard beside the foundation was strewn with pallets holding stacks of concrete blocks, fireplace bricks, and chimney stones. In the back and to the side of the main foundation was another small foundation with a wooden skeleton of two-by-fours rising from it. A guest cottage? Servants quarters? A horse shed? Anything was possible. In the water in front, two new moorings had been planted, with white, beach ball–sized floats and little white buoys with long pickup antennae. These were big floats, the size Hinckley and Northeast Harbor used to moor major yachts. Was our new neighbor a two-boat person? Maybe he had both a sailboat and a motorboat. Would it be polite to ask him to moor the sailboat in our view and hide the motorboat? A cormorant sat on one of the balls trying to dry off by holding its wings outstretched.

The telephone rang far less after Labor Day. Lynda Hamor called from the post office. She and her colleague Linda Lauriat were about as ideal a pair of civil servants as the federal bureau-cracy could have. They were friendly, helpful, efficient, hard-working, and just a bit too punctual for my taste. Sometimes they would phone minutes after opening up at eight in the morning. If a piece of overnight mail had arrived that looked important, we heard about it. On occasion we got a call from one of them to tell us our box was overflowing and we might want to come and empty it. This time Lynda told me that an Express Mail envelope had arrived.

I was expecting a package from a friend at the *Wall Street Journal* who had helped me do a little research on the man who was building the castle next door. Over the years I had done a fair amount of reporting that required me to find out about other people, but I never had a reason to do it on Mount Desert Island, until now. I started by asking friends at porch-benders and din-ners if they knew him. Nobody did, but a few people had heard his name and knew that he ran a big European company. With the name, I went to work, first checking the files of the *Journal* and then the electronic databases of hundreds of other news-papers and magazines. What I found out warmed me toward him—up to a point.

He was not, I learned, some young shake-'n-bake computer millionaire. Neither was he Old Money. He was sixty years old and self-made. Born and raised in New York City to immigrant parents, he went to Harvard, studied law at Columbia Univer-sity, and joined the firm of Shearman & Sterling. Four years later he veered into chemicals and then joined a big natural gas corpo-ration in Europe. He became managing director, chief executive officer, and chairman. He helped privatize the company and gained notoriety for being the highest-paid executive around, and he was a very spiffy dresser. One newspaper reported that he was nicknamed Movie Man by his staff "for his aging matinee idol looks." Another newspaper called him "wealthy, charming, tal-ented and when he has to be, ruthless," adding that he had "the hide of a rhinoceros."

When I told Frankie what I had found out, she said, "Sounds like an interesting guy."

At the post office, Lynda handed me an enormous pile of mail. I thumbed through it and found an envelope from Ahuan's insurance company, tore it open, and found a check for $780: rear bumper replacement money.

Back home, I called the insurance company and got Ahuan's case officer. I thanked her for the check, then asked when the alleged perp would be hauled into court. Maybe never, she told me. Collecting from her insurance company might cost more than it was worth, she said. Outrageous, I told her. I wanted justice! She said she'd keep me posted. It was the last I heard from her.

Next I called our Volvo repairman in Ellsworth and asked him how soon he could get a new rear bumper. He said he could have it in a week. I told him to order one. Then I thought about how Ahuan would look with a new rear bumper and an old front bumper with its pitted and peeling chrome.

"Make it two!" I told him. "Let's do this right. Get a front bumper too."

I'd pay for the second bumper. One new bumper, I figured, was like half a face-lift.

Runoff from the rain was so heavy that it turned Somes Sound a yellow-brown from freshwater colored by dead pine needles. "Pine-needle pee," I called it.

NOAA Weather Radio reported record rainfall across much of the state, including more than ten inches in two days in Rockland. The salt in the shaker was so congealed that we took to pouring salt out of the big blue Morton's container into our palms to sprinkle on our eggs. Towels stayed so wet that we tossed them unwashed into the dryer.

One morning deep into this rainy season we woke up to find that the sun was out and the clouds had disappeared.

"After work, why don't we take the boat over to Abel's and buy a couple of lobsters for dinner?" Frankie said.

"Good idea," I said nonchalantly, trying not to show my astonishment.

This was heretical to Frankie's lobster logic. We didn't have houseguests. We hadn't done anything particularly worthy that I could remember. I wanted to mention that she was proposing heresy and tick off all the principles she was proposing to violate. But I also wanted lobster. I stayed mum.

After work, we bailed out *Scoop* and cruised up the sound to Abel's dock, walked up to the pound, and bought two one-clawed lobsters that cost an arm and a leg.

We cruised home in a magical light. The sun was setting under a huge bank of deep gray clouds, and its light coated the underside in pinks and oranges. Frankie pronounced it "ethereal." Below the clouds, the light reflected off trees as a sparkling green all the way up Norumbega Mountain. Beams of the sun's setting rays hit the shore like spotlights. The storm and rain and winds and fog had sent the last summer people fleeing and we were being rewarded for sticking in, holding out, for believing that under the gloomiest cloud a magnificent sunset —and lobsters— awaited!

Back home, I built a fire, set the table, and retired to my laptop. Eventually I heard pounding in the kitchen.

"Okay, lobster," she shouted. I came in. There on our plates, upside down, sat two red, one-clawed lobsters. Sitting beside them were the world's tiniest bowls of melted butter. They were, in fact, those mini-bowls Chinese restaurants use to serve soy sauce.

"What's this?" I asked.

"Yeah, I should have used more butter," Frankie said.

"This is ridiculous," I said. Here I was, about to feast on a succulent lob, and we're into butter rationing?

"I meant to melt more."

"No, that's the way you planned it, I'm sure," I said, launching into a tirade. "You think that if we're going to break down and have lobster, then we're going to suffer through a rationed supply of butter. Secretly you believe that if we are going to eat lobster, we shouldn't enjoy ourselves too much doing it."

It was, in any case, delicious, with oven-roasted corn, then salad. Back at my laptop, I couldn't concentrate. I felt bad about my outburst. I got up and walked to the kitchen, where Frankie was standing before the sink washing dishes. I put my arms around her from behind and hugged, saying nothing, just holding on to her and swaying gently.

"Thank you," she said. "I think I'll skimp on butter more often."

Northeast Harbor had become, for all but the most practical of purposes, a ghost town. The tourists were gone and most of the shops were closed. What had been a village of busy summer people, boaters, and sightseers had gone into hibernation. I thought of the village as a stage set for a lively summer opera. Now the opera was over and its stage set had been struck, folded up, and trucked to some warehouse for the winter.

A few stores, those that catered to year-round residents as well as summer people, remained open. A handwritten "Open" sign was taped to the window of Mr. Stanley's fish store, but there was no trace of him inside, no Red Sox game playing on the radio.

We ran into Bob Pyle in front of the post office.

"Ah," he said, "the summer-people season is over and the real-people season has begun."

The Pine Tree Market was open, but there was no surer sign of summer's demise than the radical change of its fresh vegetable cooler. Where once sat four varieties of fresh lettuce and other gourmet salad greens now rested four heads of iceberg lettuce wrapped in cellophane. In the back of the store, the cheese cooler was empty and dark, its electrical cord unplugged.

McGrath's Store, run by Dorothy Renault and her children, Terry, David, and Sandra, was open. But their newspaper distributor had switched over to his winter schedule, delivering the *Times* and *Journal* a day late, meaning that we would be reading them two days late. We picked up the latest *Bar Harbor Times* and

Ellsworth American. Out front I flipped through the *American* to find Russ Wiggins's latest offering.

"Listen to this," I said to Frankie and anyone else who happened by the sidewalk:

> *Why doesn't the woodpecker*
> *Rattle his brains*
> *When he hammers a tree*
> *Or the windowpanes?*
> *How does a woodpecker*
> *Who is black or red*
> *Keep from the scramble*
> *Of what's in his head?*
> *Why does the woodpecker*
> *Make life a melee*
> *Digging out worms to*
> *Put into its belly?*
> *Like many dear people*
> *His life is so hollow*
> *You must let him beat things*
> *To get him to swallow.*

Our Volvo repairman called the next morning to say Ahuan's new bumpers had arrived. I dropped off Ahuan at noon, feeling like I'd just left a dear friend at the hospital. The phone rang three days later. Time to take the patient home. I sped to Ellsworth. Ahuan was sitting outside the garage, utterly transformed. She looked twenty years younger, with two pristine new bumpers—not a scratch, a nick, or a smudge on them. The bumpers gave her a new personality: perky and pristine but also regal, a restored antique motor vehicle.

I tooled around Ellsworth, doing chores, to show off Ahuan. At Downeast Office Products, I bought two replacement ribbons for Frankie's ancient Remington.

"Nice car," said the salesman.

At Life Sports, a man watched me pull in, park, and get out of Ahuan.

"Beautiful car," he said. I bought a hundred-dollar set of the Patagonia underwear for Frankie.

Next, I pulled up beside a truck selling seafood, lured by a hand-lettered sign reading: "Lobster, $3.49 lb. Hardshells." Hard-shell lobsters at $3.49 a pound were a bargain compared to the $7 a pound we paid for them at Abel's and Mr. Stanley's on the island. Once parked, I saw some fine print on the sign. Right next to, "Lobsters, $3.49 lb.," were two tiny words: "and up." Next to the word "Hardshells" were two more tiny words: "also available." The sign read: "Lobsters, $3.49 lb. And up. Hardshells also available." Once I'd turned in, I couldn't simply roar back out on to the highway. A man emerged from the back of the truck and starting ogling Ahuan. So I went in and looked over the price list. The $3.49 a pound price was for shedders—that is lobster that had shed their old hard shells and were growing new shells back, which for the first weeks were soft and thin. Prices quickly escalated to $6.99 a pound for pound-and-three-quarters lobsters with hard shells, virtually the same as Mount Desert Island prices. I nonchalantly backed out, thinking that I'd be rewarding a kind of bait-and-switch operation. Besides, we'd eaten lobsters so recently that if I showed up at Frankie's place with more, I'd probably have to eat them alone.

Doug's Shop'N'Save came next. I proudly drove Ahuan around the parking lot once after a young man saw Ahuan and gave me a thumbs up.

I stopped at J&P's farm stand. Jill and Pete still had lots of fruits and vegetables. They also stocked lobsters, crabmeat, steamers, and other seafood. I regularly consulted with Pete Mayo about such important local matters as where fishermen were catching strippers, when, and on what kind of bait. He knew lots of local gossip, too, and he often had a new batch of homemade beans or a new recipe for pickles for me to try. When I pulled into his lot in Ahuan, he stepped out from behind his counter to take a good look.

"Wow," he said. "Beautiful—a work of art."

I bought twenty-five dollars' worth of vegetables and fruit that I didn't really need: apples, beets, escarole, even squash—and I dislike squash intensely. Then I asked him about tomatoes. Pete told me the tomato season was over for him, he'd stopped selling them. All he had left, he said, were the ugly ducklings he couldn't sell.

"They're perfectly good tomatoes, mind you," he said, reaching below a counter. He pulled out a cardboard box two-thirds full of scarred, unripened, hard, geen and oddly shaped specimens. "Load 'em up, get 'em outta here," he said. "No charge."

The fresh, local tomato is a wondrous orb. When we left New York in early July, local tomatoes were beginning to appear at the farmers' markets in Manhattan. They whetted our appetites for more. But in Maine tomatoes usually didn't ripen until the end of August, so we suffered from tomato envy all summer, longing for a few big beefsteak specimens from New Jersey but doing without.

Back home, Frankie opened the box of tomatoes, took a big sniff.

"Thrilling!" she said. We carried them inside, packed some of them into paper bags, stacked others on the desk in the back bedroom, and left the hard green ones in the box.

By the middle of September, Frankie had exhausted the books and files she had brought to Maine and the resources of the Northeast Harbor Library. She had to go to New York to collect some more of her files. She'd mine New York's libraries as well. I decided to go too. As much as I disliked going, I disliked staying even more. I'd stayed behind at Frankie's place before. I had gone on walks alone, played tennis and golf with friends, attended porch-benders and dinners, and done a lot of reading and writing. But I had been lonely. Staying at Frankie's place without

Frankie wasn't very much fun. So while she worked in New York, I'd visit my mother in Michigan and my father in Florida. We'd be back in less than a week.

The Bangor airport was empty, the plane half full.

After two and a half months in the woods at Frankie's place, the first thing I noticed about New York City was that it was hard, very hard. So much concrete and stone, so little moss and lichens. Manhattan had no cushion of pine needles, no place to get away from people, nowhere beyond commerce except for Central Park. I went for a run in the park that afternoon.

The air was warm and breezy as I crossed to the park side of Fifth Avenue and jogged to the park's 79th Street entrance. I ran beside the Metropolitan Museum of Art and up to the track around the reservoir. Then I headed down to the Great Lawn, where a few softball games were under way. I circled them on a concrete roadway.

Central Park was a maelstrom of sights and smells, full of people and dogs. If the *Bar Harbor Times* thought people were overrunning Acadia National Park, I thought, it ought to check out Central Park.

By the time I got to the pond at the south end of the Great Lawn, a tendon in my calf hurt. So I stopped running and walked. I came upon a movie set. There were trailers, trucks, lights, cables, cameras, and people along with a big table to one side stacked with snacks and soft drinks. I asked a man what was being filmed. He pointed to a sign: "Pre-Operative Trans-Sexual Lesbians." I was a long way from Somes Sound.

Five Maine lobsters that I had air-freighted to Michigan arrived at my mother's house on the morning of her birthday. My half brother, Ken, his wife, Patty, and their young daughter, Anne, pulled in at noon from Iowa City, where Ken worked as a hospital pharmacy administrator. I flew into Detroit and drove to Owosso in a rented car that afternoon. Frankie's lobster rules had no jurisdiction in Michigan. The live lobsters came in a

Styrofoam box swathed in seaweed and cooled by a frozen gel pack. I steamed them and roasted corn on the cob. We toasted Mom.

My mother and the man I called Dad lived in a small house in the country just outside of Owosso. They were both in their seventies and in poor health, so Ken and I found plenty of chores that needed doing. We pruned the trees, mowed the lawn, weeded the garden. Gert and Fred lived on ten acres that had been part of a forty-acre farm his parents had bought when they came to this country from the Bohemian region of Czechoslovakia just before World War I. Fred was born the youngest of five children—three daughters and two sons—in a poor farm family. He dropped out of school after the sixth grade to work the family farm. The family raised sugar beets during the Depression and barely survived.

The Depression had a scarring effect on Fred. For example, he wouldn't throw anything away. He spent a lifetime acquiring things that might come in handy some day. "You never know," was his motto. He was prepared for rough times. You never knew when the next Depression was going to come along. He knew it would come sooner rather than later, and he would be prepared as others would not. In the meantime, he had the steel, the brackets, the connectors, the nuts and bolts, and the lumber somewhere in his barn or stacked around it to build almost anything. If you had to go to a store and buy the things he could build, they would cost you an arm and a leg and would be flimsy junk, he liked to say. He built boat trailers and truck racks and benches that were much stronger than the ones they sold in the stores. The fact that they weighed ten times more than the store-bought items didn't bother him.

His barn, in back of the house, was a marvel of disorder. Fred had amassed enormous quantities of either junk or treasure, depending on the person doing the marveling. Inside were two pickup trucks, two tractors, four riding lawn mowers, and a dozen other lawn mowers in varying states of repair. Along one wall stood two welders, an acetylene cutting and welding torch and tanks, and two standing drill presses. Benches were laden with sanders, grinders, and iron vices, and piled high with tools, bolts, and pieces of steel and iron. The walls were lined with shelves holding car, tractor, and lawn mower parts. I found Briggs & Stratton engines I had worked on back in our farm days.

Family conversation didn't get beyond small talk, as usual. Fred reminisced about bad times and good. The bad times were "hard times," which the spoiled younger generation couldn't possibly conceive of and certainly never could have survived. The good times were fishing trips to Ontario. Ken and I had been on many of these trips as children, but Fred recounted them as if we were hearing about them for the first time. Those were the days, he told us. Nobody would ever catch walleyes like that again.

Fred was still very much the ruler of his family. Ken took me aside at one point and told me our mother wanted to use our get-together to have a heart-to-heart talk about the future and what should be done when she and Fred could no longer care for themselves. She wanted to talk about medical needs, nursing costs, and legal issues, including wills and powers of attorney. But when she tried to talk about these things, Fred angrily cut her off. The idea of having a conversation about a future in which he wouldn't be in charge was threatening to him. We never had the talk.

I left Michigan for Florida.

After that first meeting with James Walter Watts in Ocala, I returned two or three times a year to visit him and play golf. I phoned Walter every month or so to see how he was doing. We became friends. He always went out of his way not to make any demands on me. The only time he seemed disappointed with me was when I missed a short putt or put a drive deep into the woods.

I arrived in the midafternoon, jumped out of my car, and Walter came out to greet me, patting me on the shoulder, grabbing my arm. He looked alert and healthy for an eighty-three years old. I asked about his golf game.

"I'm still whacking it good enough to beat you," he laughed. To make sure things stayed that way, he said, he'd been taking lessons to improve his swing.

Agnes called us to the dinner table at six o'clock, a concession, she said, to my late eating habits. They normally ate at five and were in bed by seven-thirty. Agnes pulled a big ham out of the oven, along with scalloped potatoes crusted with cheese. She said she and Walter normally ate small, simple dinners. I said I liked small, simple meals, too. This had no effect on Agnes, who continued to serve rich, heavy meals because that's what her family always did when company came.

Walter and Agnes rose at four-thirty. Walter banged on my door at five.

We ate breakfast and the two of us headed off to the Marion Oaks Golf Club, where Walter still played three mornings a week. Walter was strong for his age. The golfers he played with told me that he was cagey and shrewd, too. He was older than most of the retirees he played with, but he usually won money. He couldn't hit the ball very far, but he was remarkably consistent at punching it down the middle of the fairway and staying out of the rough. And he was very good with a putter.

The regulars at Marion Oaks were retirees, most of them former blue-collar workers from the Northeast and Midwest, factory workers, postmen, car salesmen, plumbers, career military men, and mechanics. Their golf games seemed to substitute for their old jobs. Showing up at Marion Oaks on time was the closest thing they had left to punching the time clock.

Walter and I walked into the locker room. There each golfer playing that morning put four dollars into a kitty. Walter said hello to his pals and introduced me to those I had not met.

"Well, Walter, I'm on Medicare now," said Buddy Ray, a strapping man with a young face and a gentle demeanor. "Yeah, I turned sixty-five."

"Sixty-five?" said Walter, feigning astonishment. "Why, that makes you one of the youngest around here. Ain't too many that young."

Other regulars arrived out of the morning darkness into the clubhouse in varying states of sleepiness and mobility. They joked about aging, about their bodies falling apart and their golf games going to hell. They talked about George, who had died, and about John, who was going in for an operation.

"Yeah, they found some spots on his liver and want to take a look," Ralph said.

Walter and I teed off in the first foursome.

"Ta' heck," Walter said, smashing his tee shot into dense, weedy rough that his pals called "broccoli" alongside the first fairway. He chopped his ball back into the fairway on his second shot, hit it to the green on his third, and two-putted for a bogey five.

The more I played golf with Walter and his pals, the more I saw him as a gentle, old man, unthreatening and polite, a nice guy liked by all. At the same time, he won a lot of money. Ten bucks was a lot of money at Marion Oaks.

At the end of our Monday game, our foursome added up its scores and mine was lower than Walter's. I had beaten him for the first time. I asked him to autograph the scorecard. He seemed pleased.

I flew to New York, picked up Frankie and her new files, and we headed for Bangor. We were back at Frankie's place in time for dinner.

The September gloom held, and we found ourselves sitting at our desks at opposite ends of the house day after day putting down words, building sentences, and constructing paragraphs like piece-work veterans in a shirtwaist factory. The Jurassic Park carpenters pounded away next door, but we were otherwise very much alone on the peninsula. Some neighbors would come back for Columbus Day weekend, but at the moment the neighborhood was left to us and to the wildlife.

White-tailed deer, having taken their annual summer leave when the dogs had arrived in July, were back in force. Rabbits, too. Chipmunks and red squirrels toiled, gathering their acorns and shredding pinecones with what appeared to be a mounting sense of urgency. The crows' morning cabal in the pines by the shore seemed to get louder. The osprey cruised by more frequently. The bald eagle alighted often on the pine branch out front.

On the last Sunday in September the sun peaked through the clouds at exactly 2:07 P.M. and was back in hiding four minutes later. Its rays were a sight so rare that I stopped working, looked at my watch, dashed onto the porch, and shouted, "What's this?" It turned out to be the beginning of Indian summer. By three o'clock, sunlight pierced the clouds in a dozen places over Somes Sound. By three-thirty, it was shining brightly. This was worth celebrating.

"Let's go," I prodded Frankie.

But before we could get organized, I heard some steps on the porch and saw a figure walking toward the door. Then some knocking. I got up, walked over, and opened the screen door.

"Hi, I'm the appraiser," he said.

The WHAT? He had come, he said, to estimate the value of the house and property. He explained that he would have to take a look around, inside and outside of the house and walk around the property. Then he would compare what he found to similar houses and pieces of property that had sold in recent months or years and come up with a value for it.

An appraiser! I had forgotten about the FitzGerald house-selling talk. That was loose talk. Sending an appraiser was a serious move.

"Oh, didn't I tell you," Frankie said. "We decided to get a few appraisals to have a more specific idea of how we might want to handle this."

How to handle what? Selling out? Moving away?

"In case somebody wants to sell," she added.

"Because a couple of more houses are going up? This is lunacy," I said. "As far as I'm concerned, a nine-story condo wouldn't be a disaster. They could build a Miami Beach hotel next door and I'd still live here. It would still be a wonderful place. It's just not the place it was when you were children."

"Calm down," Frankie said. "We need to know what the various shares of land and house are worth in case somebody decides they need to sell."

The appraiser did his job and left, but his appearance hung over me like a cloud.

Nineteen

October was, in many ways, the best month to be at Frankie's place. The cloud blankets of September dissolved into deep blue skies of Indian summer dotted with cotton-puff clouds. The air turned cold and crisp. The leaves on the beech trees, oaks, and maples turned bright shades of yellow, orange, and red. They sparkled in the October sun, creating great swaths of warm color between stands of evergreens and outcroppings of granite.

A few summer people stayed on. Busloads of leaf peepers arrived on the island on fall foliage tours, but Mount Desert felt empty. Instead of feeling left behind, as I had after the exodus of summer people around Labor Day, I now felt as though we had the island and the park to ourselves.

Parkman Mountain was transformed in October. At its summit the air was so clear that we thought we could see the entire state of Maine. Over on Bald Mountain patches of blueberry bushes, turned scarlet, cascaded over the granite like waterfalls.

The Canadians were winning the weather wars. The cold fronts they threw at us stayed put longer. There were none of those wimpy one-day wonders that they had sent down in July and August. The Bermudans were in retreat.

The enormous toupee of frigid air that covers the Arctic expands each winter, turning Siberia, Norway, and Canada into the superpowers of cold. Canada was on the verge of reasserting its hegemony over Mount Desert and the northern tier of the United States. Bermuda and the wet, warm fronts from the equatorial region were in full retreat. Before much longer, Canada's weather would rule. Only the ocean, with its relatively constant temperature, kept Mount Desert from becoming a polar bear habitat.

My indoor war was history. The mice, with their chorus lines and droppings, were gone. I had won the battle—but the war? The mice could be reproducing quietly. Producing litters averaging 6.7 babies, according to *Common-Sense Pest Control*.

"You can't win, you know," Frankie said over breakfast one morning. "You can hold them off but in the end they're going to win."

She was right, of course. We would soon be gone. The house would be theirs again. I had fought the good fight, but I was abandoning the place. Hamburger Hill all over again. All they had to do was wait us out and they would win. Classic Sun Tzu: ". . . those who render others' armies helpless without a fight are the best of all."

The truth was that I was tired of war. The ardor of my inner field marshal had flagged. The onset of cold weather made me feel closer to the animals around me. Eventually it was going to get a lot colder. Before long, the Canadians would be lobbing cold front after cold front at us. Faced with those possibilities, I couldn't help but have feelings of solidarity toward the living creatures around me, two-legged, four-legged, or six legged. We were, after all, in this together. Extra mammals inside was beginning to seem like a good idea. The house could use all the BTUs our collective body heat could muster.

Frankie's place had all the comforts of home save one: it wasn't winterized. It had no central heating and no insulation. The temperature outside was more or less the temperature inside. To keep warm, we added layers of clothing and built a fire. The big stone fireplace was elevated eighteen inches off the floor. In front of it was a stone deck with cushions. We'd sit in front of the flames until one side of us was hot, then turn to the other side, marshmallow-style.

Daytime temperatures didn't get above the fifties now. At night the thermometer would plunge into the thirties. With this kind of cold would come thick cloud blankets.

At noon one day Frankie was warming her hands on the tea kettle heating up some water for instant tomato soup.

"Where's global warming when we need it?" I said, holding my hands over the toaster while browning some bread for a sandwich.

We had other sources of heat. Each room had a small electric heater built into the wall. But turning on those electricity guzzlers was an act of surrender. Before we surrendered, we had fallback options: flannel shirts and wool sweaters and long underwear.

Another line of defense against the cold was giving up indefensible territory. We used the second bedroom in the back of the house as guest quarters and a storage place, and there was no reason to let heat from the fireplace into it. By closing its doors and sealing it off, we had one less room into which our precious BTUs could migrate. The fireplace didn't have to do quite as much work.

At night we added more blankets and a quilt to our bed. Our body heat kept us toasty. Breathing through a hole in the covers, my nose drew in cold air and put me on notice that any expedition to the bathroom in the middle of the night was going to be a polar adventure. The distance to that little room seemed to extend in direct proportion to the decline in temperature. Under the cozy quilt I would turn over my options again and again. Do I put this trek off, stay warm, and feel bladder buildup or do I dash forth and freeze? When the inevitable could no longer be put off, I'd leap up, pad across the icy floors in the dark, go about my business, and pad back. Sliding back under the quilt, I had to be careful because my feet had become ice cubes. At least that was the way they felt to Frankie when they accidentally touched her legs.

"EEEeeeeeahhhhh!"

Eventually we surrendered to the gods of electricity and turned on the heaters—but only in the bathrooms. Those warm bathrooms soon became sanctuaries. If you were in one, you didn't rush. A warm bathroom was an invitation to read on. I devoured old *New Yorkers*.

Daylight, too, was in retreat. Back in July, darkness didn't descend until just before nine o'clock. Soon it would be getting dark at four-thirty, the result of a tilting planet. But, as Susan Mary had laughingly reminded us before she decamped for Washington, there was one advantage in the sun setting in the middle of the afternoon. Those people on the island who traditionally had their first drink at sunset got a head start as winter closed in. They could mix their first batch of martinis at four-thirty and be completely pickled by six o'clock.

From deep within the *Times* one morning, Frankie emerged, turned to me, and said, "So why don't you go to the post office."

"Sorry," I announced. "I have to work."

That was Frankie's line, not mine. It contradicted my modus operandi. I spent the summer looking for excuses to rest my computer. Frankie had just lobbed a softball of an excuse right over the plate and I watched it sail by. Naturally, when I sat down to work, I thought of nothing but the post office. I hadn't been to the post office in a week. Our box must be stuffed with important communications from the world: notices of literary prizes won, invitations to weddings, dividend checks from accountants, requests for speaking engagements, a certified letter informing us we had won a million dollars in the National Publishers Sweepstakes! I listened to my computer hum. I looked at the words on the screen. Finally, when I figured Frankie was so deep into concentration that I wouldn't immediately lose face, I slipped out of the house.

A familiar pickup was parked at the Somesville light. A man I recognized was selling vegetables out of the back of it. He noticed Ahuan and waved. I pulled over. He'd been a regular at that spot over the summers but this was the first time I'd seen him this year. For good reason, he said as I bought a sack of potatoes and some squash. He told me of his travails with the local law enforcement authorities, how he could get arrested any minute, how the code-enforcement officer was on his case.

"Says you're not 'sposed to sell anywhere on Mount Desert," he said. "In Southwest Harbor, they don't give me no trouble. But I like it here, and I get along fine with them," he said, pointing next door to Fernald's gas station.

"They say I should just get arrested and be done with it. Go from there."

I nodded sympathetically. As I saw it, not far down the road was the alleged perpetrator of a heinous hit-and-run crime, witnessed and documented, against Ahuan, running around loose, unhampered by the authorities. Meanwhile, the same authorities were harassing a lowly, roadside practitioner of the free enterprise system! Didn't seem right. I thought about parking Ahuan next to his truck in a show of solidarity, maybe selling articles on the dangers of big government out of the back.

One afternoon Frankie wandered into the back bedroom on her way to the linen closet and saw tomatoes everywhere. Tomatoes filled fourteen brown paper bags on the desk. Hard green tomatoes sat shoulder to shoulder in cardboard boxes. Bright red tomatoes lined the windowsill. Splotchy pink, red, and green tomatoes sat piled in a box on the bed.

"We don't have enough meals left to eat all the tomatoes, even if we had them for breakfast," she said.

I went into the tomato bedroom and had a look. She had a point. I took a tomato census. We had eighty-one. It wasn't that we hadn't been eating them. Frankie fried green tomatoes so often that I felt like a stuffed tomato worm. I made fresh tomato pasta sauce. We sliced tomato after tomato into our sandwiches for lunch. We popped small tomatoes directly into our mouths. Yet we were still up to our keisters in tomatoes.

I vowed to make lots more tomato sauce, *cioppino,* and tomato soup. Frankie found a recipe for tomato sorbet. One evening, surveying the contents of the refrigerator, I got an idea. In so-called fusion cooking, some chefs blend ingredients from the West with ingredients from the East. The result: Cuban-Chinese, or Polish-Thai. Why not Somes Sound fusion: fried green tomato fried rice. It could be a fusion breakthrough. It could be confusion glop.

FRIED GREEN TOMATO FRIED RICE

Into a hot oiled wok toss ¼ onion, chopped, and half a 2-inch-long fresh jalapeño pepper, finely chopped. Sizzle for a minute or so. Add 1 cup of leftover chicken, cut into bite-sized pieces, and sizzle for another minute. Add 1 medium green tomato, chopped, and ¼ cup of fresh cilantro, chopped. Stir this mixture a couple of minutes, until the tomatoes steam and sizzle but are still firm. (If you happen to have any leftover beans, add half a cup at this point.) Finally, add 1½ cups of leftover cooked rice, stirring it into the mixture. Just before serving, shake in a little soy sauce and squeeze in the juice of ¼ lime and stir to a final steamy crescendo!

Sometimes Frankie's reactions to my experimental dishes are less than wildly enthusiastic. In this case, she banished me from the kitchen the next evening and set to work on a basic marinara using a recipe given her by an old friend.

RENEE'S MARINARA

Chop 3 large onions and sauté them in a heavy pot with olive oil until they become translucent. Add 3 cloves of chopped garlic. Take 8 large tomatoes, section them, squeeze out the seeds, and add them to the pot. Add two bay leaves and a teaspoon of dried basil, marjoram, or both. Simmer this mixture for two hours, or until the tomato sauce has been reduced to a syrup and the onions have melded into it. (At this point, you can let it cool or even freeze it for later use.) To eat immediately, chop some fresh basil, cilantro, or other fresh herbs and add just before serving.

Frankie served her marinara with fresh herbs over pasta shells. Wonderful. Frankie said she hadn't liked tomato sauces until she began tasting ones made out of fresh tomatoes. But what she especially liked about Renee's marinara recipe was that it was possible to cook and type at the same time.

The next morning in bed Frankie stirred and stirred, then announced, unusually early for her: "I have to get up. All I can think about is tomatoes."

We began liquidating tomatoes in a hurry. I started on the front porch, where a local chipmunk had become something of an overseer. I offered him an apple, a graham cracker, and two small green tomatoes. The graham cracker went first. He carried it off as though it were a miniature piece of plywood, stopping every few steps to catch his balance. He then wrestled the apple as if it were a giant bowling ball, knocking it off the rail onto the porch.

"With skills like that," I said, "this chipmunk could come in handy next door."

He left the green tomatoes for a time, but he came back later and made off with one. One less tomato at this stage was a blessing.

One morning I heard and then spotted a downy woodpecker hard at work on a dead tree trunk, mimicking the pounding of the workers at Jurassic Park.

The metal dinosaurs were still afoot on our peninsula. A red Velociraptor, parked for several days at the head of the lane, was gone when I got up to the main road. In its place sat a giant yellow Tyrannosaurus rex, the big steel teeth on its shovel folded neatly under its craning neck. Its engine was running and it was getting ready to move. I grabbed an apple off the tree by the roadside and watched. Soon, a man got out of a pickup, boarded T. rex and eased it, beeping and growling, down the lane. I watched it go, then wandered over to a little creek nearby to finish my apple and let the fumes clear. On my way back down the lane, I passed T. rex turning into Jurassic Park.

The construction uproar ebbed and flowed. Sometimes the pounding stopped. Sometimes we heard very little, the sounds having gone on for so long that they had become part of our background noise. Then a carpenter would plug in a power saw and the whine of its teeth chewing into wood would rattle my fillings.

On our final inspection of the summer we discovered that the framed parts of the house were going up fast. The skeletons of two-by-fours on the first and second stories were completely enclosed with plywood sheeting, and two-by-four frames for a third floor were partly in place. Plywood had been laid on the second floor.

As we wandered around the lumber and studs and across the floors, I realized that my perception of what was going on at Jurassic Park had changed. My knee-jerk condemnation of it as a castle in the forest, insulting the neighborhood and assaulting our lives, was giving way to a critic's-eye view. Frankie said she felt the same way. We began to notice design features we liked. On the waterside of the house, for example, something that looked like an old-fashioned front porch was taking shape. We were struck by the nice view whoever sat on that porch was going to have looking down Somes Sound. Inside, we found a kitchen perfectly situated. In front of the sink space a large window overlooked the sound. This, I thought, was a kitchen-person's touch.

"Maybe this guy is a cook," I said. "Maybe he's a good cook!"

The outside walls of the bottom two stories were half covered in an insulating wrap. Inside, the cement-block bases of fireplaces were going in. Alongside the house, rafters for a roof were taking shape. Out in back and to one side of the main structure, what looked like a small guest house was under construction. It had walls of plywood on three sides without windows. It dawned on us that this could be a bathhouse for the rumored swimming pool!

Winter advanced into October and we prepared for the end. The days got still shorter, temperatures lower. NOAA Weather Radio announcers talked of snow in the northern mountains.

In a few days we would close up Frankie's place and leave. As I sat in front of my computer I thought about things I hadn't noticed in a while. I couldn't remember the last time I heard the sound of canvas sail flapping in the wind as a boat came about on a tack out on the Sound. I hadn't seen a boat under sail in the sound for the longest time. Not many motorboats either. Fewer birds were around, fewer insects too. I hadn't seen or heard a mosquito in weeks. Itinerant spiders turned up in the bathtub or kitchen sink now and then, and some others took up residence in webs they had spun on a windowsill. Indoor flies buzzed against the windowpane, or they wound up in a web.

I swept the roof on the eve of our departure. The pitch on the roof of the house wasn't steep enough for gravity and wind to work their magic. Pine needles stacked up, forming little beds on the cedar shingles. The beds held moisture. Moisture helped lichens and moss to grow on the shingles. The shingles gradually rotted. To hold off the rot, I swept.

I transplanted the porch crops, moving chives, thyme, and other herbs that could survive the winter from pots to a small rock garden in back of the house. I removed our porch umbrella from its hole in the table on the porch and took it inside for storage.

"It's like striking the colors," Frankie said.

I called Charley Bolger at Manset Boat House and told him *Scoop* was ready to be picked up, washed down, and stored for the winter. I told Bob Young at Northeast Plumbing his men could drain the pipes. I ordered a cord of firewood. I called Ahuan's garage in Ellsworth and discussed summer glitches and winter repairs. I called for a taxi in Ellsworth to pick us up at Ahuan's garage and drive us to the Bangor airport. I stacked the porch furniture under the house.

Frankie did the laundry and wrote a note to Tammy Sprague, who would come after we'd left and button up the house for the winter. We picked up our last newspapers in town, and then walked up Norumbega. For dinner, we cleaned out the refrigerator and had ourselves a kitchen-sink festival. I popped the casserole dish of leftover beans into the oven to warm up. I brought out our last fifty-two tomatoes.

"Toss them," Frankie said. "I refuse to eat another one."

While Frankie did the dishes, I thumbed through a stack of old vinyl LPs, pulled out Bob Seeger, turned on the record player, put the needle down on "Old Time Rock and Roll," and turned up the volume.

Frankie danced away from the dishes into the living room and began gyrating in front of the Buddha. We bounced like teenagers. We held each other and kissed. It was a one-song party. Frankie went back to the dishes. I went back to packing.

The next morning, we were up before eight. I rolled up the blinds to a startling sight. Out front, planted in the sound like a giant rubber ducky in a small bathtub, was a huge cruise ship. Time to go, I thought. We split the last waffle and the last banana, downing them with coffee. We turned off the wall heaters, locked the windows, loaded Ahuan with suitcases, garbage, and bottles, and left. We stopped at the Town Garage and deposited our last refuse. We stopped at the post office, got our last mail, and gave Lynda our change-of-address forms. The taxi in Ellsworth took us to the Bangor airport. An hour and half later we landed in a New York haze.

The passage from Mount Desert to Manhattan in the middle of October is a short trip back in time. Mount Desert's foliage was turning brown; its mountainside canvases of yellow, orange, and red blotches had been slowly sapped of color and the slightest breeze sent leaves fluttering to the ground, leaving the gray, skeletal branches of maples and oaks, beeches and birch. Winter waited in the wings.

New York City, four hundred miles to the southwest, was weeks behind Mount Desert. We found a second autumn, as though we were watching a videotape rewind of Indian summer. New York in late October was warm by day and cool by night, like Maine in August. The leaves on the trees in Central Park were green.

In a taxi into Manhattan, I got to thinking about our last supper, kitchen-sink pasta, and . . . Suddenly I remembered.

"Frankie," I said. "We didn't eat the beans. We forgot the beans. The beans are in the oven."

Twenty

We came back to Frankie's place the next summer and in the summers that followed like a pair of migrating birds returning to a nest. Our summer rituals stayed much the same, but many things changed.

The Luddite in residence finished her book on a computer! It was something to behold. Over the summer and fall I showed her a few things that my laptop could do. I could move around paragraphs or pages with a few clicks of my computer mouse.

"Oh, that's nice," Frankie would say, as if she had no interest. Then I noticed a change. With her previous three books, she had had to retype her manuscript to make revisions and prepare a clean copy for her publisher. Now, facing this laborious task on her typewriter once again, she began to reconsider the virtues of my laptop, with its ability to revise on screen, store on hard drive and on backup disks, and print out clean copies at will.

I gave her an IBM Thinkpad for her birthday. She complained about its screen. She complained about its typefaces and font sizes. She complained about its blinking cursor. She complained that it was too easy to hit a wrong key and lose entire paragraphs. She complained about having to rewrite revisions because the computer forgot to save the ones she had already done. She complained and complained. But her Remington fell silent. She wasn't for-

saking it, she insisted. She was saving time. She would go back
to it, she vowed, but she never did.

We gamely pushed the mycological envelope, finding wild
mushrooms that were new to us every summer, combing through
our guidebooks in search of the perfect match and finding dev-
ilish ambiguity as often as not. But we got better at sorting the
kickers from the pickers, and slowly our list of keeper shrooms
grew.

One summer I picked up the *Bar Harbor Times* and saw a front-
page headline that read, "Plant Poachers Pose Problem." The story
was about Acadia National Park rangers cracking down on visitors
filching beach stones, sea heather, and other plants from the park.
I read on: "Mushrooming has also become a problem in recent
years—especially on the western side of the park and at Schoodic
Point. Although it used to be legal, it is now prohibited."

Prohibited? Just like that? Since when? Why? I was outraged.
Picking mushrooms is like picking apples off a tree. They are the
fruit of the fungus. The park rangers didn't seem to have a problem when visitors plucked an apple off one of the trees in the
Jordan Pond House parking lot. The story continued, "Although
mushrooming seems like harmless activity, park botanist Linda
Gregory explains that a park is a preserve where natural processes
can go through their cycle relatively undisturbed. Those processes
are changed and can even be stopped entirely when the fruits of
nature's labor are not allowed to complete the regenerative func-
tion and instead end up on the dinner table or in Christmas
wreaths."

Fair enough, I thought, but what about all the "natural processes" that were disturbed by the so-called improvements to the
carriage roads? Miles and miles of pristine mushroom habitat
alongside the roads was torn up, gouged out, covered over, and
wiped out. This was profoundly more damaging than picking the
odd chanterelle. This was like clear-cutting an entire orchard of
fruit trees; the only difference was that the mushroom trees are
called mycelium and grow underground. Why was this under-

ground orchard being destroyed? So the carriage roads could be improved for bicyclists to go faster? This was unfair. Later that summer the local newspapers began printing on their crime pages the names, ages, and addresses of nabbed mushroom poachers.

The editor of the *Ellsworth American,* J. Russell Wiggins, continued to remind readers of the need for a strong North Atlantic Treaty Organization and to warn of the perils of a mounting national debt. I was tempted to write him another letter complaining that the very government that was piling up the debt was also throwing its weight around in a very heavy-handed manner as far as shroomers were concerned. I held off, however, not wanting to alert park authorities to the fact that Frankie and I were mushroom poachers.

Wiggins also continued to remind his readers of the ongoing plight of Maine's seagulls deprived of town dumps in which to forage. On August 21, 1997, came this offering:

Mr. and Mrs. Seagull should file a brief complaint:
City dumps were everywhere and now they ain't.
The welfare changes that are made by Congress and the state
Have closed all dumps at which, not long ago, they ate.
They all grew up on city dumps, but, as the summers pass,
Each town burns up its city dump, and plants the place in grass.
They've fought for months about relief, in far off Washington,
And no one but the seagulls is aware of what they've done.

The Camden Marine Radio operators kept their friendly neighborhood on the air year after year, "holding traffic" for passing boats, patching calls from ship to shore, lending a hand to boaters in distress, finding doctors or florists who could deliver a bouquet for a friend's birthday. They told boaters where to get repairs near Stonington, whether a restaurant was open in Blue Hill, the name of the hardware store in Southwest Harbor, and the telephone numbers of everyone from the Coast Guard commander to the meat purveyor.

Then on Tuesday, August 10, 1999, Camden Marine Radio went out of business, its operators silenced when Coastal Communications turned over its license and transmitting facility to the Maritel Marine Communications System, a nationwide, semiautomated ship-to-shore phone service headquartered in Gulfport, Mississippi.

"It was the end of an era," said owner, Charley Foote. "I wanted to keep it going, but my accountant had been telling me for three years to cut my losses."

Now, instead of calling Camden Marine operators in Camden, boaters tuned their radios to Channel 28, then held down their transmit buttons for five seconds and got an automated voice: "This is KBS 856 Maritel Channel 28 at Southwest Harbor. To place a call please key your microphone for an additional five seconds now." That action triggered another automated voice telling a caller to wait while the call was forwarded to operators in Gulfport. The service operated twenty-four hours a day.

NOAA Weather Radio continued to broadcast the latest zone weather forecasts, extended forecasts, offshore forecasts, the water temperatures, wave heights, and tidal times. The haying advisory however, gave way to tallies of mysterious "heating degree days." These reports were offered summer after summer by men with familiar and reassuring voices. But then one morning in the summer of 1999, I tuned in to WX2 while shaving and heard a female announcer reciting water temperature data. Progress, I thought. As I listened, I realized she was very new to the job. She announced southwest winds of five to fifteen knots at MUNT-i-cus Rock, an embarrassing mispronunciation of Ma-TIN-a-cus Rock. A few days later, a different female voice came on and pronounced it Ma-TINK-us Rock. These gaffes were the talk of boaters all summer. But I got used to the female voices in no time. They were music to my ears compared to what I heard the next summer: a synthesized voice! Difficult to understand, it sounded like a drugged robot, a metallic Swede. I couldn't imagine how a sailor in a storm could understand its singsong delivery. I thought of it as a perfectly representative voice for a distant, bureaucratic federal government.

Lugnut compiled a record for stopping giant trucks and heavy machinery that may never be equaled, then one day disappeared. We feared the worst. We feared that he had been squashed by some mammoth dump truck! We feared that he'd been nabbed by Officer Arthur Lawrence, known to dog owners as "Lawrence of Acadia" because of his vigilance in keeping canines within the law. As it turned out, Lugnut had retired to a leafy suburb of Boston and was living a quiet life as Bentley once again.

The alleged perp got off. My insurance company declined to pursue a claim against hers. They did, however, note her collision with Ahuan on my permanent insurance record as my "hit-and-run" incident, which always took lots of explaining.

The manuscript sent by Frankie's agent sat unread and un-blurbed on the table in front of the fireplace all winter and spring while it was published, got rave reviews, and was awarded a Pulitzer Prize for biography.

Talk of selling Frankie's place didn't come up again among the FitzGerald siblings. Perhaps my offerings to the Buddha helped.

Construction at Jurassic Park lasted through two summers. On one workday the next July, I counted sixteen pickup trucks and vans parked in the driveway. Huge dump trucks came and went all day delivering dirt and landscaping supplies. A new layer of gravel was put down on the lane, making it still smoother and wider. Cars and trucks went faster, kicking up more dust. Trucks brought in hundreds of trees and shrubs, along with large granite stones.

What emerged from this labor would have seemed a bit snug for either the sultan of Brunei or the Mount Desert Moules. It was a wooden frame house of six thousand square feet with fif-teen rooms, including six bedrooms and seven and a half bath-rooms on two floors; plus an attic, a full basement, a three-car garage, and a large front porch made of cut granite. Beside the house toward the back of the property was a large heated outdoor saltwater swimming pool, also made of cut granite, with a pool house that doubled as an efficiency apartment. A carriage house was built on the other side of the pool from the main house. It had a three-car garage below and a two-bedroom apartment above.

Herb Watson was called in to manicure the property. He cut away every dead branch on every tree within sight, biting his tongue all the time, and creating a landscape as alien to the Maine woods as the house itself.

The owner arrived with four boats and a 1936 Packard Super Eight convertible. The boats included a big, beautiful Hinckley yawl, a smaller wooden sailboat, a fancy stinkpot called a picnic boat, and an outboard utility boat like *Scoop* except newer.

We didn't see much of him. He didn't come very often, usually spending a few days or weeks at a time. We ran into him and his girlfriend occasionally when they went on walks.

Three summers later, Frankie and I ran into them on the lane.

"Have you heard the rumor that our place is for sale?" she said. "Well, it's true. It's about to go on the market."

"It's just too much house for us," he said. "We expected to spend more time up here than we do."

That fall, Jurassic Park went on the market for $5.6 million and sold within two months for $5,035,000, a record, at the time, for a piece of residential shorefront property in the state of Maine.

Improvements to the Peabody plot came slowly. A linden sapling Frankie had planted opposite the birches didn't last its first winter. It was replaced by a red maple that deer stripped of bark the next winter and killed. Another red maple replaced it, this one's tender bark shielded by plastic tubing.

A suitable stone of red granite was found among the Gott Heavy Construction holdings and trucked to Ellsworth for engraving. It came back reading, simply, PEABODY and was installed in the center of the plot.

The clump of wild roses thrived. Indeed, in a few years, they were colonizing bigger and bigger chunks of the plot, sending out roots and popping up everywhere. Frankie's uncle Sam declared them out of control. Frankie and I dug them up and replaced them with a flowering shrub that the deer demolished in days.

In one corner of the plot, I planted two native bayberry bushes. They thrived.

To me, the most important development in the tortuous history of the Peabody plot occurred at a lobster dinner at the Peabody house one August several years after the death of Frankie's mother. The subject of the plot came up. Frankie's uncle George was asked how many members of the family had chosen it as their final resting place. He listed them, counting on his fingers. Then he looked up at me and, with a smile, asked, "Would you like to join us?"

I was taken aback. My first thought was that it was very sweet of George to offer me a spot. He was asking me to join the family not just for "as long as you both shall live," but for eternity.

My second thought was that this was Forest Hill Cemetery, not Forest Lawn. This wasn't sunny California. This was Mount Desert Island, where the weather got bleak and the winters long, dark, and cold. What would an eternity in the Peabody plot be like?

"Well, how about it?" George asked.

"I would consider it an honor," I said.